Tarot

OF THE

Bohemians

The Most Ancient Book in the World

for the Use of Initiates

(1914)

Absolute Key to Occult Science

Papus

(Dr. Gerard Encausse)

ISBN 0-7661-0367-6

ABSOLUTE KEY TO OCCULT SCIENCE

THE TAROT

OF THE BOHEMIANS

The Most Ancient Book in the World

FOR THE USE OF INITIATES

By PAPUS

TRANSLATED BY A. P. MORTON

SECOND EDITION REVISED, WITH PREFACE BY

A. E. WAITE

ILLUSTRATED WITH NUMEROUS PLATES AND WOODCUTS

LONDON
WILLIAM RIDER & SON, LIMITED
1914

ABSOLUTE KEY TO OCCULT SCIENCE

Frontispiece

PREFACE TO THE ENGLISH TRANSLATION

AN assumption of some kind being of common con-
venience, that the line of least resistance may be
pursued thereafter, I will open the present consideration by assuming that those who are quite unversed in
the subject have referred to the pages which follow, and
have thus become aware that the Tarot, on its external
side, is the probable progenitor of playing-cards; that,
like these, it has been used for divination and for all
that is understood by fortune-telling; but that behind
this it is held to have a higher interest and another
quality of importance. On a simple understanding, it
is of allegory; it is of symbolism, on a higher plane;
and, in fine, it is of secret doctrine very curiously
veiled. The justification of these views is a different
question; I am concerned with the statement of fact
that such views are held; and this being said, I can
pass to my real business, which is in part critical
and in part also explanatory, though not exactly on
the elementary side.

It should be understood that there are several
methods of constructing the hieroglyphic emblems
of the Tarot into a definite language of symbolism.
Setting aside the school of ordinary research, which
has naturally met with these pictures in elucidating

the antiquities of playing-cards, there is the school
of vulgar divination, working on the traditional lines
of printed books or on uninstructed intuition—using,
however, as a rule both these aids to interpretation,
and having, as there is little need to add, no canon
of criticism regarding them. Outside this there are
certain occult or mystic colleges which claim to possess
a true key to the symbolism; and there is another,
more withdrawn, school, the existence of which has
not so far transpired in the external world. It is
affirmed to possess the final meanings, of which all
others are a shadow, and it differs to this extent
from anything that has been put forward recently
under the pretext of occult revelations.

M. Gérard Encausse, most of whose works have
appeared under the name of Papus, is the head of the
school of Martinism in Paris and is a member of the
modern Kabalistic Order of the Rose-Cross. Neither
of these colleges has any heritage in tradition, but both
are indefatigable in research of one kind or another,
and within the measure of their respective spheres,
which in the ultimate are a single sphere, they deserve
and should receive reasonable praise. Whatever human
patience, equipped with some leaven of learning, can
devise regarding the Tarot will be found in *The Tarot
of the Bohemians*, a second edition of which, in its
English form, is being prefaced by these few words.

So far as history is concerned, the thesis of Papus
depends from whatever is regarded as of authority
among French occult writers; but as to this there are
a few points over which I must act as a moderator.
In respect of philosophical construction, the author
has his own lights, and the fact that he has done the

best that could be expected in virtue of a general
equipment only is to be inferred from the further
fact, by way of antithesis, that there is no living
person who seems to have done so well. I do not
propose to exhaust and shall hardly have recourse
to criticism on this side of the subject, but there are
a few things which will be added. In the matter of
divinatory methods, and such offices of vanity, Papus,
in so far as I am qualified to judge, has all the knowledge that can be needed, or in fact desired, by those
who are interested in proceedings of this kind. It
is probable that in his heart he appraises them at
their proper value, and it may be observed that his
seven lessons on the Divining Tarot occupy a small
portion only of his not unambitious work. But at
a later period he has thought fit to attempt a wider
appeal in this particular direction, and it is really
out of this fact that these prefatory remarks arise;
for seeing that he has just issued *Le Tarot Divinatoire*, it seems desirable, while reserving a proper
spirit of detachment, to say something—if one word
only—concerning it in producing a reprint of *The
Tarot of the Bohemians*. I have thus secured an
excuse to speak of matters more serious, and I now
take them in their order.

The chief point regarding the history of Tarot
cards, whether used as pretexts for fortune-telling or
as symbols for philosophical interpretation, is that
such history does not in fact exist. There are tan-
gible symbolical reasons for believing that some part
of them is exceedingly old in conception, though not
in form, and perhaps, in the last resource, they can
be held to rank as the more interesting and curious

on this account. The earliest cards which are extant
belong to the late fourteenth century, but the question whence they came, or where they originated,
offers, in the absence of any certitude, only a field
for speculation, and this has been industrious, as
usual, opening the debate at Byzantium and closing
it, to the satisfaction of several makers-in-chief of
reverie, somewhere in the great refuge of China, where
that cohort of which it might be said *omnia exeunt in
mysterium* seems to pause always on its way through
the unknown.

This is my first act of moderation in respect of
the apparent conviction with which *The Tarot of the
Bohemians* speaks of the " primeval hieroglyphs of
the Book of Thoth." *Omne ignotum pro antiquis-
simo*, and this is how history is made in the French
occult circles. I mention the point that I may do
something to exonerate Papus, who has followed a
very strong lead of antecedent writers among those
who confess to his predispositions. First in the point
of time is Court de Gébelin, who published, between
1773 and 1782, the nine great quarto volumes of *Le
Monde Primitif*. It is not so very long after all since
he used to be termed a great archæologist; but there
has risen up in Paris—say, yesterday or thereabouts
—a new authority on *L'art de tirer les Cartes*, and
he is of opinion that Court de Gébelin was a denizen-
elect of Bicêtre, who perished through his utter dis-
traction in the matter of animal magnetism. I have
been at the pains to consider, and I find that this
putative authority is qualified to tell a few light
stories concerning cartomancists; that he has thrown
into his pot some dictionaries of occult science, and

has so produced a compilation on divinatory arts. But I find further that he knows nothing of Tarot symbolism, and for this reason, and for all others that I have cited, he has elected to call himself M. Antonio Magus, which title he shall hold · in perpetuity without let or taxation. But his strictures demonstrate nothing, and as there is no reason why experiments in animal magnetism should not open the gates of eternity even for an illustrious archæologist, I will again act as a moderator. Ruling as such, there can, I suppose, be no question that Court de Gébelin was a most considerable savant for his period, or that he was especially instructed in things Egyptian a generation or so before Egyptology first came into being. On these warrants he affirms the Egyptian origin of Tarot cards, and the mode of demonstration which he adopts, to render his conviction contagious, centres in their alleged allegorical conformity with the civil, religious and philosophical doctrine of the old world of the Delta. But if we ask for some details of the conformity, we shall find that we must be content with what we have—that is to say, with the simple affirmation, *ex sede sapientiæ*. The circumstances under which the savant attained his certitude are briefly that he saw the game of Tarot played at the house of a friend, and he there and then declared (*a*) that it was one of the Egyptian books, and (*b*) that it was the sole remaining vestige of the superb libraries and literature which once flourished in the valley of the Nile. And this is precisely what, it seems to me, falls short of plenary persuasiveness. I respect M. de Gébelin for having conceived Egyptology by an act of the mind so long before it could have been conceived in any body of research; I respect him also for having had, out of previous expectation, a vision concerning the Tarot, but as he did not marry his vision to any facts on this earth, I think that he has only begotten a phantom son of the fancy. But, to do him the better justice, let me add that he does offer one typical illustration in detail. The fifth major trump, in the series called Greater Arcana, is the high priest, pope or hierophant, but the second is the high priestess, and it is obvious for Court de Gébelin that these are husband and wife— I know not why, unless it is that they have done what they could to get away from each other in the series. But the point is that the alleged fact shows the Egyptian origin, seeing that the chiefs of the priesthood —sometimes, generally, always; again I do not know— had a way of being married in Egypt. Now, from all this it seems to follow for Doctor Papus that the Tarot is the Bible of Bibles, the Book of Thoth and of primitive revelation. But so sharp an indication may appear to the careful reader a little more than true and less than kind, for Papus has many authorities besides the first French savant who spoke of the Tarot. There are J. A. Vaillant, Éliphas Lévi, William Postel, Jerome Cardan, and L. C. de Saint-Martin. But whatever has been said by the first of these writers regarding the Egyptian origin of the cards depends not from his knowledge of antiquities, to which he made no claim, but from his borrowed theory that the Gypsies—whom he knew at first hand—came from Indo-Tartary through the valley of the Nile, and it stands or falls therewith. Now, I believe that in later knowledge it has some time since fallen like Babylon. In respect of Éliphas Lévi, it is a matter of common familiarity that his opinion on any question of fact was sometimes more than worthless, and occasionally a little bit less than intellectually honest. He affirms (*a*) that the Tarot is possibly anterior to the Book of Enoch—not any apocryphal work which passes under that name, but something "ecstatic and undemonstrable," something which is of mystic rumour wild—so wild indeed that the name proves in the end to be a synonym for the Tarot itself, suggesting thus an inscrutable verbal *impasse*. He affirms further (*b*) that it is the symbolical summary of primitive tradition; (*c*) that it is the keystone of occult science; (*d*) that it is the Book of Hermes. Views of this kind —and thus arbitrarily expressed—seem obviously of the order of revelation, and are to be taken or left according to the disposition of the recipient. In the case of Éliphas Lévi, they have obtained considerable vogue, in the circle to which he appeals, because of the authority ascribed to him.

It remains only to deal with the other witnesses for the defence, and this can also be done shortly. Dr. Papus dreams stertorously when he says that Raymond Lully—who was termed in his day the illuminated doctor of Majorca—based his *Ars Magna* on the Tarot Keys, and I suggest that he has omitted to read the colossal sheaf of treatises which are included under that title: he may be forgiven in advance for the fact, but all the same he is not entitled to speak. The genuine Raymond Lully knew as much of the Book of Thoth as he did of those operations in alchemy which are also ascribed to him.

The statement that Jerome Cardan developed his work *De Subtilitate* from the same source depends from

Éliphas Lévi, and has the advantage of his imagination to support it. When Cardan was excogitating the plan of this curious product of his genius, he dreamed that it should be in twenty-one parts, which is good enough for French occultists to connect it with the Trumps Major, *hormis le fou*, as a kind of ineffable in zero. It treats of the earth and mountains, of celestial and atmospheric phenomena, of metallic substances, of botany, of animate creation, of man, angels and demons.

The report that Postel—who wrote, among other tracts, a *Key of Things kept Secret from the Foundation of the World*—discovered in the Tarot the elements of all mysteries, derives also from Lévi, who forgot that the allegorical key prefixed to the work in question was not the device of Postel, but, as I have shown elsewhere, a reverie by way of explanation contrived by one of his editors. Finally, the statement that Saint-Martin found his doctrine of the correspondences between God, man and the universe in the twenty-two Trump Cards is the masterpiece of Lévi's intuition, and has the great justification that the mystic *Tableau Naturel*, like the *Apocalypse* itself, happens to have twenty-two sections or chapters. Taking all the circumstances into consideration, and the fact that the names here cited are those of the masters of Papus — De Gébelin, Lévi, Vaillant—I think that it is much to his credit that he has not increased the confusion by adding historical considerations of his own, but has simply reproduced his precursors.

One important point remains to be added—that the presence of certain crude semi-Egyptian figures, in some extant Tarot cards—for example, the Sphinx—

signifies imported symbolism unknown to Court de Gébelin, who would only have rejoiced at the opportunity. I conclude generally that the cards are prior to the end of the fourteenth century, and that we know nothing further concerning them. I regard them personally as much older, because of their symbolism, and the fact that they were widely diffused in Southern France at the end of the eighteenth century may, even at that late time, indicate the line of their transmission to us. Many things which came from far away entered Western Europe by the port of Marseilles.

Now it should be clear, even to the casual reader, that in *The Tarot of the Bohemians* nothing depends from the historical side, which is a matter of simple assumption, on the warrants that have come into the author's hands, apart from anything that can be called research on his own part. It carries no consequence in respect of his later considerations. I am anxious to establish this fact, even at the risk of some verbal repetition, so that no prejudice may be taken over to the philosophical interpretation which is the real concern of Papus. The Egyptian derivation of Tarot symbols is, in respect thereof, in much the same position as their use in cartomancy; it is something entirely extrinsic.

And now regarding his construction of the whole symbolic language, this is largely the result of first-hand thinking, though again he has used materials which he has inherited from his school. As such, it demands herein that which it has received in France, namely, our serious consideration, because it is sincere after its own kind, has been worked out with modesty in respect of the final issues, while it exhibits there and

here some qualities of insight. It may be convenient
to summarise shortly the ruling plan of the procedure.
This begins and ends in a particular form of Kabalism
married to a mysticism of numbers which is not exactly
Kabalistic but has analogies or reflections of this kind,
and is otherwise of some antiquity. Once more, it is
not the invention of Papus. The one and the other are
centralised in a theosophic doctrine concerning the
Divine Name יהוה = JOD, HE, VAU, HE = JEVE =
Jehovah. From the mystery of this Name there depends the whole theosophy of Jewry as it is developed
in the *Sepher Ha Zohar*, or *Book of Splendour*, and the
commentaries thereon. Papus allocates the four suits
which comprise the Lesser Arcana of the Tarot to the
four letters of this Name, and the twenty-two Trumps,
which comprise the Major Arcana, he also allocates
thereto, and to the letters of the Hebrew alphabet.

We are concerned, however, more especially with the
Divine Name. The first letter, or *Jod*, represents, as he
tells us, the principle or origin of all things, and hence
eternal force. It is also, as we may learn from more
authoritative sources, the symbol of the Divine Royalty;
it is the occultation of wisdom and embodies its concealed things. It is represented as corresponding in the
Tarot to the suit of Wands or Sceptres and to the Kings
in the court cards. The second letter is *He*, which signifies substance in contradistinction to essence. It is said
by the Kabalists that the creation took place therewith:
it is the principle of production, and is thus termed
the mother. It corresponds in the Tarot to the suit of
Cups and to the Queens in the court cards. The third
letter is *Vau*, which signifies the affinity that subsists
between the first two letters, and it completes with

these the root-idea of the Trinity. In pure Kabalism, it is the bond of love, the mystery of union and of the intercommunication and superincession of the celestial virtues. It is also the Tree of Life. It corresponds in the Tarot to the suit of Swords and to the Knights in the court cards. The fourth letter is *He*, and it represents the transition from the metaphysical to the physical worlds, from the noumenal to the phenomenal. Christian Kabalism says that it is Divinity united hypostatically to a terrestrial body, or more literally, it is the Word made flesh; and although there is no question that nearly everything which has been put forward in this interest must be withdrawn, the doctrine of Messias in Jewry calls for reconsideration in the light of Christian Trinitarian doctrine. The second *He* corresponds in the Tarot to the suit of Pentacles, and to the Esquires, Pages or Knaves in the court cards. Kindred analogies are established in respect of ten numbered cards, and M. Charles Barlet, for whose authority Dr. Papus seems to assume responsibility, has contrived to connect them after another fashion with the letters of the Divine Name, through the court cards of their respective suits, by the help of an attribution which is specified in an essay on *The Initiative Tarot*.

So long as Papus has the obvious similitude of four suits to connect with four letters, his task has an air of simplicity, though its involved extensions may persuade few of his readers who are not otherwise persuaded previously. But while he recognises that it is still more important to establish the same analogies in respect of the Major Arcana, he passes of necessity among them into a region of greater uncertainty. However, as the result of his efforts, he has excogitated a septenary

application and finds that in each septenary it is possible to establish a dual correspondence with the Divine
Name by making the No. 4, which completes the first
tetrad, act as the first number which enters into the
second tetrad, thus: 1, 2, 3, 4=*Jod, He, Vau, He;*
4, 5, 6, 7 =*Jod, He, Vau, He.* To complete his analogy,
he adopts another method, explaining that in any
septenary of Trumps Major the cards 1 and 4 correspond to *Jod,* 2 and 5 to *He,* 3 and 6 to *Vau,* and the
7th card to the second *He.* The scheme is arbitrary
enough, as it is also contradictory enough. In the second
septenary he makes a second act of reversion, and thus
the correspondences to the 4 letters are 7 and 10 =*Jod;*
8 and 11=*He;* 9 and 12= *Vau;* 13 =*He* final. In
the third septenary, cards 13 and 16 =*Jod;* 14 and
17=*He;* 15 and 18=*Vau,* and he is then left with
the Trumps Major 19, 20 and 21, and with the Zero or
Fool. With these he does what he can, making a
brave struggle, but the result is not convincing.

I will now give a casual indication of his whole
difficulty: he does not know what to do with the card
which is numbered 0 in the Major Trump series, and
his septenary distribution leaves him therefore in the
lurch, while his allocation to the Hebrew letters outside those of the Divine Name is also open to question.
The attempt to connect the symbols of the Tarot with
the system of Kabalistic theosophy will seem in itself
arbitrary, but it can, under certain circumstances, produce very curious results. It did not, as I have said
originate with Papus, who follows the attribution given
by Éliphas Lévi; some vestiges of another scheme have
appeared in recent times, but they are also an imperfect
reading; the true reading has long been held in reserve,

and this so strictly that many who believe that they possess it have only been passed through one of the veils which conceal it. If ever the whole system contained in the Tarot came to be worked out, which will scarcely be in our time, it might even prove that its attribution to the Hebrew alphabet obtains only in the lesser degrees. To those, however, it is important. It is time otherwise to say that the connection with Kabalism may be in some respects like the Egyptian connection; as the latter is arbitrary and apart from evidence in history, so the other is also factitious and apart from final warrant in the highest world of symbolism. The work of Papus will appeal only to serious students, and it will be worth their while to take up his elements and seek to construct them independently Let them remember that there are four worlds in Kabalism, as there are four suits in the Tarot. One indication more: the Tarot in its proper understanding contains catholic symbolism, and when Papus says that it expresses the combinations of JEVE, this means that it typifies the elements and mysteries of the Divine Immanence. These are the true letters of the True Word, and as things without correspond to things within—that which is below to that which is above—so the characters which represent the human word are in certain respects their analogy.

In his later work, *Le Tarot Divinatoire*, published at Paris in the course of the last year, Papus dwells on the necessity of taking the Major and Minor Arcana in connection one with another, as distinguished from several French methods which lay stress on the major only. He affirms that the minor are as important for the study of the subject as are the Houses of the

Heavens for that of astrology. In respect of cartomancy at least, there is no question that he is right,
and this is his concern in the work. In respect of the
higher constructions, he promises a new edition of his
previous book, about which I do not think that we
need feel especially disturbed, since he gives ample
evidence that he adheres to the same system. As
regards divinatory methods, he draws his materials
from Moreau, from the cartomancist Etteila and from
D'Odoucet—from Etteila more than all. For those
who are concerned with such matters the result seems
therefore exhaustive, and it includes the modifications
of the root-meanings by the various combinations of
the cards in their apposition to one another as the
result of dealing. The Tarot cards have, however, just
been issued in England by the publishers of the present
work, together with their advanced interpretation on
mystic lines and a corrected mode of divination which,
so far as I am aware, has not been printed previously.
It will form an essential supplement to *The Tarot of the
Bohemians,* and will dispense with all need of reference
to *Le Tarot Divinatoire.*

The opportunity of the present edition has been
taken to revise the translation, which had certain
imperfections as it stood, owing to unfamiliarity with
the terms of occult literature.

A. E. WAITE.

PREFACE TO THE FRENCH EDITION

The Tarot pack of cards, transmitted by the Gypsies from generation to generation, is the primitive book of ancient initiation. This has been clearly demonstrated by William Postel, Court de Gébelin, Etteila, Éliphas Lévi and J. A. Vaillant.

The key to its construction and application has not yet been revealed, so far as I know. It is therefore my proposal to fill up this deficiency by supplying Initiates, or, in other words, those who are acquainted with the elements of occult science, with an accurate guide, which will assist them in the pursuit of their studies.

The uninitiated reader will find herein the explanation of the exalted philosophy and science of ancient Egypt, whilst ladies will be enabled to practise the use of the divining Tarot by methods which are rendered easy in Chapter XX.

The book has been so arranged that each part forms a complete whole, which can, if necessary, be studied separately.

I have used every effort to be as clear as possible; the public that has warmly welcomed my other books will, I hope, forgive the imperfections inherent to a work of this kind.

PAPUS.

PAPUS

CONTENTS

CHAPTER I

PART I

THE GENERAL KEY TO THE TAROT, GIVING THE ABSOLUTE KEY TO OCCULT SCIENCE

CHAPTER II

CHAPTER III

CHAPTER IV

CHAPTER V

CHAPTER VI

CHAPTER VII

PART II

SYMBOLISM IN THE TAROT. APPLICATION OF THE
GENERAL KEY TO THE SYMBOLISM

CHAPTER VIII

CHAPTER IX

CHAPTER X

CHAPTER XI

CHAPTER XII

CHAPTER XIII

CHAPTER XIV

PART III

APPLICATIONS OF THE TAROT

CHAPTER XV

CHAPTER XVI

CHAPTER XVII

CHAPTER XVIII

CHAPTER XIX

CHAPTER XX

CONTENTS xxvii

INTRODUCTION

TO

THE STUDY OF THE TAROT

A

THE TAROT

CHAPTER I

INTRODUCTION TO THE STUDY OF THE TAROT

Approaching End of Materialism—Synthesis—Occult Science—
The Secret Societies—The Cultus—*The People*, as an Organ
for the Transmission of Secret Knowledge—The Gypsies—
The Sacred Word of Freemasonry—Our Work.

"Therefore you must open the book and carefully weigh the statements
made in it. Then you will know that the drug within is of very different
value from the promise of the box, that is to say, that the subjects treated in
it are not so frivolous as the title may imply."—RABELAIS.

WE are on the eve of a complete transformation of our
scientific methods. Materialism has given us all that
we can expect from it, and inquirers, though disappointed as a rule, hope for great things from the future,
and are unwilling to spend more time in pursuing
the path adopted in modern days. Analysis has been
carried, in every branch of knowledge, as far as possible,
and has only deepened those moats which divide the
sciences.

Synthesis becomes necessary; but how can we realize
it?

If we would condescend to waive for one moment our
belief in the indefinite progress and necessary superiority

of later generations over the ancients, we should at once perceive that the colossal civilizations of antiquity possessed Science, Universities and Schools.

India and Egypt are even now strewn with valuable remains, which reveal to archæologists the existence of this ancient science.

We are in a position to affirm that the dominant character of its teaching was synthesis, which condenses in a few very simple laws the whole of acquired knowledge.

But the use of synthesis has been almost entirely lost, through several causes, which it is important to enumerate.

Amongst the ancients, knowledge was only transmitted to men whose worth had been proved by a series of tests. This transmission took place in the temples, under the name of Mysteries, and the adept assumed the title of Priest or Initiate.[1] This science was therefore secret or occult, and thus originated the name of Occult Science, given by our contemporaries to the ancient synthesis.

Another reason for the limited diffusion of the higher branches of knowledge, was the length and difficulty of the journeys involved before the most important centres of initiation could be reached.

However, as the Initiates found that a time was approaching when their doctrines might be lost to humanity, they made strenuous efforts to save the law of synthesis from oblivion. Three great methods were used for this purpose—

1. Secret societies, as a direct continuation of the Mysteries;

[1] See Jamblichus, Porphyry and Apuleius.

2. The cultus, as a symbolic translation of the higher doctrines, for the use of the people;

3. Lastly, the people itself became the unconscious depository of the doctrine.

Let us now see what use each of these groups made of the treasure confided thereto.

THE SECRET SOCIETIES

The school of Alexandria was the principal source from which the secret societies of the West arose.

The majority of the Initiates had taken refuge in the East, and recently (in 1884) the West discovered the existence in India, and above all in Thibet, of an occult fraternity, which possessed, practically, the ancient synthesis in its integrity. The Theosophical Society was founded with the object of uniting Western initiation with Oriental initiation.

But we are less interested in the existence of this doctrine in the East than in the history of the development of the initiatory societies in the West.

The Gnostic sects, the Arabs, Alchemists, Templars, Rosicrucians, and lastly the Freemasons, form the Western chain in the transmission of occult science.

A rapid glance over the doctrines of these associations is sufficient to prove that the present form of Freemasonry has almost entirely lost the meanings of those traditional symbols which constitute the trust that it ought to have transmitted through the ages.

The elaborate ceremonials of the ritual appear ridiculous to the vulgarian good sense of a lawyer or grocer—those actual modern representatives of the profound doctrines of antiquity.

We must, however, make some exceptions in favour of great thinkers, like Ragon and a few others.

In short, Freemasonry has lost the doctrine confided to it, and cannot by itself provide us with the synthetic law for which we are seeking.

THE CULTUS

The secret societies were designed to transmit in their symbolism the scientific side of primitive initiation, and the religious sects were to develop the philosophical and metaphysical aspects of the doctrine.

Every priest of an ancient creed was one of the Initiates; that is to say, he knew perfectly well that only one religion existed and that the cultus merely served to translate this religion to the different nations according to their particular temperaments. This fact led to an important result, namely, that a priest, no matter which of the gods he served, was received with honour in the temples of all the other deities, and was allowed to offer sacrifice to them. Yet this circumstance must not be supposed to imply any idea of polytheism. The Jewish High Priest in Jerusalem received one of the Initiates, Alexander the Great, into the Temple, and led him into the Holy of Holies, to offer sacrifice.

Our religious disputes for the supremacy of one creed over another would have caused much amusement to any of the ancient initiate-priests; they were unable to suppose that intelligent men could ignore the unity of all creeds in one fundamental religion.

Sectarianism, chiefly sustained by two creeds, equally

blinded by their errors, the Christian and the Mussulman, was the cause of the total loss of the secret doctrine, which gave the key to Synthetic Unity.

Still greater labour is required to re-discover Synthesis in our Western religions than to find it in Freemasonry.

The Jews alone possessed no longer the spirit but the letter of their oral or Kabalistic traditions. The Bible, written in Hebrew, is marvellous from this point of view, for it contains all the occult traditions, although its true sense has never yet been revealed. Fabre d'Olivet commenced this prodigious work, but the ignorant descendants of the Inquisition at Rome have placed such studies on the list of things prohibited.[1] Posterity will judge them.

Yet every cultus has its tradition, its book, its Bible, which teach those who know how to read them the unity of all creeds, in spite of the difference existing in the ritual of various countries.

The *Sepher Bereshith* of Moses is the Jewish Bible; the *Apocalypse* and the *Esoteric Gospels* form the Christian Bible; the *Legend of Hiram* is the Bible of Freemasonry; the *Odyssey* is the Bible of the so-called polytheism of Greece; the *Æneid* that of Rome; and lastly the *Hindu Vedas* and the *Mussulman Koran* are well known to all students of ancient theology.

To any one possessing the key, all these Bibles reveal the same doctrine; but this key, which can open Esotericism, is lost by the sectarians of our Western creeds. It is therefore useless to seek for it any longer amongst them.

[1] See Fabre d'Olivet, *La Langue Hébraïque Restituée.*

THE PEOPLE

The Sages were under no illusions respecting the possible future of the tradition which they confided to the intelligence and virtue of future generations.

Moses had chosen a people to transmit through succeeding ages the book which contained all the science of Egypt; but before Moses, the Hindu Initiates had selected a nation to hand down to the generations of the future the primitive doctrines of the great civili-zations of the Atlantides.

The people have never disappointed the expectations of those who trusted them. Understanding none of the truths which they possessed, they carefully abstained from altering them in any way, and treated the least attack made upon them as sacrilege.

Thus the Jews have transmitted intact to us the letters which form the *Sepher* of Moses. But Moses had not solved the problem so authoritatively as the Thibetans.

It was a great thing to give the people a book which it could adore respectfully, and always guard intact; but to give it a book which would enable it to live, was yet better.

The people intrusted with the transmission of occult doctrines from the earliest ages were the Bohemian or Gypsy race.

THE GYPSIES

The Gypsies possess a Bible which has proved their means of gaining a livelihood, for it enables them to tell fortunes; at the same time it has been a perpetual source of amusement, for it enables them to gamble.

Yes; the game of cards called the Tarot, which the Gypsies possess, is the Bible of Bibles. It is the book of Thoth Hermes Trismegistus, the book of Adam, the book of the primitive Revelation of ancient civilizations.

Thus whilst the Freemason, an intelligent and virtuous man, has lost the tradition; whilst the priest, also intelligent and virtuous, has lost his esotericism; the Gypsy, although both ignorant and vicious, has given us the key which enables us to explain all the symbolism of the ages.

We must admire the wisdom of the Initiates, who utilized vice and made it produce more beneficial results than virtue.

The Gypsy pack of cards is a wonderful book according to Court de Gébelin[1] and Vaillant.[2] This pack, under the name of TAROT,[3] THORA,[4] ROTA,[5] has formed the basis of the synthetic teachings of all the ancient nations successively.[6]

In it, where a man of the people only sees a means of amusement, the thinker will find the key to an obscure tradition. Raymond Lully based his *Ars Magna* upon the Tarot; Jerome Cardan wrote a treatise upon subtility from the keys of the Tarot;[7] William Postel found therein the key to the ancient mysteries; whilst

---

[1] Court de Gébelin.—*Le Monde Primitif.*
[2] Vaillant.—*Les Rômes, Histoire des Bohémiens.*
[3] Éliphas Lévi.—*Rituel de la Haute Magie.*
[4] Vaillant.—*Op. cit.*
[5] William Postel.—*Clavis.*
[6] Vaillant.—*Op. cit.*
[7] Éliphas Lévi.—*Op. cit.*

Louis-Claude de Saint-Martin, the Unknown Philosopher, discovered within it the mysterious links which unite God, the Universe and Man!

Through the Tarot we are now able to discern and develop the synthetic law, concealed in all these symbolisms.

The hour is approaching when the missing word will be restored. Masters, Rosicrucians and Kadosh, you who form the sacred triangle of Masonic initiation, do you remember!

Remember, MASTER, that illustrious man, killed through the most cowardly of conspiracies; remember Hiram, whose resurrection, promised by the Branch of Acacia, thou art looking for in faith!

Remember, ROSICRUCIAN, the mysterious Word which thou hast sought so long, of which the meaning still escapes thee!

Remember, KADOSH, the magnificent symbol which radiated from the centre of the luminous triangle, when the real meaning of the letter G was revealed to thee!

HIRAM—INRI—YOD-HE-VAU-HE—indicate the same mystery under different aspects.

He who understands one of these words possesses the key which opens the tomb of Hiram, the symbol of the synthetic science of the Ancients; he can open the tomb and fearlessly touch the heart of the revered Master, the symbol of esoteric teaching.

The whole Tarot is based upon the word ROTA, arranged as a wheel.

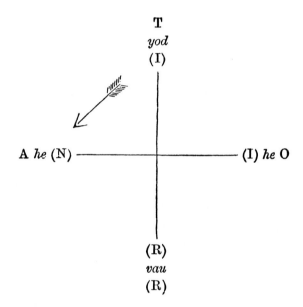

INRI is the word which indicates the Unity of your origin, Freemasons and Catholics! *Igne Natura Renovatur Integra; Iesus Nazareus Rex Iudeorum;* are the opposite poles, scientific and religious, physical and metaphysical, of the same doctrine.

YOD-HE-VAU-HE (יהוה) is the word which indicates to you both, Freemasons and Kabalists, the unity of your origin. TAROT, THORA, ROTA are the words which point out to you all, Easterns and Westerns, the unity of your requirements and of your aspirations in the eternal Adam-Eve, the source of all our knowledge and of all our creeds.

All honour, therefore, to the Gypsy Nomad, to whom we are indebted for the preservation of this marvellous instrument, the synthetic summary of the whole teaching of antiquity.

OUR WORK

We will commence by a preliminary study of the elements of the Kabalah and of numbers.

Supplied with these data, we will explain the construction of the Tarot in all its details, studying separately each of the pieces which compose our machine, then studying the action of these pieces upon each other. Upon this point we shall be as explicit as possible. We will next touch upon some applications of the machine, but upon a few only, leaving to the genuine inquirer the work of discovering others. We must confine our personal work to the gift of a key, based upon a synthetic formula; we can only supply the implement of labour, in order that those who wish for knowledge may use it as they like; and we feel assured that they will understand the utility of our efforts and of their own.

Lastly, we will do our best to explain the elements of divination by the Tarot as practised by the Gypsies.

But those who think that occult science should not be revealed must not be too angry with us. Experience has taught us that everything may be fearlessly said; those only who should understand can understand; the others will accuse our work of being obscure and incomprehensible.

We have warned them by placing at the head of this volume—

For the exclusive use of Initiates.

It is one characteristic of the study of true occult science that it may be freely explained to all men. Like the parables, so dear to the ancients, it appears to many as only the expression of the flight of a bold imagination: we need, therefore, never be afraid of speaking too openly; the Word will only reach those who should be touched thereby.

To you all, philosophers of Unity, enemies of scientific, social and religious sectarianism, 1 now address myself, to you I dedicate this result of several years' study. May I thus aid in the erection of the temple which you are about to raise to the honour of the UNKNOWN GOD, from whom all the others emanate throughout Eternity!

PART I

GENERAL KEY TO THE TAROT
GIVING THE ABSOLUTE KEY TO OCCULT SCIENCE

CHAPTER II

יהוה

THE SACRED WORD YOD-HE-VAU-HE

The Kabalah and the Sacred Word—The Yod—The He—The Vau
—The second He—Synthesis of the Sacred Word.

ACCORDING to the ancient oral tradition of the Hebrews,
or *Kabalah*,[1] a sacred word exists, which gives to the
mortal who can discover the correct way of pronouncing
it, the key to all the sciences, divine and human. This
word, which the common people of Israel never uttered,
and which the High Priest pronounced once a year,
amidst the shouts of the laity, is found at the head of
every initiatory ritual; it radiates from the centre of
the flaming triangle in the 33rd degree of the Scottish
Rite of Freemasonry; it is displayed above the gate-

---

[1] " It appears, according to the most famous rabbis, that Moses
himself, foreseeing the fate which awaited his book, and the false
interpretations which would be given to it in the course of time,
resorted to an oral law, which he delivered verbally to reliable
men, whose fidelity he had tested, whom also he charged to transmit it to others in the secret of the sanctuary; these in their
turn, transmitting it from age to age, secured its preservation
even for the most distant posterity. This oral law, which modern
Jews still flatter themselves that they possess, is called the
Kabalah, from a Hebrew word which signifies that which is received, that which comes from elsewhere, that which passes from
hand to hand."—FABRE D'OLIVET, *La Langue Hébraïque Restituée*,
p. 29.

ways of our old cathedrals; it is formed of four Hebrew letters, and reads thus, *Yod-he-vau-he*, יהוה.

It is used in the *Sepher Bereshith*, or Genesis of Moses, to designate the divinity, and its grammatical construction recalls even by its formation[1] the attributes which men have always delighted to ascribe to God. Now, we shall see that the powers attributed to this word are real up to a certain point, for with its aid the symbolical gate of the arch, which contains the explanation of the whole doctrine of ancient science, is easily opened. It is therefore necessary to enter into some detail respecting it.

The word is formed of four letters, *Yod* (י), *he* (ה), *vau* (ו), *he* (ה). The last letter *he* is thus repeated twice.

A number is attributed to each letter of the Hebrew alphabet. We must look at those which relate to the letters that we are now considering.

$$
\begin{array}{lll}
\text{י} \quad \text{Yod} & = & 10 \\
\text{ה} \quad \text{he} & = & 5 \\
\text{ו} \quad \text{vau} & = & 6 \\
\end{array}
$$

---

[1] "This name presents first the sign which indicates life, repeated twice, and thus forming the essentially living root EE (הה). This root is never used as a noun, and is the only one which enjoys such prerogative. It is from its formation not only a verb, but an unique verb, from which all the others are merely derivations; in short, the verb הוה (ÉVÉ), to be, being. Here, as we can see, and as I have carefully explained in my Hebrew grammar, the sign of intelligible light ו (VÔ) is placed in the midst of the root of life. Moses, when using this unique verb to form the proper name of the Being of Beings, added to it the sign of potential manifestation and of eternity, י (I); he thus obtained יהוה (IEVE), in which the facultative Being is placed

The total numerical value of the word יהוה is therefore

$$10 + 5 + 6 + 5 = 26.$$

Let us now study each letter separately.

THE YOD

The *Yod*, shaped like a comma or a dot, represents the principle or origin of all things.

The other letters of the Hebrew alphabet are all produced by different combinations of the letter *Yod*.[1] The synthetic study of nature had led the ancients to conclude that one law only existed, and ruled all natural productions. This law, the basis of analogy, placed the Unity-principle at the origin of all things, and regarded them as the reflections at various degrees of this Unity-principle. Thus, the *Yod*, which alone forms all the other letters, and therefore all the words and all the phrases of the alphabet, was justly used as the image and representation of this Unity-principle, of which the profane had no knowledge.

Thus also the law which presided over the creation of the Hebrew language is the same law that presided over the creation of the Universe, and to know the one is to know the other, unreservedly. The *Sepher Yetzirah*,[2] one of the most ancient books of the Kabalah proves this fact.

Before proceeding any further, let us illustrate the definition which we have just given of the *Yod* by an

---

between a past tense without origin, and a future without limit. This admirable word thus exactly signifies the Being who is, who was and who will be."—FABRE D'OLIVET, *La Langue Hébraïque Restituée.*

[1] See the *Kabbala Denudata.*

[2] Translated into English by Dr. Wynn Westcott.

example. The first letter of the Hebrew alphabet, the *aleph* (א), is composed of four *yods* placed opposite to each other; the other letters are all formed on the same basis.[1]

The numerical value of the *yod* leads to other considerations. The Unity-principle, according to the doctrine of the Kabalists, is also the Unity-end of beings and of things, so that eternity, from this point of view, is only an eternal present. The ancients used a dot in the centre of a circle as the symbol of this idea, the representation of the Unity-principle (*the dot*) in the centre of eternity (*the circle*, a line without beginning or end).[2]

According to these demonstrations, the Unity is regarded as the whole, of which all created beings are only the constituent parts; just as the Unity-man is formed of an agglomeration of molecules, which compose his being.

The Kabalah, therefore, places at the origin of all things the absolute assertion of the being by itself, of the Ego-Unity, which is represented by the *yod* symbolically, and by the number 10. This number 10,

[1] See the *Kabbala Denudata.*
[2] See Kircher, *Œdipus Ægyptiacus.*
   „ Lenain, *La Science Kabbalistique.*
   „ J. Dée, *Monas Hieroglyphica.*

representing the All-principle 1 with the Zero-nothing 0, well supplies the requisite conditions.[1]

THE HE [2]

But the Ego cannot be realized except through its opposition to the Non-Ego. The assertion of the Ego is scarcely established, when we must instantly realize a reaction of the Ego, or Absolute, upon itself, from which the conception of its existence will be drawn, by a kind of division of the Unity. This is the origin of duality, of opposition, of the Binary, the image of femininity, even as the Unity is the image of the masculine. Ten, divided by itself, in opposition to itself, then equals $\frac{10}{2} = 5$, and five is the number of the letter *He*, the second letter of the Great Sacred Name.

The *He* therefore represents the passive in relation to the *Yod*, which symbolizes the active; the Non-Ego in relation to the Ego, the woman relatively to the man; the substance relatively to the essence; life in its relation to the soul, &c., &c.

THE VAU [3]

But the opposition of the Ego and the Non-Ego immediately gives rise to another factor, which is the Affinity existing between this Ego and this Non-Ego.

Now the *Vau*, the sixth letter of the Hebrew alphabet,

[1] See Saint-Martin, *Tableau Naturel des rapports qui existent entre Dieu, l'Homme et l'Univers.*
See Lacuria, *Harmonies de l'Être exprimées par les nombres.*
[2] See Éliphas Lévi, *Dogme et Rituel de la Haute Magie; la Clef des Grands Mystères;*—Lacuria, *op. cit.*
[3] See Fabre d'Olivet, *La Langue Hébraïque Restituée.*

produced by 10 (yod) + 5 (he) = 15 = 6 (or 1 + 5), signifies link or analogy. It is the link which, uniting antagonisms in the whole of nature, constitutes the third word of this mysterious Trinity: Ego —Non-Ego; affinity of the Ego with the Non-Ego.

THE 2ND HE

Nothing can exist beyond this Trinity, considered as a law.

The Trinity is the synthetic and absolute formula to which all the sciences converge; and this formula, forgotten with regard to its scientific value, has been transmitted to us integrally by all the religions of the world, those unconscious depositaries of the SCIENCE-WISDOM of primitive civilizations.[1]

Thus, the Great Sacred Name is formed of three letters only. The fourth term of the Name is produced by the repetition of the second letter, the *He*.

This repetition indicates the passage of the Trinitarian law into a new application—that is, to speak correctly, a transition from the metaphysical to the physical world, or generally, of any world whatever to the world that immediately follows it.[2]

The knowledge of the property of the second *He* is

---

[1] See Louis Lucas, *Le Roman alchimique.*

"*Præter hæc tria numera non est alia magnitudo, quod tria sunt omnia, et ter undecumque, ut pythagorici dicunt; omne et omnia tribus determinata sunt.*"—ARISTOTLE. (Quoted by Ostrowski, page 24 of his *Mathèse.*)

[2] Ostrowski has seen this clearly. "The passage of 3 into 4 corresponds to that of the Trimurti in Maïa, and as the latter opens the second ternary of the pregenesetic decade, so the figure 4 opens the second ternary of our genesetic decimal."—*Mathèse.* p. 25.

the key to the whole Divine Name, in every application of which it is susceptible. We shall presently see the proof of this statement.

SUMMARY CONCERNING THE WORD YOD-HE-VAU-HE

Now that we have separately studied each of the letters that compose the Sacred Name, we will apply the law of synthesis to them, and sum up the results obtained.

The word *Yod-he-vau-he* is formed of four letters, signifying :

The Yod The active principle pre-eminent.
The Ego = 10.

The He The passive principle pre-eminent.
The Non-Ego = 5.

The Vau The Median letter, the *link*, which unites the active to the passive.
The Affinity between the Ego and the Non-Ego = 6.

These three letters express the Trinitarian law of the Absolute.

The 2nd He The second *He* marks the passage from one world to another. The Transition.

This second *He* represents the complete Being, comprising in one Absolute Unity the three letters which compose it : Ego, Non-Ego, Affinity.

It indicates the passage from the noumenal to the phenomenal or reciprocal; it serves as the means of ascension from one scale to another.

REPRESENTATION OF THE SACRED WORD

The word *Yod-he-vau-he* can be represented in various ways, which are all useful.

The circle can be drawn in this way—

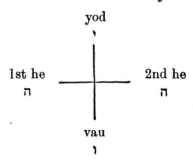

But since the second *He*, the sign of transition, becomes the active entity in the following scale, *i.e.*, since this *He* only represents a *yod* in germ,[1] the Sacred Word can be represented, with the *second he under the first yod*, thus—

> *yod*   1*st he*   *vau*
> 2*nd he*

Lastly, a third method of representing the word consists in enveloping the Trinity, *Yod-he-vau*, with the tonalising letter, or second He, thus—

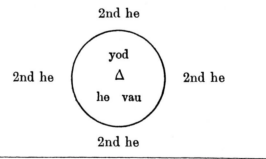

---

[1] The second He, upon which we are intentionally dwelling at some length, may be compared to *a grain of wheat* relatively to the

Now we will leave these data, to which we must return later on, and speak of the occult or Pythagorean conception of numbers.

---

ear. The ear, the Trinity manifest, or *yod-he-vau,* exerts all its activity in the production of the grain of wheat, or second *He.* But this grain of wheat is only the *transition* between the ear which gave it birth and the ear to which it will itself give birth in the following generation. It is the transition between one generation and another, which it contains in germ; this is why the second *He* is a *Yod* in germ.

CHAPTER III

THE ESOTERICISM OF NUMBERS

The Theosophic Numbers and Operations—Signification of the Numbers.

THE NUMBERS

THE ancients had a conception of numbers which is almost lost in modern times.

The idea of the Unity in all its manifestations led to numbers being considered as the expression of absolute laws. This led to the veneration expressed for the 3 or for the 4 throughout antiquity, which feeling is so incomprehensible to our mathematicians.

It is however evident that if the ancients had not known how to work any other problems than those that we now use, nothing could have led them to the ideas which we find current in the Hindu, Egyptian and Greek Universities.[1]

What then are these operations, that our savants do not know?

They are of two kinds: theosophic reduction and theosophic addition.

These operations are theosophic because they cause the essential laws of nature to penetrate throughout

---

[1] See Fabre d'Olivet, *La Langue Hebraïque Restituee* and Saint-Yves d'Alveydre, *Mission des Juifs.*

the world; they cannot be included in the science of phenomena, for they tower above it, soaring into the heights of pure intellectuality.

They therefore formed the basis of the secret and oral instruction confided to a few chosen men, under the name of Esotericism.

1. *Theosophic Reduction*

Theosophic reduction consists in reducing all the numbers formed of two or several figures to the number of a single figure, and this is done by adding together the figures which compose the number, until only one remains.

EXAMPLE :

$$10 = 1 + 0 = 1$$
$$11 = 1 + 1 = 2$$
$$12 = 1 + 2 = 3$$
$$126 = 1 + 2 + 6 = 9$$
$$2488 = 2 + 4 + 8 + 8 = 22 = 2 + 2 = 4$$

This operation corresponds to that which is now called the proof by 9.

2. *Theosophic Addition*

Theosophic addition consists in ascertaining the theosophic value of a number, by adding together arithmetically all the figures from unity to itself inclusively.

Thus, the figure 4, in theosophic addition, equals all

the figures from 1 to 4 inclusively, added together—
that is to say, $1+2+3+4=10$.

The figure 7 equals—

$$1+2+3+4+5+6+7=28=2+8=10.$$

Theosophic reduction and addition are the two operations which it is indispensable to know, if we would understand the secrets of antiquity.[1]

Let us now apply these rules to all the numbers, that we may discover the law which directs their progression.

Theosophic reduction shows us that all numbers, whatever they may be, are reducible in themselves to the nine first, since they are all brought down to numbers of a single figure.

But this consideration is not sufficient, and theosophic addition will now furnish us with new light.

Through it we find that 1, 4, 7, 10 are equal to 1.

for : $1=1$
$4=1+2+3+4=10=1$
$7=1+2+3+4+5+6+7=28=10=1$
$10=1$

Hence all the three numbers ultimately return to the figure 1, thus—

1. 2. 3   4. 5. 6
$4=10=1$ $7=28=10=1$

<hr>

[1] See for more details : *Traité Élémentaire de Science Occulte*, by Papus, chap. ii.

.. 3

i. 6

etc.

eration are : (1) That all the numbers, in their evolution, reproduce the 4 first ;

(2) That the last of these 4 first, the figure 4, represents the unity at a different octave.

The sequence of the numbers may therefore be written in this way—

$$
\begin{array}{ccc}
1. & 2. & 3 \\
4. & 5. & 6 \\
7. & 8. & 9 \\
10. & 11. & 12 \\
13. & 14. & 15 \\
16. & 17. & 18 \\
19 & \cdots & \\
\end{array}
$$

We may notice that 4, 7, 10, 13, 16, 19, etc., are only different conceptions of the unity, and this may be proved by the application of theosophic addition and reduction thus—

$$
\begin{aligned}
1 &= 1 \\
4 &= 1+2+3+4 = 10 = 1 \\
7 &= 1+2+3+4+\ 5+6+7 = 28 = 10 = 1 \\
10 &= 1 \\
13 &= 4 = 10 = 1 \\
16 &= 7 = 28 = 10 = 1 \\
19 &= 10 = 1, \text{ etc., etc.}
\end{aligned}
$$

We see that in every three numbers the series reverts to the unity abruptly, whilst it returns to it progressively in the two intermediate numbers.

Let us now repeat that the knowledge of the laws of numbers and the study of them, made as we have here indicated, will give the key to all occult science.

We can sum up the preceding statements in the following conclusion : that all numbers may be reduced, in a final analysis, to the series of the 4 first, thus arranged—

1. 2. 3

4

THE SIGNIFICATION OF NUMBERS

But our knowledge of the numerical science of the ancients does not end here. That science also attributed a meaning to each number.

Since we have reduced the series of all the numbers to the 4 first, it will suffice for us to know the meaning attributed to these 4 first.

The Unity represents the creative principle of numbers, since the others emanate therefrom ; it is the pre-eminent active principle.

But the Unity alone cannot produce anything except by opposing itself to itself, thus $\frac{1}{1}$. From this proceeds duality, the principle of opposition represented by two, the pre-eminent passive principle.

From the union of the Unity and Duality proceeds the third principle, which unites the two opposites in one common neutrality, $1+2=3$. Three is the pre-eminent neuter principle.

But these three principles reduce themselves into

the fourth, which merely represents a new acceptation
of the Unity as an active principle.[1]

The law of these principles is therefore as follows :—

Unity or return to unity	Opposition antagonism	Action of opposition upon the unity
Active 1	Passive 2	Neuter 3
Active 4	Etc.	

Active
1

Passive   Passive-Active
2   4

Neuter
3

---

[1] See for further enlightenment the *Traité Élémentaire de Science Occulte*, p. 49 and following.

CHAPTER IV

ANALOGY BETWEEN THE SACRED WORD AND NUMBERS

The Kabalistic Word and the Series of Numbers—Explanation of the *Tretractys* of Pythagoras—Plan of the General Law

NUMBERS AND THE KABALISTIC WORD

THIS sequence of numbers 1, 2, 3 and 4, representing the active, the passive, the neuter and a second active principle, corresponds in all points with the series of the letters of the Sacred Name, so that the latter may be thus written—

$$\text{Yod — He — Vau}$$
$$\text{2nd He} = \text{Yod, etc.,}$$

which demonstrates analogically that—

1	represents	Yod
2	—	He
3	—	Vau
4	—	The 2nd He

We can prove the truth of these analogies by the identity of the action of the number 4, which becomes an unity ($4 = 10 = 1$), and of the second *He*, which represents the Yod of the following sequence.

In comparing the two identical series we obtain the following figures—

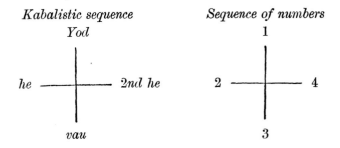

Kabalistic sequence   *Sequence of numbers*

Identity of the two sequences

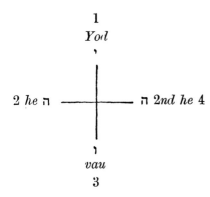

We can now understand why Pythagoras, initiated in Egypt into the mysteries of the sacred word *Yod-he-vau-he*, replaced this word in his esoteric teachings by the sequence of the 4 first numbers or tetractys.

This sequence of numbers is, in all points, identical with the sequence of the letters of the Sacred Name, and the tetractys of Pythagoras, 1, 2, 3, 4, equals and absolutely represents the word *Yod-he-vau-he*.

The sequence of the numbers, or the sequence of the

c

letters, therefore, resolves itself definitely into the following data —

 1 Term positive and generator.
        The *Yod* or the 1.

 1 Term negative or generant.
        The *He* or the 2.

 1 Term neuter or generated proceeding from the two preceding.
        The *Vau* or the 3.

 1 Term of transition individualizing itself in the following sequence,
        The *2nd He* or the 4.

Provided with these preliminary data, which are absolutely indispensable, let us now take our pack of cards, or Tarot, and see if we cannot find the universal law therein—

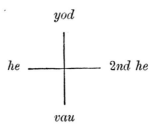

symbolized through antiquity by the Cross.

CHAPTER V

THE KEY TO THE MINOR ARCANA

Formation of the Tarot—Study of a Suit—The Four Court Cards
—The Ten Numbers—Affinity between the Court Cards and
the Numbers—Study of the Four Suits—General Study of
the Minor Arcana.

THE KEY TO THE MINOR ARCANA

THE Tarot is composed of 78 cards, divided as follows—

56 cards called the minor arcana.
22 cards called the major arcana.

The 56 minor arcana are formed of 4 series of 14
cards each.

The 22 major arcana are formed of 21 numbered
cards and of 1 un-numbered.

In order to study the Tarot with success, we must
then arrange the following packets—

4 packets of 14 cards each.
$$14 + 14 + 14 + 14 \quad = \quad 56$$
1 packet of 21 cards............ $=$ 21
1 packet of 1 card.............. $=$ 1
___
78

We shall return to the origin of this marvellous conception of the human mind, but for the present we

must confine ourselves to the dissection of the machine, and the display of its mysterious arrangement.

Starting from a fixed and immovable principle, the constitution of the Sacred Tetragrammaton, *Yod-he-vau-he*, the Tarot develops the most diverse combinations, without one departure from its basis. We shall now unveil this wonderful construction, which confirms in its application the universal law of analogies.

The explanations which follow may appear dry to some persons; but they must remember that we are here giving them an almost infallible key to the ancient or occult science; and they will understand that they must open the door of the sacred arch for themselves.

STUDY OF A SUIT

Let us now take one of the packets of fourteen cards and analyze its construction.

This packet, taken as a whole, corresponds to one of the suits of our pack of cards. The 4 packets respectively represent the Wands or Sceptres, corresponding to our clubs; the Cups or Goblets, corresponding to our hearts; the Swords, corresponding to our spades; and Money or Pentacles, corresponding to our diamonds.

We shall now study one of these packets, for instance that of Sceptres.

The packet consists of 4 figures: the king, queen, knight and knave, and of ten cards which simply bear numbers:—The ace, two, three, four, five, six, seven, eight, nine and ten.

QUEEN of SCEPTRES

KNAVE of SCEPTRES

KNIGHT of SCEPTRES

To face page 36

THE FOUR PICTURES

We must first consider the court cards—

The king represents the active, the man, or male.

The queen represents the passive, the woman, or female.

The knight represents the neuter, the adolescent.

Lastly, the knave represents the 4th term of the sequence, which may be figured in this way—

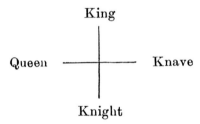

This sequence is only an application of the general law *Yod-he-vau-he*, which we already know, and the analogy is easily established—

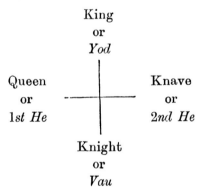

The knave therefore corresponds with the *second He*, i.e. it is only a term of transition; but transition between what? Between the four figures and the ten numbers following.

THE TEN NUMBERS

Let us next study these numbers. We are acquainted with the Law of numbers, or law of the sequences, which we have already stated in these terms—

$$1 - 2.\ 3$$
$$4 - 5.\ 6$$
$$7 - \text{etc.}$$

The ten cards cannot escape from this law, and we may at once arrange them in series.

The first series will be formed of the ace, or 1, representing the active; of the 2, personating the passive; of the 3 for the neuter; and lastly of the 4, which represents the transition from one series to another.

1, 2, 3, 4 therefore correspond also with the *Yod-he-vau-he*, and are thus formulated—

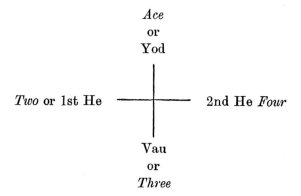

The other series follow the same rule exactly, the second *He* of the preceding series becoming the *Yod* of the following series: thus 4, the fourth term of the first series, becomes the first term of the second series;

7, the fourth term of the second, becomes the first term of the third, as follows—

THE SERIES OF NUMBERS

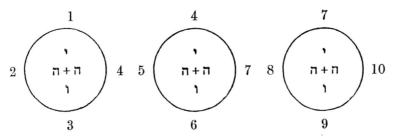

We see that the same law, *Yod-he-vau-he*, can be applied to these series. Since this law is also applicable to the four figures, we can make a comparison based on the following proposition—

Two terms (the numbers and the figures) equal to a same third (the law *Yod-he-vau-he*) are equal between themselves.

THE SEQUENCE IN ONE SUIT

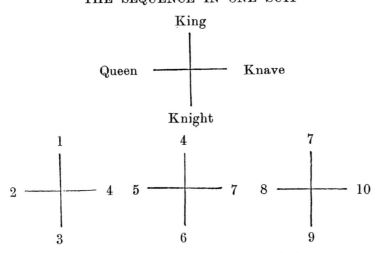

If we now group all the numbers of the sequence

according to that letter of the Tetragrammaton to which they are analogous, we shall find—

Representing *Yod*   1 — 4 — 7
Representing the 1*st He*   2 — 5 — 8
Representing the *Vau*   3 — 6 — 9
Representing the 2*nd He*   10

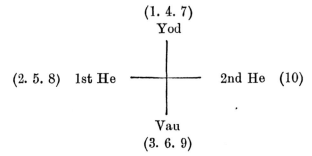

$$(1.\ 4.\ 7)$$
$$\text{Yod}$$

$(2.\ 5.\ 8)$ 1st He ——|—— 2nd He (10)

$$\text{Vau}$$
$$(3.\ 6.\ 9)$$

The figure 10 therefore acts for the numbers as the knave acts for the figures, that is to say, it serves as a transition. Between what? Between one suit and another.

AFFINITY BETWEEN THE PICTURES AND THE NUMBERS

We have already studied both the pictures and the numbers separately; let us now see what connection exists between them.

If we group the similar terms according to the identical Law which rules them, we shall find them as follows—

The King is the   *Yod* of 1. 4. 7
The Queen —   *He*   of 2. 5. 8
The Knight —   *Vau* of 3. 6. 9
The Knave — 2*nd He* of   10

The sequence of the pictures is reproduced three times in the series of numbers, that is to say, each series of numbers represents a conception of the pictures in each of the three Kabalistic worlds.

To face page 40

The series 1, 2, 3, 4 represents the emanation of the sequence king, queen, knight, knave, in the divine world.

The series 4, 5, 6, 7 represents this evolution in the human world.

The series 7, 8, 9, 10 represents this evolution in the material world.

Each suit is a complete whole, formed like intelligent beings:—

Of a material body:

(Knight — 7.8.9)

Of a vital force:

(Queen — 4.5.6)

Of an intellect:

(King — 1.2.3)

Of reproductive organs:

(Knave — 10)

Each of these parts can subdivide itself into three others, as the numbers indicate.[1]

Let us, however, return to our deduction, and by summing up the results obtained, we shall find—

Representations of the *Yod*:

The King
The 1 or Ace
The 4
The 7

Representations of the *He*:

The Queen
The 2
The 5
The 8

---

[1] This application of the Tarot will explain to Initiates the results consequent on the laws which govern the Tarot system.

Representations of the *Vau:*

> The Knight
> The 3
> The 6
> The 9

Representations of the *2nd He:*

> The Knave
> The 10

DIAGRAM OF ONE SUIT

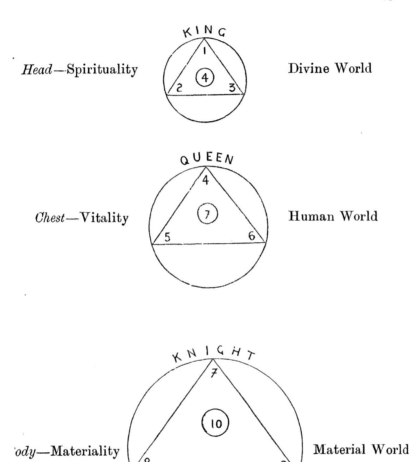

Head—Spirituality   Divine World

Chest—Vitality   Human World

Body—Materiality   Material World

Transition from
one being to
another

Transition from
one world to
another

STUDY OF THE FOUR SUITS

Supplied with these data, let us continue our study and apply the same principle to the other cards.

The laws which we have defined for the constitution of one suit, apply in the same way to the other three suits.

But when we consider the four suits of the Tarot, new deductions will be called forth. We must remember that these suits are: the Sceptre, the Cup, the Sword, and the Money or Pentacles.

The Sceptre represents the Male or the Active.

The Cup is the image of the Passive or Feminine.

The Sword represents the union of the two by its crucial form.

Lastly, the Pentacles represent the second *He*.

The authors who have philosophically studied the Tarot are all unanimous in asserting the analogy that exists between the Tetragrammaton and the four suits. William Postel[1] and above all Éliphas Lévi[2] have developed these studies with important results, and they show us the four letters of Tetragrammaton applied in the symbolism of every cultus.

We must pause one moment to notice the analogy between these letters and the symbols of the Christian religion.

The Yod or Sceptre of the Tarot is represented by the episcopal crosier;

The 1st He or Cup is represented by the Chalice;

The Vau or Sword by the Cross, bearing the same form;

The 2nd He or Pentacles by the Host, the transition from the natural to the Supernatural world.

---

[1] *Clavis absconditorum a constitutione mundi.*

[2] Éliphas Lévi, *Dogme et Rituel de la Haute Magie.*

To face page 44

The series which we have studied in one suit is defined with equal strictness in the four suits regarded as a whole, thus—

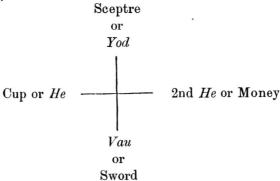

Sceptre
or
Yod

Cup or *He* ———————— 2nd *He* or Money

Vau
or
Sword

A COMPREHENSIVE GLANCE AT THE MINOR ARCANA

If we look back a little, we can easily judge the road so far traversed.

The four suits considered *in globo* have shown us the application of the law *Yod-he-vau-he.*

But the same law is reproduced in each of the suits taken separately.

The four court cards represent *Yod-he-vau-he ;*

The four series of numbers represent the Sacred Name in like manner.

Let us now arrange all the cards according to their affinities, and we shall obtain the following results—

The 4 Kings ⎫
The 4 Aces ⎬ = *Yod*
The 4 Fours ⎪
The 4 Sevens ⎭

The 4 Queens ⎫
The 4 Twos   ⎬ = *He*
The 4 Fives ⎪
The 4 Eights ⎭

$$
\left.\begin{array}{l}
\text{The 4 Knights} \\
\text{The 4 Threes} \\
\text{The 4 Sixes} \\
\text{The 4 Nines}
\end{array}\right\} = Vau
$$

$$
\left.\begin{array}{l}
\text{The 4 Knaves} \\
\text{The 4 Tens}
\end{array}\right\} = He
$$

If we wished to represent this arrangement by a synthetic diagram, we should place the Sacred Name in the centre of a circle divided into four parts, which respectively correspond with each of the letters *Yod-he-vau-he*. In each of the quarters, the cards that are analogous to the letters of Tetragrammaton will radiate from the centre. See the diagram on page opposite.

The pictures have the same connection with the suits as the numbers have with the pictures.

The sequence of the pictures is reproduced in the three worlds by the numbers; the same thing takes place in the sequence of suits: Sceptre, Cup, Sword, Pentacles are reproduced in the pictures.

The Sceptre is the *Yod* of the 4 Kings.
The Cup is the *He* of the 4 Queens.
The Sword is the *Vau* of the 4 Knights.
The Pentacles is the *He* of the 4 Knaves.

And just as each suit is a complete whole, formed of a body, of a soul, and of a mind or vital force, so the four suits constitute together a complete whole as follows :—

The material body of the minor arcana:

The 4 Knights
The 4 Sevens
The 4 Eights
The 4 Nines

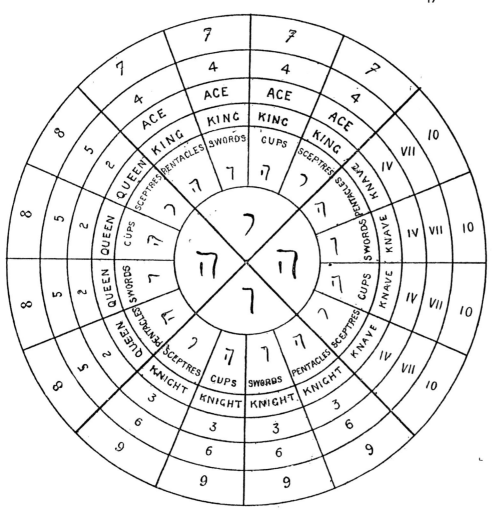

GENERAL FIGURE OF THE MINOR ARCANA.—*Disposition of Series.*

The vital body of the minor arcana :

           The 4 Queens
           The 4 Fours
           The 4 Fives
           The 4 Sixes

To face page 48

The intellectual body:

> The 4 Kings
> The 4 Aces
> The 4 Twos
> The 4 Threes

Reproductive organs:

> The 4 Knaves
> The 4 Tens

It is possible only to indicate the instructive affinities shown in these figures; they can be developed at great length.

We give the bare outlines to demonstrate the method of analogy, the method of occult science, to which we have so frequently alluded in our preceding works.

We need only compare this last diagram, which represents the four suits, with the first, which depicted one of them only, to see at once that the law upon which both diagrams are constructed is the same, though its applications are varied.

It is the same law by which the cells that form the human being group themselves to constitute organs; the organs group themselves to form members; and the grouping of the latter produces the individual.[1]

We may draw the following conclusion from all that we have already stated—

The Pentacles, responding to the second *He*, indicate a transition. Between what? Between the minor and major arcana.

---

[1] See the *Traité Élémentaire de Science Occulte*, chap. iii.

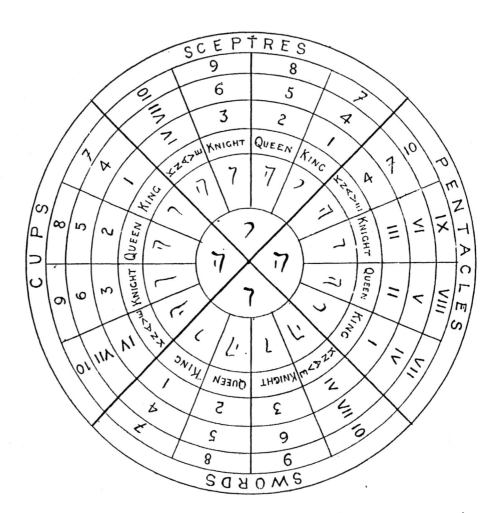

GENERAL KEY TO MINOR ARCANA

CHAPTER VI

THE KEY TO THE MAJOR ARCANA

The Major Arcana—1st Ternary—2nd Ternary—1st Septenary—
2nd Septenary—The Three Septenaries and the Ternary of
Transition.

THE MAJOR ARCANA

THE fundamental difference which exists between the
minor and major arcana is that in the latter the pictures and numbers are united, whilst in the former they
are distinct.

There are 22 major arcana, but one of them bears
a 0, so that, in reality, there are only 21 great or major
arcana.

Most of the authors who have studied the Tarot have
devoted all their attention to these 22 cards, without
noticing the others, which, however, contain the real
key to the system.

But we will leave these digressions and commence
the application of the law *Yod-he-vau-he* to this portion
of the Tarot.

A little reflection will suggest to us that there should
be some sequence in the major arcana as well as in the
minor arcana.   But how are we to define the limits of
the respective series ?

Each card of the minor arcana bears a symbol which
easily connects it with the whole scheme (Sceptre, Cup,

Sword, or Pentacles); it is different in the alternative case. Each card bears a different symbol. Therefore it is not symbolism that can guide us here, at all events for the moment.

Besides the symbol, each card expresses an idea. This idea is of itself a better guide, for it is easier to classify than the symbol; but such guide does not yet offer all the security that we could desire, for it may be read differently by various persons. Again, the idea proceeds from the action of the symbol upon the other term expressed by the card—the number.

The number is certainly the most reliable element, the easiest to follow in its evolutions; it is, therefore, the number that will guide us; and through it we shall discover the two other terms.

Let us now recall our explanation of the numbers, and we shall easily define the series of the major arcana.

However, from the commencement we must make one great reservation. The series which we are about to enumerate are the most usual, but they are not the only ones.

This said, we will now study the four first major arcana.

The numbers 1, 2, 3, 4 at once indicate the classification to be adopted and the nature of the terms.

1 corresponds to *Yod*, and is active.
2   „   to *He*,   „   passive.
3   „   to *Vau*,   „   neuter.
4   „   to the 2nd *He*, and indicates transition.

This 4th arcanum corresponds to the Knave and to the 10 of the minor arcana, and becomes *Yod* in the next or following series.

If we wish to make a figure of the first ternary 1, 2, 3, we should do it in this way—

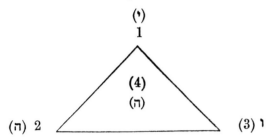

The active term 1 is at the head of the triangle, the two other terms are at the other angles.

This ternary can also be represented in its affinities with *Yod-he-vau-he*—

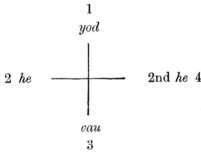

SECOND TERNARY.—We have stated that the 4 becomes the *Yod* or active term in the following sequence. This is exhibited in the figure below—

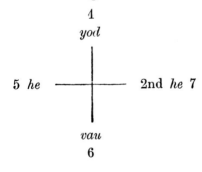

The 4, representing the *Yod*, therefore acts with regard to 5 and 6 as the 1 acted with regard to 2 and 3, and we obtain another ternary.

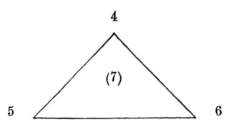

The 7 acts here as the 4 acted previously, and the same rule applies to all the series in the arcana.

FIRST SEPTENARY.—The application of one law to very different terms has led us so far; we must not abandon this system, but persevere and say—

If in one ternary exist an active term = *yod*, a passive term = *he*, and a neuter term = *vau*, resulting from the two first, why should not the same result be found in several ternaries taken together?

The first ternary is active and corresponds to *yod;* the second ternary is passive and corresponds to *he;* the reaction of one ternary upon another gives birth to a third ternary, or *vau*.

Let us make a figure representing this—

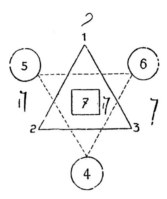

The 7 therefore forms the element of transition between one septenary and another.

If we define the analogy between this first septenary and the *Yod-he-vau-he*, we shall find—

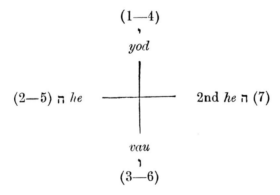

A deduction may be made in passing from which a great deal of information will be derived, if it be carefully studied: the 4 is only the 1, considered negatively, the 5 is only the 2 considered negatively, whilst the 6 is the negative of 3. It is always the same number under different aspects.

We have therefore defined a first septenary, formed of two opposing ternaries.

We have seen that this septenary also reproduces *Yod-he-vau-he.*

SECOND SEPTENARY.—The law that applies to the first ternaries is also true for the others, and following the same method we obtain a second septenary, thus formed—

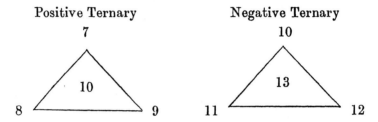

The two ternaries, positive and negative, will balance each other to give birth to a second septenary and to its term of transition, 13.   Thus—

General figure—

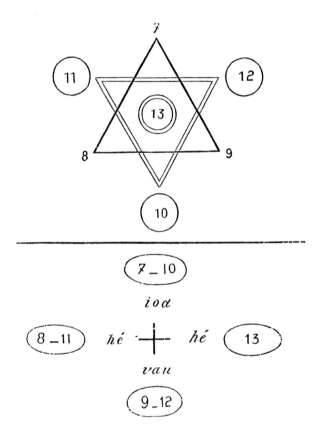

But if the two ternaries respectively act as positive and negative, why should not the two septenaries do the same ?

The first septenary, taken as a whole, will therefore be positive, relatively to the second septenary, which will be negative.

The first septenary corresponds to *yod*, the second to *he*.

THIRD SEPTENARY. The third septenary is thus formed—

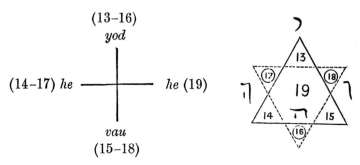

If the first septenary is positive and the second negative, the third will be neuter, and will correspond with *vau*.

We should have therefore, definitely—

1st, A POSITIVE SEPTENARY = *Yod*.
2nd, A NEGATIVE SEPTENARY = *He*.
3rd, A NEUTER SEPTENARY = *Vau*.

Yet each septenary contains one term which belongs to the preceding septenary, and one which belongs to the following septenary.

Thus the 7 is the 7th term of the first septenary and the 1st term of the second. 13 is the last term of the second septenary and the 1st of the third, etc.

The result is that three terms remain to be classed. These are—

$$19 - 20 - 21$$

These three terms form the last ternary, the ternary of transition between the major arcana and the minor arcana, a ternary which corresponds to the second *he*, and which may be thus represented—

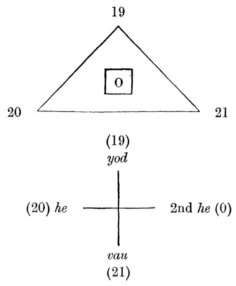

The last numbered card, which ought correctly to bear the number 22 (or its Hebrew correspondent), closes the Tarot by a marvellous figure, which represents its constitution to those who can understand it. We will return to it presently. Therefore, in the major arcana, the great law is thus definitely represented :—(See next page.)

The first septenary corresponds to the Divine World, to God;

The second to Man;

The third to Nature;

Finally, the last ternary indicates the passage from the creative and providential world to the created world of destiny.

This ternary establishes the connection between the major and minor arcana.

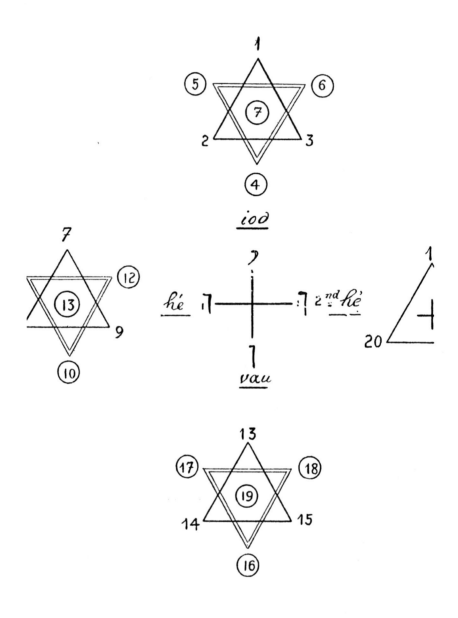

CHAPTER VII

CONNECTION BETWEEN THE MAJOR AND MINOR ARCANA: GENERAL AFFINITIES

KEY OF THE TAROT

Domination of the 1st Septenary—Affinities of the 2nd Septenary in the Tarot, Card by Card—Ditto of the 3rd Septenary—General Affinities—Affinities of *Yod, He, Vau,* and of the 2nd *He*—General Table giving the Key to the Tarot.

CONNECTION BETWEEN THE MAJOR AND MINOR ARCANA

THE Pentacles on one side, the Ternary of transition on the other, establish the connection between the major and minor arcana.

This connection is found in the general affinities of the four letters of the tetragrammaton.

The 1st septenary, which corresponds to *yod*, governs all the correspondences of *yod* in the minor series, that is to say—

> The 4 Kings.
> The 4 Aces.
> The 4 Fours.
> The 4 Sevens.

Each element of the septenary governs different terms, thus—

1st Septenary.

The arcana 1 and 4 govern *King*-1.4.7 of Sceptres.
    ,,   2 and 5   ,,   ,,   of Cups.
    ,,   3 and 6   ,,   ,,   of Swords.
The arcanum 7   ,,   ,,   of Pentacles.

Moreover—

The 1st arcanum especially governs the positive terms of the series, *i.e.*—

| Arcanum | The King of Yod or of Sceptres (+).[1] |
| 1 (+) | The King of Vau or of Swords (−). |

The 4th arcanum especially governs the negative terms of the series—

| Arcanum | The King of He   ... Cups (+). |
| 4 (−) | The King of the 2nd He + Pentacles (−-). |

By applying the same law to the other arcana we find—

| Arcanum | Ace of Yod (+) Sceptres. |
| (+) 2 | Ace of Vau (−) Swords. |

| Arcanum | Ace of He (+) Cups. |
| (−) 5 | Ace of He (−) Pentacles. |

| Arcanum 3 | 4 of Sceptres (+). |
| (+) | 4 of Swords (−). |

| Arcanum 6 | 4 of Cups (+). |
| (−) | 4 of Pentacles (−). |

| Arcanum 7 | All the transitional terms. |
| (∞) | 7 (∞). |

---

[1] The signs +, −, ∞ indicate: the sign + the *positive* terms, the sign − the *negative* terms, the sign ∞ the *neuter* terms.

SECOND SEPTENARY.—The second septenary, corresponding to *He,* governs all the correspondences of the first *He,* in the minor series, that is to say—-

> The 4 Queens.
> The 4 Twos.
> The 4 Fives.
> The 4 Eights.

Each element of the second septenary has the following dominations :—

Arcanum 7 (+) { Queen of Sceptres, (+) / Queen of Swords, (−) }   Arcanum 10 (−) { Queen of Cups, (+) / Queen of Pentacles, (−) }

Arcanum 8 (+) { Two of Sceptres, (+) / Two of Swords, (−) }   Arcanum 11 (−) { Two of Cups, (+) / Two of Pentacles, (−) }

Arcanum 9 (+) { Five of Sceptres, (+) / Five of Swords, (−) }   Arcanum ·12 (−) { Five of Cups, (+) / Five of Pentacles, (−) }

Arcana 13 (♏) { All the 8, (♏) }

THIRD SEPTENARY.—The third septenary corresponds to *Vau,* and rules over—

> The 4 Knights.
> The 4 Threes.
> The 4 Sixes.
> The 4 Nines.

Each element of this septenary thus rules over—

Arcanum 13 (+)
{ Knight of Sceptres, (+)
  Knight of Swords, (−) }

Arcanum 16 (−)
{ Knight of Cups, (+)
  Knight of Pentacles (−) }

Arcanum 14 (+)
{ Three of Sceptres, (+)
  Three of Swords, (−) }

Arcanum 17 (−)
{ Three of Cups, (+)
  Three of Pentacles, (−) }

Arcanum 15 (+)
{ Six of Sceptres, (+)
  Six of Swords, (−) }

Arcanum 18 (−)
{ Six of Cups, (+)
  Six of Pentacles, (−) }

Arcanum 19 (∞)
{ All the nines, (∞) }

TERNARY OF TRANSITION.—The ternary of transition rules over—

The 4 Knaves.
The 4 Tens.

Each of its elements thus rules over—

Arcanum 19 (∞) (+)
{ Knave of Sceptres, (+)
  Knave of Swords, (−) }

Arcanum 20 (∞) (−)
{ Knave of Cups, (+)
  Knave of Pentacles, (−) }

Arcanum 21 (+)
{ All the 10, (∞) }

Value of the signs +, −, and ∞.

The signs which follow each card in the preceding lists define the exact value of the card. One example will suffice to make this clearly understood.

Each term can be taken in two principal acceptations: in the positive ($+$) or in the negative ($-$). The same rule applies to the sub-divisions of these terms.

For instance, the correspondences of the first septenary are 1 and 4.

> 1 is the positive ($+$).
> 4 is the negative ($-$).

1 governs two minor arcana: the King of Sceptres and the King of Swords.

> The King of Sceptres is positive.
> The King of Swords is negative.

The definite value of these terms would therefore be—

1st King of Sceptres.

> Positive ($+$) of the Positive ($+$);
> or
> King of Sceptres
> $+$ $+$

2nd King of Swords.

> Negative ($-$) of the Positive ($+$);
> or more simply
> King of Swords
> $+$ $-$

The same rule applies to the other terms in combining the sign which follows the major arcanum with that which follows the term under consideration.

The value of each of the 78 cards of the Tarot is thus defined.

E

GENERAL AFFINITIES

AFFINITIES TO *Yod*

		Positive.	*Negative*
Major Arcana		Arcanum 1	Arcanum 4
		,, 7	,, 10
		,, 13	,, 16

	King of Sceptres	*King of Cups*
	Ace ,,	Ace ,,
	4 ,,	4 ,,
Minor Arcana	7 ,,	7 ,,
	King of Swords	King of Pentacles
	Ace ,,	Ace ,,
	4 ,,	4 ,,
	7 ,,	7 ,,

AFFINITIES TO THE 1ST *He*

		Positive.	*Negative.*
Major Arcana		Arcanum 2	Arcanum 5
		,, 8	,, 11
		,, 14	,, 17

	Queen of Sceptres	Queen of Cups
	Two ,,	Two ,,
	Five ,,	Five ,,
	Eight ,,	Eight ,,
Minor Arcana	Queen of Swords	Queen of Pentacles
	Two ,,	Two ,,
	Five ,,	Five ,,
	Eight ,,	Eight ,,

AFFINITIES TO *Vau*

		Positive.	*Negative.*
Major Arcana		Arcanum 3	Arcanum 6
		,, 9	,, 12
		,, 15	,, 18

Minor Arcana	Knight of Sceptres	Knight of Cups
	Three ,,	Three ,,
	Six ,,	Six ,,
	Nine ,,	Nine ,,
	Knight of Swords	Knight of Pentacles
	Three ,,	Three ,,
	Six ,,	Six ,,
	Nine ,,	Nine ,,

AFFINITIES TO THE 2ND *He*

Positive.	*Negative.*
Arcanum 19	Arcanum 20
Knave of Sceptres	Knave of Cups
,, Swords	,, Pentacles

Equilibrium.

Arcana | 21—22 |

Ten of Sceptres
,, Swords
,, Cups
,, Pentacles

GENERAL FIGURE OF THE CONSTRUCTION OF THE TAROT,
SHOWING ALL AFFINITIES

The absolute law :—

Yod He Vau He

is in the centre of the figure.

Each of the letters of Tetragrammaton governs one quarter of the circle which contains its affinities.

The different suits indicate the especial dominion of each arcanum.

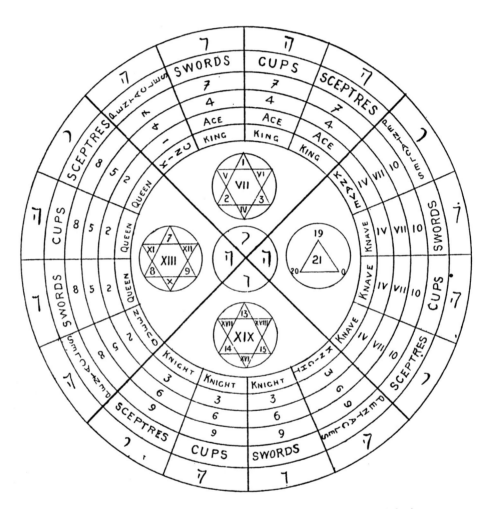

GRAND GENERAL FIGURE OF THE TAROT.—*Arrangement of Series.*

PART II

SYMBOLISM IN THE TAROT
APPLICATION OF THE GENERAL KEY TO SYMBOLISM

CHAPTER VIII

INTRODUCTION TO THE STUDY OF SYMBOLISM

The Symbols — The Primitive Terms — Key of Symbolism —
Definition of the Sense of one of the Symbols—The General
Law of Symbolism.

INTRODUCTION TO THE STUDY OF SYMBOLISM IN THE TAROT

OUR study of the Tarot and its numerical arrangement
has given us the general key, which should be applied
to all the further developments of which our subject
may be susceptible.

The symbols should therefore exactly follow the
evolution of the numbers, and this we shall find them
do. However, as we shall now study each of the cards
of the Tarot in turn, and as the reader's attention may
be a little diverted by all these details, we have determined to commence by a short introduction to the
study of the symbolism of the Tarot, an introduction
in which we shall say a few words upon the grouping
of the symbols.

This point explained, we can pass on to further
details, which we shall terminate by a synthetic
recapitulation. We thus hope to obtain the greatest
possible light upon these difficult subjects.

The analysis of the word *Yod-he-vau-he* has given

us the general law upon which the whole Tarot is constructed. This law is thus represented—

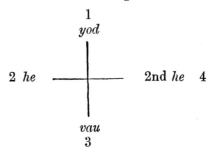

We must therefore first define the four primitive terms in our symbols, which form the law exactly applicable to the whole symbolism.

And, in fact, we find these four terms in our four first cards ; the general sense of these terms being—

1 — Creator or Divine.
2 — Preserver or Astral.
3 — Transformer, or Physical, and Diffuser.
4 — Generator or Transitional becoming Creator.

This law corresponds in all points with our sacred word, thus—

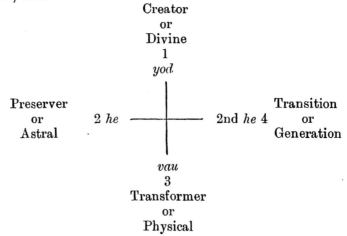

We shall see that this law applies exactly to each of the cards, which possess three meanings :—

A superlative or Divine meaning.
A comparative or Magic-Astral meaning.
A positive or Physical meaning, responding to a transition.

GENERAL STUDY OF THE FOUR FIRST CARDS

Key to the Symbolism of the Tarot

The four first cards of the major arcana form, symbolically as well as numerically, a complete sequence, which corresponds with the sacred word *Yod-he-vau-he*.

For the first card expresses the active absolute, and corresponds with *Yod*.

The second card denotes the reflex of the first, the passive absolute ; it corresponds with the first *He*.

The third indicates the median term, the convertible transforming term, corresponding to *Vau*.

Lastly, the fourth card is a term of transition between the preceding series and the one that follows it.

The symbolic series of the Tarot is therefore completely represented by the four first cards, exactly as the numerical sequence is represented by the four first numbers. This fact produces a very important consideration, namely, that all the symbols of the Tarot are but transformations of the three first, and that the latter will supply us with the general law of symbolism, a law which will enable us to determine mathematically the sense of each card that follows.

But we can go still further.

Since the second card is the reflex of the first, and

is formed by the first considered negatively, and since the third card results from the two others, it suffices to be perfectly acquainted with the first card of the Tarot to determine mathematically the sense of all the others.

Some details upon this subject are necessary.

The general law of the four first cards is as follows—

1 — Positive. Creator.
2 — Negative. Reflex of the first. Preserver.
3 — Neuter, enveloping the two others. Transformer.
4 — Passage from one series to another.

We can then represent the series in this way.

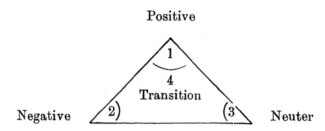

And what is true for each of the terms of a ternary is also true for the ternary taken as a whole, and this leads us to new considerations.

The first ternary would be positive, corresponding to *Yod*, the active, the creator.

The second ternary would be negative, and would correspond to the first *He*. In other words, all the terms of this ternary would be reflections of the terms of the first, just as the second card was the reflex of the first card.

This gives us—

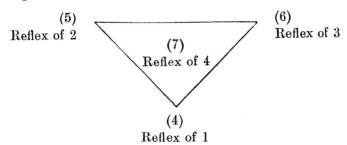

We can thus determine the meaning of the arcana 4, 5, 6, 7 in the three worlds, since we know the meaning of the arcana 1, 2, 3, 4.

We need only refer to the study of the Tarot by numbers, to find the symbols, which correspond respectively to *Yod*, to *He*, to *Vau*, and to the second *He*.

But if the second ternary is the reflex of the first, the same rule applies to the septenaries.

All the cards of the second septenary will therefore be the symbolical reflection of those of the first.

All the cards of the third septenary are representatives of the third term, or of transformation.

We have then—

The 1st septenary,
> Which represents the *active Creation*. The Divine Osiris-Brahma, or the Father.

The 2nd septenary,
> Which represents *Preservation*. The Astral, Isis, Vishnu, the Son.

The 3rd septenary,
> Which represents *Transformation*, Physics, Horus, Siva, the Holy Spirit.

The three first arcana will therefore give the sense of all the others according to the following tabulation:

FIGURE

SHOWING THE SENSE OF EACH OF THE 22 MAJOR ARCANA.

yod positive or creative series	1.	4.	7.	10.	13.	16.	19.
1st *he* negative or preservative series	2.	5.	8.	11.	14.	17.	20.
vau neuter or transforming series, equilibrium	3.	6.	9.	12.	15.	18.	21.
2nd *he* transitional series	$4 = (1)$						
	+ positive	− negative	+	−	+	−	∞
	yod positive or creative series		*he* negative or preservative series		*vau* neuter or transforming series equilibrium		2nd *he* transitional series

This tabulation is very important, for it enables us to see at once the symbolical value of any card in the Tarot, by working in the following way—

TO DISCOVER A PRIORI THE SYMBOLICAL VALUE
OF ANY CARD IN THE TAROT

We must see—

(*1st*) Which Hebrew letter is written to the left in the horizontal column, which contains the card under consideration.

(*2nd*) Which Hebrew letter is written at the foot of the vertical column, containing the card.

(*3rd*) Which sign (+ or −) governs the secondary vertical column, containing the card in question.

EXAMPLE

I wish to determine the sense of the 5th arcanum.

I look to the left and find the Hebrew letter *he*.

This shows that the 5th arcanum is the *he* of what?

In order to know, I look at the vertical column and find *yod*.

The 5th arcanum is the *he* of *yod*, but that is not enough, so I look at the secondary column which contains the sign (−) negative.

I thus obtain a definite description of the 5th arcanum.

The fifth card of the Tarot is—

The He of Yod considered negatively.

This is a synthetic formula comprehensible to those only who are used to manipulating the sense of the word *Yod-he-vau-he*.

It is therefore necessary to give further explanations.

He represents the *reflex*.

We may therefore say, more explicitly—

The 5th arcanum is:

The reflex of *yod* considered negatively.   But what is *yod* considered negatively?

To ascertain this, I look in my left column at the letter *yod*, I seek in the secondary vertical column the sign (–) negative, and at the intersection of these two lines I find the 4th arcanum.

The *yod* considered negatively is the 4th arcanum.

This leads me to conclude—

That the 5th arcanum is the reflex of the 4th arcanum.

All the arcana can be explained in this way by each other, according to the above rules.

This table is the key of the *Ars Magna* of Raymond Lully.

CORRESPONDENCE BETWEEN THE CARDS OF THE TAROT

To obtain the origin and derivation of any card in the Tarot, it suffices to take the third card before it, and the third card after it.

Thus the 8th arcanum is derived from the 5th arcanum, and gives rise to the 11th arcanum.

5	8	11
Universal life.	Elementary existence.	Reflected and transitory life.

. . . .

From this it ensues that, when two cards added together give an even number, we need only take the half of the number to discover the card which serves to unite those under consideration.

Thus, in order to discover the link which binds the 4th arcanum to the 6th, *i.e.*, the universal vivifying fluid to universal love, I add together $4+6=10$, and I take one-half of the number obtained $\frac{10}{2}=5$.

The 5th arcanum (universal life) therefore unites the two opposites.[1]

The passage of the vivifying fluid (4) into love (6) is performed through the medium of universal life (5).

Since each card of the Tarot has three meanings, it is easy to philosophize by means of our pack, without taking too much trouble about it.

. . . .

Another result of this rule is, that each card of the Tarot has a complementary in any card bearing a number which, added to its own, gives a total of 22.

For instance, what is the complementary card of the 1st arcanum?

It is the 21st arcanum, since $21+1=22$. What is the transition from 1 to 21?

According to what we have just stated it is $21+1=\frac{22}{2}=11$.

The 11th arcanum (reflected and transitory life) therefore forms the transition between the 1st arcanum (creative principle) and the 21st arcanum (universal generation).

To find the card that serves as complementary to any other, we must therefore subtract the number of the card in question from 22.

[1] The Hebrew alphabet thoroughly establishes this affiliation for the letters corresponding to these three numbers. (See 8th arcanum.)

For instance, to find the complementary card to 14—

$$22 - 14 = 8.$$

The 8th arcanum is therefore complementary to the 14th.

We have made this digression because all these details will be most useful to us presently. We can now return to the study of our major arcana.

Let us once more recall the manner in which the four first arcana have given us the key to the symbolism of all the others, according to their affinities with the sacred word, as follows—

THE GENERAL LAW OF THE SYMBOLISM OF THE TAROT

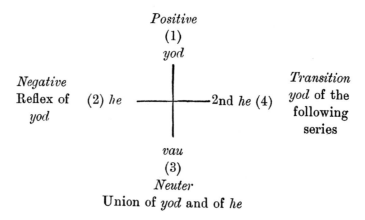

CHAPTER IX

HISTORY OF THE SYMBOLISM OF THE TAROT : INQUIRY INTO ITS ORIGIN

The Tarot is an Egyptian Book—Its Transformations—Mantegna's Pack—Venetian Tarot—Florentine Tarot—Bolognese—Hindu Tarot—Chinese Tarot—Modern Tarots—Etteila—Marseilles — Besançon — Watillaux—Oswald Wirth—Italian and German Tarots—Constitution of the Symbolism of the Tarot—The 16 primitive Hieroglyphic Signs—The 22 Hebrew Letters.

ORIGIN OF THE SYMBOLISM OF THE TAROT

As we have already stated, each card of the Tarot represents a symbol, a number and an idea.

We have endeavoured to avoid empiricism as far as possible in the course of these explanations; and therefore we first studied the numbers, for they are the most settled element and give the most unvarying results in their combinations.

Relying firmly upon the basis which we have thus constructed, we can now study the symbols with absolute assurance.

We hope that for this purpose you have procured the Tarot of Marseilles, the most correct in its symbolism,[1] or else the twenty-two keys designed by

[1] It is no longer extant, and has been superseded in all respects by the Tarot set which is issued in connection with this work. See preliminary announcement. The keys designed by Oswald Wirth are also out of print.—ED.

Oswald Wirth; perhaps—and this is really almost in dispensable—you have secured both of them.

You need, then, only deal the cards upon the table to see at once that the personages depicted upon them all wear dresses of the Renaissance period.[1]

And yet, is this pack of cards of ancient origin? I does not appear so.

Look at your figures more attentively and you will soon perceive Egyptian symbols [the triple cros (No. 5), and the ibis (No. 17)] combined with thes Renaissance costumes.

They at once prove that the Tarot of Marseille is really the exact- representation of the primitiv Egyptian Tarot, slightly altered to the epoch de noted by the costumes. Only the gypsies possess th primitive pack intact.

The studies of those learned men who have inves tigated the Tarot have confirmed this fact by th strongest evidence. And the works of Chatto,[2] Boiteau, and above all of Merlin,[4] show us that history corro borates our assertion.

Merlin conducted his researches very scientifically and succeeded in discovering the original of our Taro of Marseilles in an Italian Tarot at Venice, the fathe of all the later packs.

He believed also that he had discovered the origin

---

[1] The description does not apply to all Tarot sets.—ED.

[2] Chatto, *Facts and Speculations on the Origin and History c Playing Cards in Europe.* 8vo. London, 1848.

[3] Boiteau, *Les Cartes à Jouer et la Cartomancie.* 4to. Paris 1854.

[4] Merlin, *Origine des Cartes à Jouer, recherches nouvelles sur le Naibis, les Tarots et sur les autres Espèces de Cartes.* A worl ornamented with 70 illustrations. 4to. Paris, 1869.

of this Venetian Tarot in the philosophical pack of *Mantegna.*

But he could not determine the origin of this pack, because the one that Merlin believed to be the source of the Tarot is on the contrary a reproduction, made by one of the Initiates. The *Ars Magna* of Raymund Lully was produced in the same way; it is drawn entirely from the Tarot.

We have given for reference the pack of Mantegna, known in the trade as the cards of Baldini, as well as the packs of the Italian Tarots, from which most of ours are derived.

The table[1] which indicates the connection between the Tarot packs and the set of Mantegna ought to be reversed, and on the contrary show the cards of Mantegna derived from the Tarot, as we have stated.

Here follow the details of various Tarot sets. (See pages 84, 85.)

[1] Page 86.

MANTEGNA'S PACK

E	D	C	B	A .
1 The beggar.	11 Calliope.	21 Grammar.	31 Astronomy.	41 Moon.
2 The knave.	12 Urania.	22 Logic.	32 Chronology.	42 Mercury.
3 The artisan.	13 Terpsichore.	23 Rhetoric.	33 Cosmology.	43 Venus.
4 The merchant.	14 Erato.	24 Geometry.	34 Temperance.	44 Sun.
5 The Nobleman.	15 Polyhymnia.	25 Arithmetic.	35 Prudence.	45 Mars.
6 The Knight.	16 Thalia.	26 Music.	36 Strength.	46 Jupiter.
7 The Doge.	17 Melpomene.	27 Poetry.	37 Justice.	47 Saturn.
8 The King.	18 Euterpe.	28 Philosophy.	38 Charity.	48 8th sphere.
9 The Emperor.	19 Clio.	29 Astrology.	39 Hope.	49 Chief agent.
10 The Pope.	20 Apollo.	30 Theology.	40 Faith.	50 First cause.

E = Positions in life.
D = Muses and Arts.
C = Sciences.
B = Virtues.

A = Trumps.
B = Sceptres.
C = Cups.
D = Pentacles.

ORIGIN OF THE OTHER PACKS

Minchiate of Florence, 97 cards, of which 40 are Tarots.	Venetian Tarot, 78 cards, of which 21 are Tarots.	Tarot of Bologna, 62 cards, of which 21 are Tarots.
The Foolish Man.	0 The Foolish Man.	0 The Foolish Man.
The Juggler.	1 The Juggler.	1 The Juggler.
The Grand Duke.	2 The High Priestess.	2 The High Priestess.
The Emperor of the West.	3 The Empress.	3 The Empress
The Emperor of the East.	4 The Emperor.	4 The Emperor.
Love.	5 The Pope	5 The Pope.
Temperance.	6 The Lovers.	6 Love.
Strength.	7 The Chariot.	7 The Chariot.
Justice.	8 Justice.	8 Temperance.
The Wheel of Fortune.	9 The Hermit.	9 Justice.
The Chariot.	10 The Wheel of Fortune.	10 Strength.
The Old Man, with an Hour-glass.	11 Strength.	11 Fortune.
The Hanged Man.	12 The Hanged Man.	12 The Old Man.
Death.	13 Death.	13 The Hanged Man.
The Devil.	14 Temperance.	14 Death.
Hell.	15 The Devil.	15 The Devil.
Hope.	16 The Lightning-struck Tower.	16 Thunder.
Prudence.		
Faith.		
Charity.		
Fire.		
Water.		
The Earth.		
Air.		
The Scales.		
The Virgin.		
The Scorpion.		
The Ram.		
Capricornus.		
Sagittarius.		
Cancer.		
Pisces.		
Aquarius.		
The Lion.		
The Bull.		
The Twins.		
The Star.	17 The Star.	17 The Star.
The Moon.	18 The Moon.	18 The Moon.
The Sun.	19 The Sun	19 The Sun.
The Universe.	20 The Last Judgment.	20 The Universe.
Fame	21 The Universe	21 The Angel

CORRESPONDENCE BETWEEN THE PRIMITIVE ITALIAN PACKS
AND THE MODERN TAROT—

Modern Tarot. *Mantegna.*

The King	King		No. 8 of Mantegna
The Knight	Knight		,, 6 ,,
The Knave	Knave		,, 2 ,,
The Emperor	4 of the Tarot is the IX series E of Mantegna		
The Pope	5	,,	X ,, E ,,
Temperance	14	,,	34 ,, B ,,
Strength	11	,,	36 ,, B ,,
Justice	8	,,	37 ,, B ,,
The Moon	18	,,	41 ,, A ,,
The Sun	19	,,	44 ,, A ,,
The Foolish Man (unnumbered)	Beggar		No. 1 Mantegna
The Star	17	Venus	,, 42 ,,
The Chariot	7	Mars	,, 10 ,,
The Hermit	9	Saturn	,, 47 ,,
The Universe 21	{ Jupiter	,, 46 ,,	
	{ First cause	,, 50 ,,	

If, however, the existence of purely Egyptian symbols
in these so-called Italian Tarots do not convince the
reader, a few words on the transformation of the Taro
in the East, and in other countries of Europe besides
Italy, will completely enlighten him on the subject.

HINDU TAROTS

In spite of Merlin's assertions, the Tarot represents
the summary of the scientific knowledge of the ancients
This is unquestionably proved by Chatto's researches
amongst Orientals on this subject.

In fact, the Indians possess a game of chess, the

Tchaturanga, evidently derived from the Tarot, from the manner in which the men are arranged in four series :—Elephants, chariots, horses, foot-soldiers.

The Mussulmans of India also possess a pack of cards that is derived from the old symbols of the Tarot: the *Gungeifu* or *Ghendgifeh*.

This game is composed of eight series of twelve cards each, divided in this way—

Superior Section or Bishbur :	*Inferior Section* or Kunbur :
Crowns	Harps
Moons	Suns
Sabres	Royal Diplomas
Slaves	Bales of Merchandise.

CHINESE TAROT

An inexperienced eye might find some difficulty in recognizing the Tarot in this form, but the Chinese have given us an irrefutable argument in favour of our assertion, in the arrangement of their Tarot, which is represented by the table on page 88.

We have placed the correspondences of the minor and major arcana, and of the four letters of the Tetragrammaton, above the table in question.

A description of this Chinese pack will be found in Court de Gébelin (*Le Monde Primitif*) and in the work of J. A. Vaillant.

With regard to other European Tarots, we have copies of nearly all, and this induces us to name the various editions which we have been enabled to consult.

| MINOR ARCANA | | | | MAJOR ARCANA | |
yod	he	vau	he		
1	15	29	43	57	71
2	16	30	44	58	72
3	17	31	45	59	73
4	18	32	46	60	74
5	19	33	47	61	75
6	20	34	48	62	76
7	21	35	49	63	77
8	22	36	50	64	
9	23	37	51	65	
10	24	38	52	66	
11	25	39	53	67	
12	26	40	54	68	
13	27	41	55	69	
14	28	42	56	70	

MODERN TAROTS

The following are the most important of these modern Tarots—

The Tarot of Etteila.
The Italian Tarot.
The Marseilles Tarot.
The Tarot of Besan

The double-headed Tarot of Besançon.
The Tarot of Watillaux.
The German Tarot.
The Tarot of Oswald Wirth.

THE FRENCH TAROT PACKS

The Tarot of Etteila is of no symbolic value; it is a bad mutilation of the real Tarot.

This pack is used by all our fortune-tellers. Its sole interest lies in the strangeness of its figures. It can be obtained for 5 or 8 francs from all the great card-sellers in Paris.

The Tarot of Watillaux, or pack of the Princess Tarot, reproduces the minor arcana very correctly. It is worth consideration on this account.

The Italian Tarot, that of Besançon and of Marseilles, are unquestionably the best which we possess, particularly the last, which fairly reproduces the primitive symbolical Tarot.

THE GERMAN TAROT

Besides the Italian we must mention the German Tarot, in which the symbols of the minor arcana are different.

For

The Cups	are represented by	The Hearts
The Pentacles	,,	,,	The Bells
The Swords	,,	,,	The Leaves
The Sceptres	,,	,,	The Acorns

However, this Tarot is a very bad one.

THE TAROT OF OSWALD WIRTH

It became necessary to have a Tarot pack in which the symbolism was definitely established. This work, suggested by Éliphas Lévi, who defined the principles on which it was to be based, has been accomplished by Mr. Oswald Wirth.

This clever occultist, aided by the advice of Stanislas de Guaita, has designed the series of the twenty-two major arcana. These drawings reproduce the Tarot of Marseilles, with the symbolical modifications suggested by the researches of Éliphas Lévi upon this important question.

Owing to the kindness of M. Poirel, who assisted the work by printing these designs, we now possess a marvellous symbolic document in the Tarot of Oswald Wirth.

It is therefore wise, as we have already said, for those who wish to study the Tarot very thoroughly, to procure the Tarot of Marseilles and that of Oswald Wirth.

We shall use them both presently in our explanation of the symbolical meaning of each card.

But before passing to the study of these symbols, card by card, we must see if there are no means of positively defining the symbolism of the Tarot.

HOW CAN WE HOPE TO DEFINE THE SYMBOLISM OF THE TAROT CONCLUSIVELY?

We have already and sufficiently explained that the Tarot represents the ancient or occult science in every possible development.

If we then wish to find a solid basis for the study of

To face page 90

the symbols represented in the 22 major arcana, we may put the Tarot on one side for an instant, and devote ourselves to this ancient science. It alone can enable us to attain our end, not in finding the explanation of the symbols, but in leading us to create them one by one, deducing them from fixed and general principles.

We shall thus commence work of quite a new character, whilst avoiding, so far as possible, falling into those errors which arise from the effort to explain the symbols of the Tarot by themselves, instead of seeking for their solution at their original source.

The first step in the search for these particular symbols leads us to discuss the grave problem of the origin of symbolism itself.

We cannot enter upon, much less solve, this question by ourselves; we shall therefore quote the opinions of several writers upon the subject. Truth having Unity for its criterion, the agreement of various conclusions in one point will be a valuable guide for us.

Louis Claude de Saint-Martin, the unknown philosopher, states in his book, the *Tableau Naturel des Rapports*, that the primitive alphabet is composed of sixteen signs. He received these data, so far as we can judge, from intuitive revelation, joined to the teaching of a secret school, of which he was one of the members.

Lacour, in his book on the Elohim or Gods of Moses, has inductively determined the existence of a primitive alphabet, also composed of sixteen signs. Another author, Barrois, pursuing inquiries of quite a different nature, also reaches the conclusion of the existence of sixteen primitive signs in his system of Dactylology.

But the labours of Court de Gébelin, and above all of Fabre d'Olivet, are the most remarkable in this respect. In his *Langue Hébraïque Restituée*, the latter learned Initiate established the existence of primitive hieroglyphic signs from which the Hebrew letters are derived.

All these writers, starting from very different points, agree in their conclusions, and this gives us a strong argument in favour of the truth of their researches.

But it matters very little to us whether these 16 primitive signs are the direct origin, either of the Hebrew, Sanscrit, Chinese, or Greek letters. The identity of source tends strongly to identity of results, and any one of these derivative alphabets will answer our purpose.

The Hebrew alphabet, composed of 22 letters, seems preferable to us, on account of the concordance between the number of its letters and that of the Arcana in our Tarot.

We shall therefore adopt, as the starting-point of our study, the Hebrew alphabet of 22 letters, derived from the 16 primitive hieroglyphic signs.

This conclusion is scarcely reached, when fresh light shines upon us from all sides.

William Postel[1] reveals to us the connection between the Hebrew letters and the Tarot; Van Helmont the Younger,[2] L. C. de Saint-Martin,[3] Fabre d'Olivet,[4] all confirm our opinion; lastly, Éliphas Lévi[5] also throws

[1] *Clavis.*

[2] *Origin of Language* (Latin).

[3] *Tableau naturel des rapports qui existent entre Dieu, l'homme et l'Univers.*

[4] *La Langue Hebraïque Restituée.*

[5] *Rituel de la Haute Magie.*

the weight of his marvellous learning into the question.

But we shall be more surprised to learn that the *Sepher Yetzirah*,[1] an old book of the Kabalah, which contains a study upon the formation of the Hebrew alphabet, arrives at a division of the letters which exactly corresponds with the astrological data contained in an old manuscript in the Vatican, upon which Christian [2] based his horoscopic works.

One single and identical conclusion arises from all these different points of view: the value of the Hebrew letter as a symbol.

In it we possess a real symbol, of which we can ascertain not only the meanings but also the origin.

It would be possible, therefore, to make a Tarot exclusively composed of Hebrew letters and of numbers, but this is not our object; we are seeking to discover in the symbolism of the Hebrew characters the symbolism of the Tarot, and we shall thus realize our intention of ascertaining deductively the value of the emblems of the Tarot and the reason which actuated their choice.

THE HEBREW LETTERS AS THE BASIS OF THE SYMBOLICAL TAROT

We shall now study the Hebrew letters one by one, in determining successively—

1st. The hieroglyphic value of each one of them according to its origin (Fabre d'Olivet, Barrois);

2nd. Its symbolic value derived from this hieroglyphic (Fabre d'Olivet, Éliphas Lévi, Christian);

[1] Translated into English by Dr. Wynn Westcott.
[2] *Histoire de la Magie.*

3rd. Its astronomical value (Christian and the *Sepher Yetzirah*).

Once acquainted with these data, it will be easy for us to deduce from them the application of the letters to the symbols of the Tarot.

But before we enter upon this study, it is necessary to say a few words upon the Hebrew alphabet in general and its constitution.

The alphabet of the Hebrews is composed of 22 letters; these letters, however, are not placed by chance, one after the other. Each of them corresponds with a number according to its rank, with a hieroglyphic according to its form, with a symbol according to its affinities with the other letters.

As we have already said, all the letters are derived from one amongst them, the *yod*.[1] The *yod* has generated them in the following manner (see *Sepher Yetzirah*)—

1st. Three mothers:

The A	(Aleph)	א
The M	(The Mem)	מ
The Sh	(The Shin)	ש

2nd. Seven doubles (double because they express two sounds, the one positive and strong, the other negative and soft):

The B	(Beth)	ב
The G	(Gimel)	ג
The D	(Daleth)	ד
The Ch	(Caph)	כ
The Ph	(Pe)	פ
The R	(Resh)	ר
The T	(Tau)	ת

3rd. Lastly, twelve simple, formed by the other letters.

[1] See above (p. 19): Study upon the word *Yod-he-vau-he*.

To render this clearer, we will append the Hebrew alphabet, indicating the quality of each letter and its rank. (See Table below.)

We have now provided a fixed principle for symbolism in the Hebrew letter, and need not fear being deceived by the false interpretation of a costume, or of an incorrect figure. The Hebrew letter will be always there, to enlighten us upon obscure or difficult points.

We can therefore safely return to the Tarot, which we have left to make this digression.

Numbers in Order.	Hiero-glyphic.	Names.	Value in Roman Letters.	Value in the Alphabet.
1	א	aleph	A	mother
2	ב	beth	B	*double*
3	ג	gimel	G	*double*
4	ד	daleth	D	*double*
5	ה	he	E	simple
6	ו	vau	V	simple
7	ז	zain	Z	simple
8	ח	heth	H	simple
9	ט	teth	T	simple
10	י	Yod	I	simple and principle
11	כ	kaph	CH	*double*
12	ל	lamed	L	simple
13	מ	mem	M	mother
14	נ	nun	N	simple
15	ס	samech	S	simple
16	ע	ayin	GH	simple
17	פ	phe	PH	*double*
18	צ	tzaddi	TS	simple
19	ק	quoph	K	simple
20	ר	resh	R	*double*
21	ש	shin	SH	mother
22	ת	tau	TB	*double*

CHAPTER X

STUDY OF EACH OF THE 22 MAJOR ARCANA

Scheme of Work

WE shall now apply this general law of symbolism to
each of the twenty-two major arcana.

We must here beg for the reader's careful attention,
in spite of the length of the subject under consideration. We shall make every effort to be as clear as
possible, and therefore we shall first explain the scheme
which we have adopted in the study of each of the
cards of the Tarot.

(1st) We shall always start from the hieroglyphic
sign which has given birth to the Hebrew letter. Court
de Gébelin is the author whom we shall consult chiefly
upon this subject.

(2nd) We shall explain from the hieroglyphic character all the ideas that can be progressively deduced

therefrom, and which characterize the Hebrew letter considered as a sign. Kircher and Fabre d'Olivet are our authorities in this work.

(3rd) When we have once defined the ideas signified by the Hebrew letter, we shall search for the application of these ideas in the symbolic figure of the Tarot.

Éliphas Lévi,[1] Christian [2] and Barrois [3] will aid us in our inquiries.

(4th) Lastly, we shall determine the meaning which must be attributed to each card of the Tarot, according to its numerical and symbolical affinities with the other cards, in applying to it the general law of symbolism. This portion of our work is strictly personal.

(5th) We shall end the study upon each of the cards by a table summarising all that we have said.

We must warn the reader that the perusal of the recapitulations only will be of no use as a means of understanding any card of the Tarot, and that the best way will be to follow the successive explanations of each card, with the Tarot before him.

We cannot end this opening chapter without alluding to the basis upon which we have established the astronomical relations of each card of the Tarot.

One of the most ancient books of the Kabalah which we possess, the *Sepher Yetzirah*,[4] says that the three mother letters of the Hebrew alphabet correspond with the three worlds, the seven double with the seven planets, and the twelve simple with the twelve signs of the zodiac.[5]

[1] *Rituel de la Haute Magie.*
[2] *Histoire de la Magie.*
[3] *Dactylologie ou Langage Primitif.*
[4] Translated into French by Papus.
[5] See Franck, *La Kabbale*, Paris.

Now in studying the astrological manuscript published by Christian, we have discovered that the numbers attributed to the planets by the author of this work exactly correspond with the double Hebrew letters, and the numbers attributed to the twelve signs of the zodiac exactly correspond with the simple letters.

Considering that this absolute agreement between two documents of such different origin deserves our serious attention, we have therefore assigned to each letter its astronomical correspondence.

KEY OF THE FIRST SEPTENARY

ARRANGEMENT OF THE FIGURES FOR STUDY

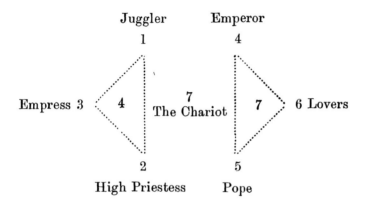

Juggler   Emperor
1   4

Empress 3 4 7 The Chariot 7 6 Lovers

2   5
High Priestess Pope

CHARACTER OF THE FIGURES

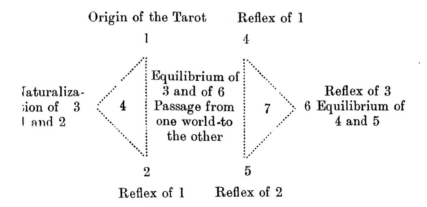

Origin of the Tarot Reflex of 1
1   4

Naturaliza-   Equilibrium of   Reflex of 3
tion of 3 4 3 and of 6 7 6 Equilibrium of
1 and 2 Passage from   4 and 5
   one world-to
   the other

2   5
Reflex of 1 Reflex of 2

THE FIRST CARD OF THE TAROT

ORIGIN OF THE SIGNIFICATION OF ALL THE OTHERS

So far as our work has proceeded, it follows that if we know the exact meaning of the first card of the Tarot we can discover therefrom the signification of all the others.

We cannot approach this subject without great hesitation. The hope of ascertaining the truth is, in fact, troubled by the possibility of making a mistake which might have very serious results.

The work which we have already accomplished will, however, enable us to decipher the meaning of the symbolism of the first card of the Tarot almost mathematically, but the general meaning only; whilst we know that each card must have not one but three meanings.

We must discover three sufficiently general principles to be applied to every order of human knowledge; for this should be the object of the Tarot.

In this case we will, as usual, resort to those eminent authors who have treated such questions from different points of view, and the agreement between their teachings will give us new light to illuminate our path.

The Pole Hœné Wronski,[1] who died of hunger in the suburbs of Paris, was perhaps one of the most powerful intellects produced by the nineteenth century. He asserted that he had discovered the formula of the absolute, and his works are unquestionably a summary of one of the most elevated syntheses that

[1] See *l'Occultisme Contemporain* (M. Carré).

we have ever seen. We need not discuss the doctrines
of Wronski, but will only say a few words upon the three
primitive elements which enter into his law of creation.

Wronski places at the origin of all creation three
elements, which he designates by the names—

Neuter Element   (N. E.)
Element of Being   (E. B.)
Element of Wisdom (E. W.)

The Neuter Element represents the Absolute, Reality
resulting from the total neutralization of the two other
elements by each other.

The Element of Wisdom represents the CREATIVE
FACULTY with its especial characteristics, autogeny and
spontaneity.

The Element of Being represents the PERMANENT
FACULTY with its characteristics, autothesis and inertia.

Principle of the Creation or Element of Wisdom.
Principle of Preservation or Element of Being.
Principle of Neutralization or Neuter Element.

These are the three terms upon which Wronski
establishes the foundations of Reality and, consequently, of all the systems of creation. We must
remember these conclusions.

FABRE D'OLIVET, in his researches upon the first
principles which direct everything,[1] determines the
existence of three elements, which he names Providence, Destiny and Human Will.

Providence is the principle of ABSOLUTE LIBERTY, of
the creation of beings and of things.

[1] See *Les Vers Dorés de Pythagore* and the *Histoire Philosophique
du Genre Humain*.

Destiny is the principle of ABSOLUTE NECESSITY, of the preservation of beings and of things.

Lastly, the Human Will is a neuter principle intermediate between the two: the principle of MOBILITY and CHANGE in all their forms. Now it is not necessary to be deeply learned in order to perceive the absolute agreement which exists between the two authors; the one, Wronski, reached his conclusions by mathematics, the other, d'Olivet, attained his own by profound study of antiquity and its mysteries. The words used may vary, but the idea is fundamentally the same.

Wronski's Element of Wisdom (E. W.), the principle of the creation, is the same thing as the Providence of d'Olivet, who thus places it as the principle of the creation.

Wronski's Element of Being (E. B), the principle of the permanent faculty, exactly represents what d'Olivet calls Destiny, and this he concludes to be the principle of preservation.

Lastly, d'Olivet's human Will corresponds in all points with Wronski's Neuter Element.

Here then are two very different systems which lead to the same signification. But our conclusions do not stop here.

If we study these three primitive principles more attentively we shall find in the first: Providence or the Element of Wisdom, represented in philosophy by the word God.

Destiny or Being shows us its identity with the immutable laws which govern the Universe.

Lastly, it does not require much study to prove to us that the human Will responds to Man.

GOD, MAN AND THE UNIVERSE

This is the basis of all the esoteric philosophy of the ancients, and not only Wronski and Fabre d'Olivet agree in their conclusions respecting this mysterious ternary; occult science itself proclaims its identity with these principles by the mouth of all its disciples. Hermes Trismegistus, the Holy Kabalah, Neoplatonism, the Alchemists through Pythagoras and all the Greek philosophers assert the division of the Great All into THREE ENTITIES OR WORLDS.

In less remote ages William Postel[1] gives the key of the Tarot without explaining it, and the basis of his key is formed by this mysterious entity—

DEUS, HOMO, ROTA

Trithemius and his pupil Cornelius Agrippa[2] also give us this fruitful and sublime trinity in all their analogical figures.

The Jesuit *Kircher*[3] describes this division into three worlds as the basis of the Egyptian mysteries.

Lastly, L. C. de Saint-Martin has written a book entirely based upon the keys of the Tarot, and it is entitled—*Tableau Naturel des rapports qui existent entre* DIEU, L'HOMME ET L'UNIVERS.

Let us question India upon the law of the Absolute; she replies—

Trimurti: BRAHMA, SIVA, VISHNU

Let us ask China for the great secret of her philosophy, and she will give us the *Tri-grams of Fo-Hi*.

[1] *Clavis.*
[2] *La Philosophie Occulte.*
[3] *Œdipus Ægyptiacus.*

Address ourselves to one of the ancient initiated Egyptians, he will tell us—

OSIRIS, ISIS, HORUS

The founder of Greek Cosmogony, the disciple of the science of Egypt, Hesiod, also transmits this law to us, and all indifferently confirm Louis Lucas when he states:[1] "I feel that hidden beneath this mystical formula of the Trinity is one of the most important scientific laws that man has ever discovered."

God, Man and the Universe—these are the most general principles that we can attain, and they constitute the three meanings of the first card of the Tarot.

It remains for us to ascertain first, whether these meanings respond to the primitive hieroglyphic, and then to determine how far they extend through the whole Tarot.

[1] See *Le Roman Alchimique.*

THE JUGGLER

THE JUGGLER

1. א

1st Hebrew letter (Aleph)

ORIGIN OF THE SYMBOLISM OF THE FIRST CARD OF THE
TAROT

The *Aleph* hieroglyphically expresses Man himself
as a collective unity, the master principle, ruler of the
earth.

From this hieroglyphic meaning are derived ideas
of the Unity and of the principle which determines it,
ideas which give to *Aleph* its value as the sign of Power
and Stability.

Man, or the Microcosm, the Unity and the Principle
in all the worlds, is the meaning of the primitive hieroglyphic, which, as we see, exactly renders the general
ideas that we have established.

But attentive consideration of this first card of the Tarot will enlighten us still further.

Symbolism of the First Card of the Tarot

THE JUGGLER

If you take the first card of the Tarot and examine it attentively, you will see that the form of the Juggler depicted upon it corresponds in all points with that of the letter *Aleph*. If we now apply to the study of this card the principles of the elucidation of symbolism, according to the *Traité Élémentaire de Science Occulte*, we at once find new explanations of it.

The top of the figure is occupied by the divine sign of Universal Life ∞ placed upon the head of the Juggler.

The bottom of the figure represents the Earth ornamented with its productions, the symbol of Nature.

Lastly, the centre is occupied by the Man himself, placed behind a table covered with divers objects.

The right and left of the figure are occupied by the hands of the Juggler, one of them bent towards the Earth, the other raised towards Heaven.

The position of the hands represents the two principles, active and passive, of the Great All, and it corresponds with the two columns *Jakin* and *Bohas* of the temple of Solomon and of Freemasonry.

Man with one hand seeks for God in heaven, with the other he plunges below, to call up the demon to himself, and thus unites the divine and the diabolic in humanity. In this way the Tarot shows us the *rôle* of universal mediator accorded to Adam-Kadmon.

If we wish to make a summary of the meaning of

the symbol, so far as we have now deciphered it, we can represent it in this way—

	Top	Divine	*Head*	
Right				Left
(*Arm lowered*)	Centre	Human	*Body*	(*Arm raised*)
Necessity				Liberty
Evil	Bottom	Natural	*Feet* .	Good

Yet the symbolism of this first card of the Tarot does not end here.

The Juggler holds the wand of the Mage in the left hand, which he raises, and the four great symbols of the Tarot are placed before him.

The Cup, the Sword, the Wand, Pentacles or Talismans, which, as we have already seen, exactly correspond with the letters of the Tetragrammaton—

> *Sceptre or Yod*, symbol of the active Principle preeminent, and of God.
> *Cup or He*, symbol of the passive Principle preeminent, or of the Universe.
> *Sword, Cross or Vau*, symbol of the Equilibrating Principle pre-eminent, or of Man.
> *Pentacles or 2nd He*, the cyclic symbol of Eternity, which unites the three first Principles in one Whole.

From the human point of view these symbols correspond with the four great human classes.

> *The men of Yod*, or the Inventors, the Producers. The Nobility of Intellect.
> *The men of He*, or the depositories of the great truths discovered by the men of *Yod* : the Savants, the Judges. Professional nobility.
> *The men of Vau*, or the guardians and defenders of the former : the Warriors. Nobility of the sword.
> *The men of the 2nd He*, the multitude, from which the other classes are continually recruited : the People.

The four great symbols are placed upon the table at random, and Man rules them and must arrange them; in the twenty-first arcana we shall find these symbols arranged in a cross.

We already know that the first card of the Tarot is completed by the twenty-first ($21+1=22$), and we see why, if this first card represents the Microcosm, the last would represent the Macrocosm, and the eleventh card, which serves as the universal link to all the complements of the Tarot, signifies the Vital reflex Current, which serves as a link between the worlds.

But we must not anticipate, so we will return to our first arcanum.

This symbol is the first of the whole Tarot,[1] and it bears Unity as its characteristic number.

The Unity-principle, the origin of which is impenetrable to human conceptions, is placed at the beginning of all things. We cannot discern the origin of this primal cause, which we are content to assert according to the absolute law of analogies so well expressed by Éliphas Lévi—

> " Je crois à *l'inconnu* que Dieu *personnifie*,
> Prouvé par l'être même et par l'immensité,
> *Idéal* SURHUMAIN de la philosophie,
> Parfaite Intelligence et Suprême Bonté." [2]

---

[1] It is curious to notice, when examining the position of the hands of the personages in the Tarot of Marseilles, how often this position represents the alphabetical letter to which the figure corresponds, according to Barrois (system of dactylology or primitive language). The arcana 1, 2 and 5 are especially noticeable in this respect.

[2]   " I believe in the unknown, which God personifies,
> Proved by existence itself and by immensity,
> SUPERHUMAN Ideal of all philosophy,
> Perfect Intelligence and Supreme Benignity."

If we cannot follow this Unknown in its principle, it is at least easy for us to follow it in its consequences, and therefore our study will be only the development of the Unity-principle in creation, according to the Cosmogony of ancient initiation.

God, Man and the Universe are, then, the three meanings of our first card, and we will now say a few words upon the application of these data to all the other cards of the pack.

EXTENSION OF THE THREE GREAT PRINCIPLES THROUGH THE TAROT

The three meanings of the first card respectively represent—

The Creator or *Yod*.
The Receiver or *He*.
The Transformer or *Vau*.

Lastly, there is transition to the second *He*, which is not under consideration at present.

But the first card of the Tarot, taken as a whole, represents the Creator or *Yod*; the second card, taken as a whole, will therefore represent the Receiver or *He*, and the third the Transformer or *Vau*. Each of them will also show the four aspects of *Yod-he-vau-he* in the idea which it expresses.

But what is true of the ternary, is also true of the Septenary, so that the first Septenary, taken as a whole, will represent the CREATOR; the second septenary will represent the RECEIVER; and the third the TRANSFORMER. Lastly, the ternary of transition will represent the return of effects to causes and of consequences to the principle.

Let as condense this all by saying—

> 1st *septenary* represents God.
> 2nd *septenary*   „   Man.
> 3rd *septenary*   „   the Universe.

Moreover, each of these elements is contained in the two others in all points of their manifestations.

GENERAL RECAPITULATION

We have now to recapitulate all the acceptations of the first card in a general figure. As each card in the Tarot will have the same recapitulation, we think that it may be useful to explain the scheme followed in this arrangement.

At the head of the figure will be found the Hebrew number and letter of the card; below it, the name usually given to the card in the Tarot. To the right of the figure are the significations in the Three Worlds: Divine, Human and Natural. Below these three significations is found the absolute key to each card, according to the table of the revolutions of the word *Yod-he-vau-he*. The Hebrew letters placed upon the upper line of this key indicate the origin of the card under consideration; the Hebrew letters placed above it indicate the exact meaning of the card.

1. א

The Juggler

AFFINITIES	SIGNIFICATIONS	
	Key to the Card	*yod* yod
Primitive Hieroglyphic Man	The divine Creator or GOD	
Kabalah Kether	the Father	
Astronomy No affinity	OSIRIS	
	yod of yod yod-yod	
	The divine preserver MAN ADAM	
	he of yod yod-yod	
OBSERVATIONS	The divine transformer THE ACTIVE UNIVERSE NATURA NATURANS[1]	
	vau of yod yod-yod	
	2nd he of yod yod-yod	

[1] According to Spinoza, the only free cause and substance of all modes or phenomena, conscious and unconscious, past present and to come. [A. P. M.]

THE HIGH PRIESTESS   THE HIGH PRIESTESS

2. ב

2nd Hebrew letter (Beth)

ORIGIN OF THE SYMBOLISM OF THE SECOND CARD
OF THE TAROT

The *Beth* hieroglyphically expresses the mouth of
man as the organ of speech. Speech is the production
of man's inner self. Therefore *Beth* expresses that
inner self, central as a dwelling, to which one can retire
without fear of disturbance. From this ideas arise of a
Sanctuary, an inviolate abode for man and for God. But
the *Beth* also expresses every production that emanates
from this mysterious retreat, every internal activity, and
from it issue ideas of Instruction, of the higher Knowledge, of Law, of Erudition, of occult science or Kabalah.

Beth corresponds with the number 2, and astronomically with the moon. This number has given birth

to all the *passive* significations emanated from the Binary; hence the ideas of reflection, of Woman, applied to the Moon relatively to the Sun and to Woman relatively to Man.

THE SECOND CARD OF THE TAROT

The High Priestess

God, understood as the Father, reflects Himself, and gives birth to God the Man, or God the Son, who is negative relatively to his Creator. As we have seen, man is the divine receiver; therefore this second card of the Tarot will express all the ideas of the first conceived negatively.

The first card represents a man standing; this, on the contrary, bears the figure of a seated woman.

> First idea of passivity by the woman and by her position.

The man, endowed with all the attributes of Power, was placed in the midst of Nature.

The woman is adorned with all the attributes of Authority and persuasion, and she is placed under the porch of the temple of Isis, between two columns.

> Idea of a sacred dwelling, of a divine recipient.
> The two columns, like the arms of the Juggler, express the Positive and the Negative.

The woman is crowned with a tiara, surmounted by the lunar crescent; she is enveloped in a transparent veil falling over her face. On her breast she bears the solar cross, and upon her knees lies an open book, which she half covers with her mantle.

This is the picture of Isis, of Nature, whose veil must not be raised before the profane. The book indicates that the doctrines of Isis are hidden; but she divulges to the magi the secrets of the true Kabalah and of occult science. Let us admire this profound symbol.

The first card expressed Osiris in the three worlds; this second conveys the signification of Isis, the companion of Osiris—

> *In God* it is the reflex of Osiris, the reflex of God the Father, Isis, or God the Son.
>
> *In Man* it is the reflex of Adam of the absolute man: Eve, the woman, life (הוה).
>
> *In the Universe* it is the reflex of *natura naturans:* it is *natura naturata.*[1]

2. ב

The High Priestess

AFFINITIES		SIGNIFICATIONS
Hieroglyphic—	The Mouth of Man	Reflex of God the Father or Osiris
Kabalah	*Chokmah*	GOD
Astronomy	*The Moon* ☽	the Son
Day of the Week	Monday	ISIS
Hebrew letter	Beth (Double)	*yod of he* he he
		Reflex of Adam EVE the woman *he of he* he he
OBSERVATIONS		Reflex of Natura naturans NATURA NATURATA *vau of he* he he
		2nd *he of he*

[1] That which follows from the divine nature.

THE EMPRESS   THE EMPRESS

3. ‎ג‎

3rd Hebrew letter (Gimel)

ORIGIN OF THE SYMBOLISM OF THE THIRD CARD OF THE
TAROT

The hieroglyphic meaning of the letter *Gimel* is the throat, the hand of man half closed in the act of prehension. Hence it signifies all that incloses, all that is hollow, a canal, an inclosure. The throat is the spot where the words conceived in the brain are formed, or I might almost say embodied; therefore the *Gimel* is the symbol of the material envelopment of spiritual forms, of organic generation in all its phases, of all the ideas springing from the corporeal organs or their actions.

Generation is the mystery by which the spirit unites itself to matter, by which the Divine becomes Human.

The signification of Venus-Urania, to which this card corresponds, is easily understood by the above explana-

THE THIRD CARD OF THE TAROT

The Empress

This symbol would therefore signify ideas of generation, of embodiment in all the worlds.

A woman seen full face

> The human being becomes corporeal in the womb of a woman.

This woman is represented with wings, or in the centre of a radiating sun.

> The idea of the spirituality of the vivifying Principle of all beings.

She holds an eagle in her right hand.

> The eagle is the symbol of the soul and of life (Holy Spirit).

In the left hand she bears a sceptre forming the astrological sign of Venus.

> The sceptre is held in the left hand to indicate the passive influence, which Nature, Venus-Urania, or the woman exercises in the generation of beings.

She wears a crown with twelve points, or twelve stars.

> The sign of the diffusion of the vivifying Principle through all the worlds, and of the sun through the Zodiac.

The third card of the Tarot shows the result of the reciprocal action of the two first terms neutralizing each other in one principle. It is the Neuter Element of Wronski, the basis of every system of reality.

The absolute creative force, or Osiris, and the absolute preservative force, or Isis, neutralize themselves in the equilibrated force, which contains in itself the two distinct properties of the two first forms.

In God this would be the equilibrium of the Father and of the Son, or—

God the Holy Ghost
HORUS
The universal vivifying force.

In Man this would be the equilibrium of the Adam-Eve—

Adam-Eve
or HUMANITY.

In the Universe this would be the equilibrium of *Natura naturans* and of *Natura naturata*—

THE WORLD
Conceived like a being.

2. ב

The Empress

AFFINITIES		SIGNIFICATIONS	*vau* vau
Primitive Hieroglyphic	{ The hand in the act of prehension	God the Holy Ghost Horus **THE UNIVERSAL** **VIVIFYING FORCE** *yod of vau* vau-vau	
Kabalah	BINAH		
Astronomy	Venus ♀		
Day	Friday		
Hebrew letter	Gimel (double)		
		Adam Eve **HUMANITY** *he of vau* vau-vau	
OBSERVATIONS		**THE WORLD** *vau of vau* vau-vau	
		2nd he of vau vau-vau	

The creative principle and the receptive principle, having, by their mutual action, given birth to the transforming principle, a complete entity is created.

The term which now follows will correspond with the *second he* of the Sacred Word, and will consequently indicate the passage from one series to the other.

THE EMPEROR   THE EMPEROR

4. ד

4th Hebrew letter (Daleth)

ORIGIN OF THE SYMBOLISM OF THE FOURTH CARD OF
THE TAROT

The hieroglyphic meaning of *Daleth* is the womb. It suggests the idea of an object giving plentiful nourishment, the source of future growth. The child is the living link, which in its neutrality reunites the opposition of the sexes; the *Daleth* therefore denotes abundance springing from division.

Like the 1, it is a sign of active creation; but this creation is the result of previous actions easily determinable, whilst the origin of the Unity is inaccessible to human conceptions. The *Daleth* expresses a creation made by a created being according to divine laws.[1]

The *Daleth* should be the image of the active vivifying principle of the Universe, Jupiter, the reflex of the Primal cause.

THE FOURTH CARD OF THE TAROT

The Emperor

This symbol should express in the active form all that the preceding card expressed in the passive.
A man seated in profile.

> The man indicates the active; his position, however, shows that this activity is engendered by a superior term. The 1st arcanum, the Juggler, the active absolute, was represented standing, looking to the front; the 4th arcanum, active relative, is seated in profile.

This man holds in his right hand the sceptre, the symbol of generation or of Venus ♀.

> The sceptre is held in the right hand, to indicate the active influence, which the vivifying principle exercises in nature, by opposition to the formative principle (arc. 3).

The man is bearded and wears a helmet with twelve

[1] See the second *He*, and the study upon the number 4.

points (six on each side). He is seated upon a cubic stone, which bears the figure of an eagle.

> The helmet indicates the rule of the Divine Will in the Universe, and its universal action in the creation of Life (eagle).
>
> The position upon the cubic stone indicates realization in all the worlds.
>
> (1st) Realization of the Divine Word by the creation.
>
> (2nd) Realization of the ideas of the creature shared by the quadruple work of the spirit—
>
> > Affirmation,—Negation,
> > Discussion,
> > Solution.
>
> (3rd) Realization of the actions conceived by the Will.

The man's legs are crossed, his body forms a triangle ♀.

> Domination of the Spirit over Matter.

Considered more attentively, the figure reproduces the symbol of Jupiter 2+, who is represented by this card.

The fourth card of the Tarot corresponds to the second *He*, and therefore bears two very distinct aspects.

It first expresses a term of transition uniting the first series (active and passive forces, the link between the two forces) to the following series; the passage from one world to the other.

But it also represents this term of transition, itself becoming the first term in the following series. As the following series, taken as a whole, is negative relatively to the first, the fourth symbol represents the active influence of the first series 1, 2, 3, in the second series 4, 5, 6.

The 4 therefore expresses the reflections of the first card in all its details. It acts towards the first series exactly as the second card acted towards the first card. This interprets its meaning—

> *In the Divine:* Reflex of God the Father—
> THE WILL.
>
> *In the Human:* Reflex of Adam—
> THE POWER.
>
> *In the Natural:* Reflex of *Natura naturans*—
> THE UNIVERSAL CREATIVE FLUID.
> The soul of the Universe.

4. ד

The Emperor

AFFINITIES		SIGNIFICATIONS
Primitive	The Womb	Reflex of God the Father
Hieroglyphic		THE WILL
Kabalah	CHESED	
Astronomy	Jupiter	Reflex of Adam
Day	Thursday	
Hebrew letter	Daleth (double)	THE POWER
OBSERVATIONS		Reflex of *Natura naturans*
		The universal creative fluid
		THE SOUL OF THE UNIVERSE

THE POPE

THE POPE

5. ה

5th Hebrew letter (He)

ORIGIN OF THE SYMBOLISM OF THE FIFTH CARD OF
THE TAROT

The hieroglyphic meaning of *He* is aspiration, breath.
It is by aspiration that life is incessantly maintained
and created.   Hence springs the attribution of all that
animates to *He.*

But life specializes being, by rendering it different
from any other; hence the attribution of being itself to
this letter.

However, the action of life does not stop here.   It
is also the mediating principle, which attaches the
material body to the divine spirit, in the same way that
man unites God and Nature; life is to the man (*aleph*)
what man is to the universe, pre-eminently the mediate

principle. Here we find the origin of the ideas of bond, of the reunion of opposing principles, of religion, attributed to *He*.

This letter is simple; astronomically it corresponds with the igneous sign of the Ram, which it explains.

THE FIFTH CARD OF THE TAROT

The Pope

This symbol expresses the following ideas—

(1st) Idea of Life, of animation,
(2nd) Idea of Being,
(3rd) Idea of Reunion.

The Initiate of the mysteries of Isis is seated between the two columns of the sanctuary. He leans upon a triple cross, and makes the sign of Esotericism with his left hand.

> The triple Cross represents the triple *Lingam* of Indian theogony; that is to say, the penetration of the creative power throughout the Divine, the Intellectual and the Physical Worlds, which causes all the manifestations of universal life to appear (first idea).

> The two columns symbolize: on the right, Law; on the left, Liberty to obey and to disobey, the essence of Being (second idea).

The Initiate wears a tiara. Two crowned men kneel at his feet, one clothed in red, the other in black.

> Here we find the active form of that symbolism which is expressed in passive form by the second card. The same idea of Esotericism, of secret Instruction, reappears; but the tuition is now practical and oral; it no longer requires a book (third idea).

As we see, this card is the complement of the second;

the same rule applies to all the cards, when the total of their number makes 7.   Thus—

3		4
The Empress	is completed by	The Emperor
	$4 + 3 = 7$	
	$7 = 28 = 10 = 1$	

2		5
The High Priestess	is completed by	The Pope
	$2 + 5 = 7$	

1		6
The Juggler	is completed by	The Lovers
	$1 + 6 = 7.$	

The fifth card of the Tarot corresponds with the letter *he* of the Sacred Word.   It is the direct reflection of the 4th arcanum, and the indirect reflection of the 2nd arcanum.   It therefore signifies—

In the Divine: Reflex of the Will—

INTELLIGENCE
(characteristic of God the Son).

In the Human: Reflex of Power—

AUTHORITY
(characteristic of the Woman).
Religion.   Faith.

In Nature: Reflex of the Soul of the World, or of the Universal creative fluid—

THE UNIVERSAL LIFE
(characteristic of *Natura naturata*).

5. ה

The Pope

AFFINITIES		SIGNIFICATIONS
Primitive ⎫ Hieroglyphic ⎬ Breath		Reflex of the Will INTELLIGENCE
Kabalah	Pechad	Reflex of Power AUTHORITY RELIGION—FAITH
Astronomy	The Ram	
Month	March	
Hebrew letter	He (simple)	
OBSERVATIONS		Reflex of the soul of the world THE UNIVERSAL LIFE

Universal life is the negative side of the vivifying universal fluid. Their reciprocal action will give rise to the universal attraction or universal Love represented by the 6th arcanum.

THE LOVERS

THE LOVERS

6. ٦

The 6th Hebrew letter (Vau)

ORIGIN OF THE SYMBOLISM OF THE SIXTH CARD OF
THE TAROT

The hieroglyphic symbol of *Vau* is the eye, all that
relates to light and brilliancy. The eye establishes
the link between the external world and ourselves; by
it light and form are revealed to us. The dominant
idea expressed by this letter will therefore be that of
a connection, of a link between antagonisms. We have
already dwelt at some length upon the *Vau*, but it
may be useful to quote Fabre d'Olivet's observations
upon this letter *in extenso :—*

"This sign is the image of the deepest and most
inconceivable mystery, the image of the knot which

reunites, or of the point which separates the nothing from being. It is the universal convertible sign, which forms the passage from one nature to the other; communicating on one side with the sign of light and of spiritual sense ꜧ (a pointed *Vau*), which is but a higher form of itself; on the other hand linking itself in its degeneration with *Ayin* (y), the sign of darkness and of the material senses, which again is but a lower form of itself."

The *Vau* is the second simple letter; astronomically it represents the second sign of the zodiac, the Bull.

THE SIXTH CARD OF THE TAROT

The Lovers

This symbol represents reunion, antagonism, with all their consequences.

A beardless youth (our Juggler of the 1st arcanum), but without a hat, is standing motionless in the angle where two roads meet. His arms form a diagonal cross upon his breast.

> The repetition of the 1st arcanum under another form. Here the man is not one of the Initiates. He does not know how to direct the magnetic currents of the Astral Light; he is therefore plunged in the antagonism of different ideas which he has no power to master.

Two women, one on his right, the other on his left, each with one hand upon his shoulder, point to the two roads. The woman on the right has a circle of

gold upon her head, the one on the left is dishevelled
and crowned with vine leaves.

> The two arms of the Juggler, expressing the positive
> and negative, the two columns of the temple of Isis,
> expressing necessity and liberty, are here personified
> by the two women, who represent Vice and Virtue.
> The future of the young man depends upon the road
> which he chooses—whether, in other words, he becomes
> one of the Initiates, the Mage of the 1st arcanum (the
> spiritual ١), or the rash, thunder-stricken personage of
> the 16th arcanum (the ﻉ).

The spirit of Justice floats above this group in a
radiant halo; he bends his bow and aims the arrow
of Punishment at the personification of Vice.

> This is a profound symbol, indicating that if man chooses
> the path of Virtue he will not be left unaided, but
> that Providence will ally itself to his will and assist
> him to overcome vice.

In short, this hieroglyph expresses the struggle
between the passions and conscience, the antagonism
of ideas.

But this antagonism is also the most powerful natural
producer that exists in the world, when it resolves itself
into Love, which attracts the opponents and unites
them for ever.

The sixth card of the Tarot must be regarded
under two aspects, which tend to the same signification.

1. As 3 of the 4, that is to say, as representing the
4th arcanum, or the reflection of 1 considered in its
relation to union;

2. As balancing 4 and 5. This is shown in the triangle formed by the second ternary—

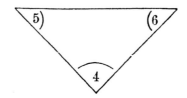

Each card balances the two others.

The 4 balances the 5 and the 6.
  „ 5   „   „ 4   „   6.
  „ 6   „   „ 4   „   5.

Its signification proceeds from this :—

In the Divine. The Equilibrium between Will and Intelligence—
BEAUTY
(characteristic of the Holy Spirit).

In the Human. The Equilibrium between Power and Authority—
LOVE
(characteristic of Humanity).
CHARITY

In Nature. The Equilibrium between the Universal soul and the Universal life—

THE UNIVERSAL ATTRACTION.
Universal Love.

6. ו

The Lovers

AFFINITIES		SIGNIFICATIONS
Primitive Hieroglyphic } The eye, The ear		Equilibrium of Will and Intelligence
Kabalah	Tiphereth	BEAUTY
Astronomy	The Bull	
Month	April	Equilibrium of Power and Authority
Hebrew letter	Vau (simple)	LOVE
		CHARITY
OBSERVATIONS		Equilibrium of the Universal Soul and the Universal Life
		THE UNIVERSAL ATTRACTION
		or
		UNIVERSAL LOVE

CONSTITUTION OF GOD

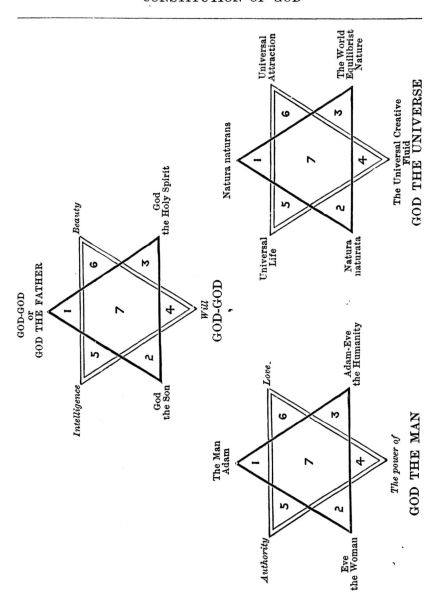

GOD-GOD
or
GOD THE FATHER

Beauty
God the Holy Spirit
Intelligence
God the Son

GOD-GOD
Will

GOD THE UNIVERSE

Universal Attraction
The World Equilibrist Nature
Natura naturans
Universal Life
Natura naturata
The Universal Creative Fluid

GOD THE MAN

Love.
Adam-Eve the Humanity
The Man Adam
Authority
Eve the Woman
The power of

CHAPTER XI

SECOND SEPTENARY: ARCANA 7 TO 13
ANDROGONY

Key to the 2nd Septenary—The Zain and the Chariot—The Heth
and Justice—The Teth and the Hermit—The Yod and the
Wheel of Fortune—The Kaph and Strength—The Lamed
and the Hanged Man. Summary of the 2nd Septenary—
Constitution of Man.

KEY TO THE SECOND SEPTENARY

ARRANGEMENT OF THE FIGURES FOR STUDY

CHARACTER OF THE FIGURES

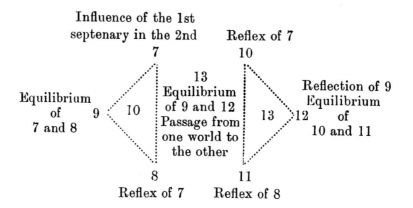

The 1st septenary has shown us the world of principles, or of the Creation under all its aspects; we shall now study the world of laws, or of Preservation.

---

7. ז

7th Hebrew letter (Zain)

ORIGIN OF THE SYMBOLISM OF THE SEVENTH CARD OF
THE TAROT

Hieroglyphically the *Zain* represents an arrow, and therefore it suggests the idea of a weapon, of the instrument which man uses to rule and conquer, and to attain his object.

The *Zain* expresses victory in all the worlds. As a simple letter, it corresponds with the astronomic sign of the Twins in the Zodiac.

THE CHARIOT   THE CHARIOT

SEVENTH CARD OF THE TAROT

The Chariot

The symbolism of this card corresponds in all points with the ideas which it expresses.

A Conqueror, crowned with a coronet, upon which rise three shining Pentagrams of gold, advances in a cubical chariot, surmounted by an azure, star-decked canopy supported by four columns.

> This symbol reproduces the 1st and 21st arcana in another order of ideas. The four columns represent the four animals of the 21st arcanum and the four symbols of the 1st arcanum, symbols of the quaternary in all its acceptations.
>
> The Conqueror, who occupies the centre of the four elements, is the man who has vanquished and directed the elementary forces: this victory is confirmed by the cubical form of the chariot, and by the Pentagrams which crown the Initiate.

The Conqueror has three right angles upon his cuirass, and he bears upon his shoulders the Urim and Thummim of the sovereign priest, represented by the two crescents of the moon on the right and left; in his hand is a sceptre surmounted by a globe, a square and a triangle. Upon the square, which forms the front of the chariot, we see the Indian *lingam*, surmounted by the flying sphere of Egypt.

Two sphinxes—one white, the other black—are harnessed to the chariot.

> This symbol represents the sacred septenary in all its manifestations. The word *Yod-he-vau-he* is portrayed upon the front of the chariot by the winged globe, to indicate that the septenary gives the key to the whole Tarot. The two sphinxes correspond to the two principles, active and passive. The Conqueror corresponds especially with the Sword and with the *Vau* of the Sacred Name.

The 7th card of the Tarot shows the influence of the creation in the preservation of the Divine in the Human. It represents the *Yod*, or the God of the 2nd septenary.

THE GOD *of the 2nd septenary.*
Man performing the function of God the Creator.

THE FATHER

The law of the 2nd septenary.

REALIZATION
(Reflex of the Power)

The Man of the 2nd septenary
Man performing the function of Adam.

THE ASTRAL LIGHT

7. ז

The Chariot

AFFINITIES		SIGNIFICATIONS
Primitive Hieroglyphic } Arrow		Man performing the function of God the creator
Kabalah	Hod	THE FATHER
Astronomy	The Twins	The Realizer
Month	May	
Hebrew letter	Zain (simple)	Law
		THE REALIZATION
OBSERVATIONS		
		Nature performing the function of Adam
		THE ASTRAL LIGHT

The passage from one world to the other is scarcely performed, before we see the same law in action that we found in the 1st septenary. The second term of this series will be the reflection of the first, just as the second term of the first series also reflected the first. However, since this 2nd septenary is the central one, we shall find, as the foundation of all its constituent arcana, the idea of mediation or equilibrium. This is shown by the eighth card.

JUSTICE

JUSTICE

8. ח

8th Hebrew letter (Heth)

ORIGIN OF THE SYMBOLISM OF THE EIGHTH CARD OF THE TAROT

Hieroglyphically the *Heth* expresses a field. From it springs the idea of anything that requires labour, trouble, an effort.

Continued effort results in the establishment of an equilibrium, between the destruction of the works of man accomplished by Nature, when left to herself, and the preservation of this work. Hence the idea of balancing power, and consequently of Justice, attributed to this letter.[1]

[1] This letter, an intermediary between ה (He) and כ (Kaph), the one designating life, absolute existence, the other the relative life, assimilated existence, is the sign of elementary existence: it is the image of a kind of equilibrium, and attaches itself to ideas of effort, of labour and of normal and legislative action.—FABRE D'OLIVET.

Astronomically the *Heth* corresponds to the sign of Cancer in the Zodiac.

THE EIGHTH CARD OF THE TAROT

Justice

The ideas expressed by this symbol are of Equilibrium in all its forms.

A woman seen full face, and wearing an iron coronet, is seated upon a throne. She is placed between the two columns of the temple. The solar cross is traced upon her breast.

> Here we find the continuation of the symbolism of the 2nd and 5th arcana. The seated woman occupies the centre between the columns, offering a first idea of the equilibrium between Good and Evil.

She holds a sword, point upwards, in her right hand, and a balance in her left.

> Occult science (2), at first theoretical, has become practical (5), and has been taught verbally. Now it appears in all the pitilessness of consequences, terrible for the false Magi (the Sword), but just toward the true Initiates (Balance). The signification of this arcanum is central between the 5th (ה *He*) and the 11th (כ *Kaph*) arcana.

This card is the complement of the eleventh, as the fifth was of the second. In the 1st septenary all the cards which, by addition, formed the number 7, completed each other; in the 2nd septenary all the cards which, added together, form 19, act in the same way.

7		12
The Chariot	is completed by	The Hanged Man

$$7 + 12 = 19$$
$$19 = 10 = 1$$

8		11
Justice	is completed by	Strength

$$8 + 11 = 19$$

9		10
The Hermit	is completed by	The Wheel of Fortune

$$9 + 10 = 19$$

The eighth card of the Tarot represents the conception in preservation of the second card. It synthesizes in itself the meaning of the second and of the fifth card of the Tarot, and represents the reflex of the seventh. It signifies—

1. *In the Divine.* God the Son of the 2nd septenary. The woman fulfilling the functions of God the Son.

THE MOTHER

Reflex of the Father. Preserver of God the Son in Humanity.

2. Passive law of the 2nd septenary.

JUSTICE

Reflex of Realization and Authority.

3. *The woman of the 2nd septenary.* Nature fulfilling the function of Eve.

ELEMENTARY EXISTENCE

Reflex of the Astral Light. Preservation of *Natura naturata* in the World.

8. ח

Justice

AFFINITIES		SIGNIFICATIONS
Primitive Hieroglyphic } A Field		The woman fulfilling the functions of God the Son THE MOTHER
Kabalah	Netsach	
Astronomy	Cancer	
Month	June	
Hebrew letter	Heth (simple)	Law JUSTICE
OBSERVATIONS		Nature performing the function of Eve ELEMENTARY EXISTENCE

The elementary existence is the means by which the astral vivifying fluid or astral light (7) manifests itself through the ether or astral matter (9). This is demonstrated by the following arcanum.

THE HERMIT   THE HERMIT

9. ט

9th Hebrew letter (Teth)

ORIGIN OF THE SYMBOLISM OF THE NINTH CARD OF THE TAROT

Hieroglyphically the *Teth* represents a roof and suggests the idea of a place of safety, a protection. All the ideas arising from this letter are derived from the alliance of safety and protection ensured by wisdom.

Astronomically the *Teth* corresponds with the zodiacal sign of the Lion.

NINTH CARD OF THE TAROT

The Hermit

The following ideas are connected with this card—

     1. Protection.
     2. Wisdom, Circumspection.

An old man walking, supported by a stick. He carries before him a lighted lamp, half hidden by the great mantle which envelopes him.

> This symbol is midway between the sixth and the twelfth.
> Protection is indicated by the mantle which envelopes the old man.
> Wisdom is suggested by the half-hidden lamp.
> The stick indicates that the Sage is always armed to fight against Injustice or Error.

By comparing this card with two others, the sixth and the twelfth, we shall see that the beardless young man in the former (6th) has chosen the right path. Experience, won in the labour of life, has rendered him a prudent old man, and prudence united to wisdom will safely lead him to the higher level, which he is anxious to attain (12th card). The arrow shot by the genius in the sixth arcanum has become his support, and the effulgent aureole which surrounded the genius is now imprisoned in the lamp which guides the Initiate. This is the result of his prolonged efforts.

The ninth card of the Tarot represents the third, conceived as preserver and recipient. It also balances the seventh and the eighth.

1. Humanity fulfilling the function of God the Holy Spirit.

The human creative force.

HUMAN LOVE

> The preserving power of Humanity. The equilibrium of the Father and the Mother.

2. Equilibrium of Realization and Justice.

PRUDENCE
(Silence)

3. Nature accomplishing the function of humanity. Equilibrium of the Astral Light and Elementary Existence.

THE NATURAL PRESERVING FORCE
The Astral Fluid

9.   ט

The Hermit

AFFINITIES		SIGNIFICATIONS
Primitive Hieroglyphic }	A Roof	Humanity accomplishing the functions of God the Holy Spirit
Kabalah	IESOD	
Astronomy	The Lion	HUMAN LOVE
Month	July	
Hebrew letter	Teth (simple)	PRUDENCE
		Silence
OBSERVATIONS		
		The natural Preserving Force
		THE ASTRAL FLUID

The astral fluid therefore represents the universal preservation of the active forces in Nature. Here ends the first ternary of the septenary of Preservation. We shall now see the reflections of all these terms in the following ternary.

THE WHEEL OF FORTUNE   THE WHEEL OF FORTUNE

10. ,

10th Hebrew letter (Yod)

ORIGIN OF THE SYMBOLISM OF THE TENTH CARD OF
THE TAROT

The hieroglyphic meaning of the *Yod* is the finger of man; the forefinger extended as a sign of command. This letter has therefore become the image of potential manifestation, of spiritual duration, and, lastly, of the eternity of time, with all the ideas relating to it.[1]

[1] See the study of the word *Yod-he-vau-he.*

The *Yod* is a simple letter; astronomically it corresponds with the zodiacal sign of the Virgin.

TENTH CARD OF THE TAROT

The Wheel of Fortune

Two principal ideas are expressed by this symbol—

1. The idea of Command, of Supremacy.
2. The idea of duration, of the eternal action of time.

The wheel of fortune suspended upon its axis. To the right *Anubis*, the genius of good ascending; to the left *Typhon*, the genius of evil descending; the *Sphinx* is balanced upon the centre of the wheel, holding a sword in its lion claws.

> The first idea is expressed by the ternary, Anubis or positive, Typhon or negative, the balanced Sphinx, the ruler.
>
> The second idea is expressed by the wheel, a line without beginning or end, the symbol of eternity.

The 10th arcanum is midway between the 7th and 13th arcana.

$$7 + 13 = 20 \quad \frac{20}{2} = 10.$$

It expresses the incessant equilibrium which modifies the creative realizations of the septenary by the necessary destruction through Death (arcanum 13). The three arcana, 7, 10, 13, correspond exactly with the Hindu trinity or *Trimurti*.

> Brahma = Creator   = Arcanum 7.
> Siva   = Destroyer = Arcanum 13.
> Vishnu = Preserver = Arcanum 10.

It represents the course of things according to the ternary law, which directs all the divine manifestations.

The tenth card of the Tarot commences the negative portion of the 2nd septenary, and expresses the notion of the septenary considered in its reflections.

It will therefore represent—

1. Reflex of will (see 4th arcanum).

NECESSITY
The *Karma* of the Hindus.

2. Reflex of power and of realization.

MAGIC POWER
Fortune.

(To will.)

3. Reflex of the universal soul.

FORCE POTENTIAL IN ITS MANIFESTATION

10. ⁷

The Wheel of Fortune

AFFINITIES		SIGNIFICATIONS
Primitive Hieroglyphic } The Forefinger		NECESSITY The *Karma* of the Hindus
Kabalah	MALKUTH	
Astronomy	The Virgin	MAGIC POWER
Month	August	Fortune
Hebrew letter	Yod (simple)	*To Will*
OBSERVATIONS		Reflection of the universal soul FORCE POTENTIAL IN ITS MANIFESTATION

The absolute creative force has varied successively in the universal vivifying Fluid (4), and the astral Light (7); now it is represented by force potential in its manifestation. We shall see this force fully displayed in the following arcanum.

STRENGTH   STRENGTH

11. כ

11th Hebrew letter (Kaph)

ORIGIN OF THE SYMBOLISM OF THE ELEVENTH CARD OF
THE TAROT

The hieroglyphic meaning of the *Kaph* is the hand of man, half closed and in the act of prehension, like the *Gimel*. But the *Kaph* is a reinforcement of the *Gimel*, so that we might say that it designates the hand of man in the act of grasping strongly. Ideas of strength are therefore applied to this letter.

The number 11, the first after the decade, gives a different value to the *Kaph*, which designates a reflected, transitory life, a kind of mould, which receives and restores every variety of form.

It is derived from the letter *Heth*, ח (8), which is itself derived from the sign of absolute life, He ה (5). Thus, allied on one side to the sign of elementary life (see the 8th arcanum), it joins to the signification of the letter *Heth* (ח) that of the organic sign ג (*Gimel*) (3rd arcanum), of which too it is merely a reinforcement.

The *Kaph* is a double letter, corresponding astronomically with March and Tuesday.

THE ELEVENTH CARD OF THE TAROT

Strength

Only two ideas are expressed by this arcanum—

1. The idea of strength.
2. The idea of vitality.

A young girl calmly closes a lion's mouth without any visible effort.

(First idea.)

This young girl wears the vital sign ∞ upon her head.

(Second idea.)

The 11th arcanum is midway between the 5th and 14th arcana. In it we find the symbolism of the 8th arcanum transferred to the physical plane. It is, in fact, an image of the power given by the sacred science (2nd arcanum) when justly applied (8).

The eleventh card of the Tarot shows us all the

negative or reflective significations of the fifth, that is to say—

    1. Reflex of Intelligence (5).

LIBERTY

    2. Reflex of Authority, of Faith.

COURAGE
(To dare)

    3. Reflex of Universal Life.   Manifestation of the strength of the preceding arcanum.

REFLECTED AND TRANSITORY LIFE

11. כ

Strength

AFFINITIES		SIGNIFICATIONS
Primitive Hieroglyphic	The Hand in the act of grasping	Reflex of the Intelligence
Astronomy	Mars ♂	LIBERTY
Day	Tuesday	
Hebrew letter	Kaph (double)	Reflex of Authority, of Faith
		COURAGE
		(*To dare*)
OBSERVATIONS		
		Reflex of Universal Life
		Reflex and Transitory Life

The strength, already potential in its manifestations, has shown its full force in the 11th arcanum; it will balance itself in the following arcanum.

THE HANGED MAN   THE HANGED MAN

12. ל

12th Hebrew letter (Lamed)

ORIGIN OF THE SYMBOLISM OF THE TWELFTH CARD OF
THE TAROT

Hieroglyphically the *Lamed* designates the arm, and therefore it is connected with anything that stretches, that raises, that unfolds like the arm, and has become the sign of expansive movement. It is applied to all ideas of extension, of occupation, of possession. As a last sign, it is the image of the power derived from elevation.

Divine expansion in humanity is produced by the

prophets and revelation, and this inspires the idea of the revealed law. But the revelation of the law involves punishment for him who violates it, or elevation for him who understands it; and here we find the ideas of punishment, of violent death, voluntary or involuntary.

The *Lamed*, a simple letter, astronomically corresponds with the zodiacal sign of the Balance.

TWELFTH CARD OF THE TAROT

The Hanged Man

A man hangs by one foot to a gibbet, resting upon two trees, each bearing six branches, which have been cut off.

The man's hands are tied behind his back, and the fold of his arms forms the base of a reversed triangle, of which his head is the apex. His eyes are open and his fair hair floats upon the wind. His right leg crosses his left and so forms a cross.

> This young man is again the Juggler whose transformations we have already followed in the 1st, 6th and 7th arcana.
>
> Like the sun placed in the midst of the signs of the Zodiac (six on each side, the lopped branches), our young hero is again suspended between two decisions, from which will spring, no longer his physical future, as in the 6th arcanum, but his spiritual future.

The 12th arcanum fills the centre between the 6th arcanum (Wisdom) and the 15th (Fatality). These arcana represent the two women of the 6th arcanum, regarded in the spiritual sense.

This Hanged Man serves as an example to the presumptuous, and his position indicates discipline, the absolute submission which the human owes to the Divine.

Considered alchemically, the Hanged Man shows the sign of personality.

In the Hermetic grade of Rose Croix (18th degree of the Ancient and Accepted Rite) one of the signs of recognition consists in crossing the legs like those of the Hanged Man. It is needless to say that the origin and meaning of this sign is quite unknown to Freemasons.

The twelfth card of the Tarot represents Equilibrated Power. It neutralizes the oppositions of the tenth and eleventh cards.

1. Equilibrium of Necessity and Liberty—

CHARITY—Grace

(Preserving power of Love)

2. Equilibrium of Power and Courage. Reflex of Prudence—

ACQUIRED EXPERIENCE

(Knowledge)

3. Equilibrium of potential Manifestation (10) and of reflected Life (11). Reflex of the astral Fluid.

EQUILIBRATED FORCE

12. ל

The Hanged Man

AFFINITIES	SIGNIFICATIONS
Primitive ⎫ The Arm out- Hieroglyphic ⎭ stretched	**CHARITY** Grace
Astronomy The Balance	
Month September	**ACQUIRED EXPERIENCE** (Knowledge)
Hebrew letter Lamed (Simple)	
OBSERVATIONS	**EQUILIBRATED FORCE**

Modifying force is the last term of the 2nd septenary. By it the Astral will realize itself, to pass into the physical, from the world of preservation and reception (2nd septenary) into the world of transformation (3rd septenary).

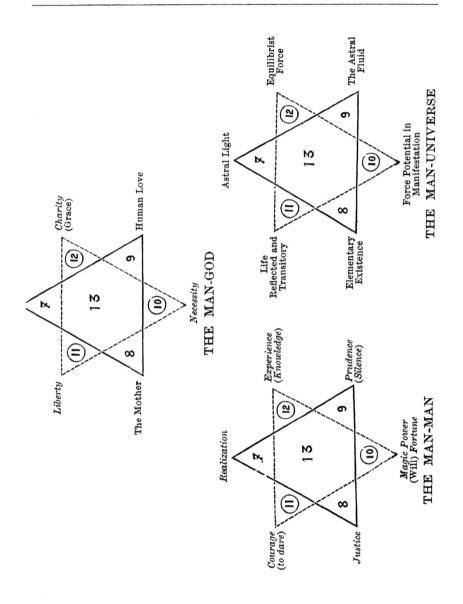

CHAPTER XII

THIRD SEPTENARY: ARCANA 13–19

Key of the 3rd Septenary—The Mem and Death—The Nun and
Temperance—The Samech and the Devil—The Ayin and the
Lightning-struck Tower—The Tzaddi and the Moon. Sum-
mary of the 3rd Septenary—Constitution of the Universe.

KEY TO THE THIRD SEPTENARY

ARRANGEMENT OF THE FIGURES FOR STUDY

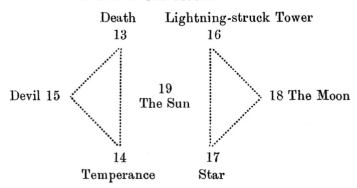

```
              Death        Lightning-struck Tower
               13                    16

                      19
Devil 15             The Sun              18 The Moon

               14                    17
            Temperance              Star
```

CHARACTER OF THE FIGURES

```
Influence of the 2nd Septenary
         in the 3rd              Reflex of 13
              13                    16

                     19
Equilibrium      Equilibrium         Reflex of 15
of 13 and 14  15  of 15 and 18    18 Equili-
                  return             brium of
                 to the world of     16 and 17
                  principles

              14                    17
         Reflex of 13          Reflex of 14
```

The first septenary has shown us the World of Principles, or of the Creation.

The second has developed the World of Laws, or of Preservation.

The third will now show us the World of Facts, or of Transformation.   We shall thus see how the circulation of the forces of the two first septenaries is established.

DEATH   DEATH

13.   מ

13th Hebrew letter (Mem)

ORIGIN OF THE SYMBOLISM OF THE THIRTEENTH CARD OF
THE TAROT

The hieroglyphic meaning of the *Mem* is a woman, the companion of man; it therefore gives rise to ideas of fertility and formation.   It is pre-eminently the maternal and female, the local and plastic sign, an image of external and passive action. Employed at the end of words, this letter becomes a collective sign ם (final *Mem*). In this case it develops the idea of being in unlimited space.

Creation necessitates equal destruction in a contrary sense, and therefore the *Mem* designates all the regenerations that have sprung from previous destruction, all transformations, and consequently death, regarded as the passage from one world to the other.

The *Mem* is one of the three Mother letters.

THIRTEENTH CARD OF THE TAROT

Death, or the Skeleton Mower

The ideas expressed by this arcanum are those of destruction preceding or following regeneration.

A skeleton mows down heads in a field, from which hands and feet spring up on all sides, as the scythe pursues its work.

> The works of the head (conception) become immortal as soon as they are realized (heads and feet).

The 13th arcanum is explained by the 10th (Fortune) and by the 16th (Destruction), between which it stands.

$$10 + 16 = 26 \qquad \frac{26}{2} = 13.$$

13 is therefore the centre between the *Yod* (Principle of the creation) and the *Ayin* (16), Principle of destruction.

The 13th arcanum is completed by the 18th, its

complementary, as the fifth was of the second, and the twelfth of the seventh. (See the 8th and the 5th arcana.)

13		18
Death	is completed by	The Moon
	$13 + 18 = 31$	
	$31 = 4 = 10 = 1$	
14		17
Temperance	is completed by	The Stars
	$14 + 17 = 31$	
15		16
The Devil	is completed by	Destruction
	$15 + 16 = 31$	

The thirteenth card of the Tarot is placed between the invisible and the visible worlds. It is the universal link in nature, the means by which all the influences react from one world to the other. It signifies—

1. God the transformer—

THE UNIVERSAL TRANSFORMING PRINCIPLE

Destructive and creative.

2. The negative of realization—

DEATH

3. The Astral light accomplishing the function of the Creator—

THE UNIVERSAL PLASTIC FORCE

(Balancing death and the transforming force.)

13. מ

Death

AFFINITIES	SIGNIFICATIONS
Primitive ⎫ Hieroglyphic ⎭ The Woman	THE UNIVERSAL TRANSFORMING PRINCIPLE Destroyer and Creator
Hebrew letter Mem (one of the 3 mothers)	
	DEATH
OBSERVATIONS	THE UNIVERSAL PLASTIC FORCE

TEMPERANCE

TEMPERANCE

14.   ﬨ

14th Hebrew letter (Nun)

ORIGIN OF THE SYMBOLISM OF THE FOURTEENTH CARD
OF THE TAROT

The hieroglyphic sense of the *Nun* is the offspring of
the female—a son, a fruit of any kind, all things produced. This letter has therefore become the image of
the being produced or reflected, the sign of individual
and corporeal existence.

As a final it is the sign of augmentation ן (*Nun* as
a final), and gives to the word which contains it all the
individual extension of which the thing expressed is
susceptible.

Astronomically the *Nun* corresponds with the
zodiacal sign of the Scorpion.

In short, the *Nun* expresses the production of any combination, the result of the action of the ascending or creative forces and of the descending or destructive forces, figured by the star of Solomon.

FOURTEENTH CARD OF THE TAROT

Temperance

The following ideas are expressed by this symbol—

    1. Combination of different fluids.
    2. Individualization of existence.

The genius of the Sun pours the fluid of Life from a golden vase into a silver one.

(First idea.)

This essence passes from one vase to the other without one drop being spilt.

(Second idea.)

The fourteenth card represents the young girl whom we have already seen in the 11th arcanum, and whom we shall see again in the 17th.

The vital current placed upon her head in the 11th arcanum here passes from one vase into another, but will spread further in the 17th arcanum.

The fourteenth card of the Tarot shows us the fluid, hitherto carefully preserved, now freely circulated in Nature.

1. Combination of active and passive fluids. Entry of Spirit into Matter, and reaction of Matter upon Spirit—

INVOLUTION

2. Reflex of Justice in the material world—
TEMPERANCE

3. Fixation of reflex Life. Incarnation of Life—
INDIVIDUAL AND CORPOREAL LIFE

14. ‫נ‬

Temperance

AFFINITIES		SIGNIFICATIONS
Primitive Hieroglyphic }	A Fruit	INVOLUTION (The Spirit descends towards Matter)
Astronomy	The Scorpion	
Month	October	
Hebrew letter	Nun (simple)	TEMPERANCE
OBSERVATIONS		
		INDIVIDUAL AND CORPOREAL LIFE

THE DEVIL   THE DEVIL

15.   ס

15th Hebrew letter (Samech)

ORIGIN OF THE SYMBOLISM OF THE FIFTEENTH CARD
OF THE TAROT

The *Samech* expresses the same hieroglyphic sign as
the *Zain* (7th arcanum), that is to say, an arrow—
a weapon of any kind; but to this idea is here added
that of the arrow making a circular movement,
or of any circle defining and delineating a circum-
scription.

This idea of an impassable circle has given birth to
that of Destiny, of Fatality, circumscribing the limits
of the circle in which the human will can act freely;
so that the Serpent forming a circle of his own body,

biting his own tail, has always been the symbol of this Fatality, of this Destiny, encircling the world in its embrace. It is the image of the year (the ring), and of the fatal and settled revolutions of time.

As a letter, the *Samech* is the link (*Zain*) reinforced and turned back upon itself. As a simple letter, it corresponds with the zodiacal sign of Sagittarius.

FIFTEENTH CARD OF THE TAROT

The Devil

In every cosmogony the Devil represents the mysterious astral force, the origin of which is revealed to us by the hieroglyphic of *Samech*.

But a little attentive consideration of the symbol will show us that it contains several of the details which we have already seen in other figures of the Tarot, though under a different aspect.

If we place the Juggler by the side of the Devil we shall see that the arms of the two personages are using the same gesture, but in an inverse sense. The Juggler points his right hand towards the Universe, his left hand towards God; on the other hand, the Devil raises his right hand into the air, whilst his left points to the earth. Instead of the magical, initiating wand of the Juggler, the Demon holds the lighted torch, the symbol of black magic and of Destruction.

By the side of the Devil, and balanced by him, are two personages reproducing the same symbolism that we find in the two women of the Lovers (6), and in the two supports of the gibbet of the Hanged Man (12).

The universal vivifying force represented by the 3rd arcanum has here become the universal destroying force. The sceptre of Venus-Urania has become the Demon's torch; the Angel's wings have changed into the hideous pinions of the God of Evil.

The 3rd arcanum symbolizes the Holy Spirit, or the Providence of Fabre d'Olivet.

The 15th arcanum symbolizes the False Spirit, or the Destiny of Fabre d'Olivet.

$$15 + 3 = \frac{18}{2} = 9.$$

The 9th arcanum, which fills the centre between the two figures, symbolizes Prudence, or the Human Will of Fabre d'Olivet.

The Devil has materialized upon his head the universal fluid which surrounded the head of the Juggler; this is indicated by the two six-pointed horns which adorn him.

He stands upon a cube, which itself is placed upon a sphere, to indicate the domination of Matter (the cube) over the Spirit (the Sphere).

The fifteenth card of the Tarot derives its signification from its own symbolism—

1. DESTINY (chance).

2. FATALITY, the result of the fall of Adam-Eve.

3. The astral fluid, which individualizes.

NAHASH, the Dragon of the Threshold.

15. ס

The Devil

AFFINITIES		SIGNIFICATIONS
Primitive ⎫ Hieroglyphic ⎰	Serpent	**DESTINY**
		Chance
Astronomy	Sagittarius	
Month	November	**FATALITY**
Hebrew letter	Samech (simple)	Result of the fall of Adam-Eve
OBSERVATIONS		**NAHASH**
		The Dragon of the Threshold

THE FIRE OF HEAVEN   THE LIGHTNING-STRUCK TOWER
(*Lightning*)

16. ע

16th Hebrew letter (Ayin**)**

ORIGIN OF THE SYMBOLISM OF THE SIXTEENTH CARD
OF THE TAROT

The *Ayin* expresses the same hieroglyphic as the
Vau (6), but materialized. It is the sign of Material
sense. Again degenerated, it expresses all that is
crooked, false, perverse and bad.

Astronomically this letter corresponds with the
zodiacal sign of Capricornus.

SIXTEENTH CARD OF THE TAROT

The Lightning-struck Tower

This card bears the picture of a tower, with its battle-
ments struck by lightning; two men, one crowned, the

other uncrowned, are falling with the fragments of broken masonry; the attitude of the former recalls the shape of the letter *Ayin*.

This card contains the first allusion to a material building in our pack, but we shall find the same symbol reproduced in the 18th and 19th arcana.

Here it signifies the invisible or spiritual world, incarnated in the visible and material world.

The 16th card represents the material fall of Adam. He will gradually become more gross and earthly, until the 18th arcanum, in which he attains the maximum of his materialization.

The significations of this figure are all derived from the idea of fall, of the materialization of the spiritual letter (*Vau*).

1. Materialization of God the Holy Spirit. (See 3rd arcanum.)

Entrance of the Holy Spirit into the visible World. The Holy Spirit acting like the God of matter.

DIVINE DESTRUCTION

2. The materialization of the Adam-Eve, who have been spiritualized until now.

Entrance of the Adam-Eve into the visible World—

THE FALL

3. Materialization of the Universe-Principle—

THE VISIBLE WORLD

16. ע

The Lightning-struck Tower

AFFINITIES		SIGNIFICATIONS
Primitive ⎫ Hieroglyphic ⎭	Link (Vau) materialized	DIVINE DESTRUCTION
Astronomy	Capricornus	
Month	December	
Hebrew letter	Ayin (simple)	THE FALL
OBSERVATIONS		
		THE VISIBLE WORLD

THE STARS

THE STARS

17. פ

17th Hebrew letter (Phe)

ORIGIN OF THE SYMBOLISM OF THE SEVENTEENTH CARD
OF THE TAROT

The *Phe* expresses the same hieroglyphic meaning as the *Beth* (2nd card), but in a more extended sense. For, whilst the *Beth* signifies the mouth of man as the organ of speech, the *Phe* represents the produce of that organ: Speech.

It is the sign of speech and of all connected with it—the Word in action in Nature with all its consequences.

Astronomically this letter responds to Mercury the God of Speech and of scientific or commercial diffusion, the God of Universal exchange between all beings and all worlds.

Phe is a double letter.

SEVENTEENTH CARD OF THE TAROT

The Star

The ideas expressed by this symbol are those—

    1. Of the expansion of fluids ;
    2. Of their eternal renewal.

A nude female figure pours the Water of Universal Life from two cups.

> The genius of the Sun (14th arcanum) has now descended to earth under the form of this young girl, the image of eternal Youth. The fluids, which she formerly poured from one vase to the other, she now throws upon the ground (first idea).

This young girl is crowned with seven stars; in the midst of them shines one which is very large and brilliant. Near her an ibis (or sometimes a butterfly) rests upon a flower (or bush).

> Here we find the symbol of immortality. The soul (ibis or butterfly) will survive the body, which is only a place of trial (the ephemeral flower). The courage to bear these trials will come from above (the stars).

The fall of the Divine and of the Human into the Material has scarcely taken place, when a mysterious voice whispers courage to the Sinner, by showing him future re-instatement through trial.

This card exactly balances the evil effects of the preceding one, and from it we derive the following significations—

1. *Opposition to destruction.* No destruction is final. Everything is eternal and immortal in God—

IMMORTALITY

Creation of the human soul.

2. The fall is not irreparable. This is whispered to us by the intuitive sentiment that we name

HOPE:

3. The Visible Universe contains the source of its Divinization in itself. This is—

THE FORCE WHICH DISPENSES THE ESSENCE OF LIFE,

which gives it the means of perpetually renewing its creations after their destruction.

17. פ

The Star

AFFINITIES		SIGNIFICATIONS
Primitive Hieroglyphic }	Speech (the mouth and the tongue)	IMMORTALITY
Astronomy	Mercury	
Day	Wednesday	HOPE
Hebrew letter	Phe (double)	
OBSERVATIONS		
		THE FORCE WHICH DISPENSES THE ESSENCE OF LIFE

THE MOON

THE MOON

18. צ

18th Hebrew letter (Tzaddi)

ORIGIN OF THE SYMBOLISM OF THE EIGHTEENTH CARD
OF THE TAROT

The hieroglyphic idea connected with the *Tzaddi* is the same as that of the *Teth* (9th card); but it chiefly signifies a term, an aim, an end. It is a final concluding sign, relating to all the ideas of term, of secession, division and aim.[1]

The *Tzaddi* is a simple letter; it corresponds with the zodiacal sign of Aquarius.

---

[1] Placed at the commencement of a word, it indicates the movement which leads towards the end; placed at the end it marks the term itself to which it has tended; it then receives this form, צ. It is derived from the letter *Samech* ס (15) and the letter *Zain* ז (7), and it marks the secession of one or the other.

THE EIGHTEENTH CARD OF THE TAROT

The Moon

We have now traversed the steps which the spirit descends in its gradual and utter fall towards the material world. All is now ended; the spirit is completely materialized, and the change is indicated by the eighteenth card.

It depicts a meadow feebly lighted by the moon.

> That light, symbol of the soul, no longer reaches us directly; the material world is only lighted by reflection.

The meadow is bounded by a tower on each side. Drops of blood are falling from the moon.

> The material world is the last point which the spirit can reach; it can descend no lower. This is shown by the boundaries of the field. The drops of blood represent the descent of the Spirit into Matter.

A path sprinkled with drops of blood loses itself in the horizon. In the centre of the field a dog and a wolf are howling at the moon; a crayfish is climbing out of the water between the two animals.

> The entry of the Spirit into Matter is so great a fall that everything conspires to augment it.
>
> Servile spirits (the dog), savage souls (the wolf), and crawling creatures (the crayfish) are all present watching the fall of the soul, hoping to aid in its destruction.

1. End of divine Materialization. Final point of involution—

CHAOS

2. End of the Materialization of man—

THE MATERIAL BODY AND ITS PASSIONS

3. End of physical Materialization—

MATTER

18. צ

The Moon

AFFINITIES		SIGNIFICATIONS
Primitive Hieroglyphic }	A Roof	CHAOS
Astronomy	Aquarius	
Month	January	THE MATERIAL BODY AND ITS PASSIONS
Hebrew letter	Tzaddi (simple)	
OBSERVATIONS		
		MATTER

Involution—that is to say, the descent of the Spirit into Matter—ends with the 3rd septenary.

The three last cards of the Tarot will show us how all the emanated forces gradually return to their common principle by evolution.

CONSTITUTION OF THE UNIVERSE

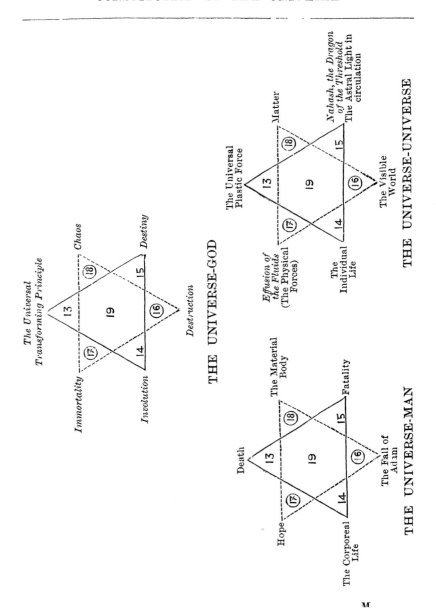

M

CHAPTER XIII

GENERAL TRANSITION: ARCANA 19 TO 21.

The Quoph and the Sun—The Resh and the Judgment—The Shin
and the Fool—The Tau and the World. The Ternary of
Transition.

THE SUN

THE SUN

19. ק

19th Hebrew letter (Quoph)

ORIGIN OF THE SYMBOLISM OF THE NINETEENTH CARD OF
THE TAROT

Hieroglyphically the *Quoph* expresses a sharp
weapon, everything that is useful to man, that de-
fends him and makes an effort for him.

178

The *Quoph* is therefore a particularly compressive, astringent and cutting sign; it is the image of agglomerative, restricting form, which gives rise to the idea of material existence.

This letter represents the letter כ (*Kaph*, 11) entirely materialized, applying itself to purely physical objects. Here is the progression of the sign—

ה (*He*, 5).   Universal life.

ח (*Cheth*, 8).   Elementary existence. The effort of nature.

כ (*Kaph*, 11).   Assimilated life, tending to material forms.

ק (*Quoph*, 19).   Material existence, becoming the medium of forms.

Quoph is a simple letter; it corresponds with the sign of Gemini.

NINETEENTH CARD OF THE TAROT

The Sun

Two naked children stand in a walled enclosure. The sun sends down his rays upon them; drops of gold escape from him and fall upon the ground.

The spirit resumes its ascendancy. It is no longer a reflected light, as in the preceding arcanum, which ilumines the figure, but the direct creative light of the God of our Universe which floods it with its rays.

The walls indicate that we are still in the visible or material world. The two children symbolize the two creative fluids, positive and negative, of the new creature.

1. Awakening of the Spirit. Transition from the

material world to the divine world.   Nature accomplishing the functions of God—

THE ELEMENTS

2. The body of man is renewed—

NUTRITION : DIGESTION

3. The material world commences its ascension towards God—

THE MINERAL KINGDOM

19. ק

The Sun

AFFINITIES		SIGNIFICATIONS
Primitive Hieroglyphic { Axe, sharp-edged weapon		THE ELEMENTS
Astronomy The Gemini		
Month February		NUTRITION
Hebrew letter Quoph (simple)		Digestion
OBSERVATIONS		
		THE MINERAL KINGDOM

THE JUDGMENT   THE JUDGMENT

20. ר

20th Hebrew letter (Resh)

ORIGIN OF THE SYMBOLISM OF THE TWENTIETH CARD OF THE TAROT

The hieroglyphic meaning of the *Resh* is the head of man, and it is therefore associated with the idea of all that possesses in itself an original, determined movement. It is the absolute sign of motion, good or bad, and expresses the renewal of things with regard to their innate power of motion.

The *Resh* is a double letter, and responds astronomically to Saturn.

TWENTIETH CARD OF THE TAROT

The Judgment

An angel with fiery wings, surrounded by a radiant halo, sounds the trumpet of the last judgment. The instrument is decorated with a cross.

A tomb opens in the earth, and a man, woman and child issue therefrom; their hands are joined in sign of adoration.

How can the reawakening of nature under the influence of the Word be better expressed? We must admire the way in which the symbol answers to the corresponding Hebrew hieroglyphic.

1. Return to the divine World. The Spirit finally regains possession of itself—

ORIGINAL DETERMINED MOTION

2. Life renews itself by its own motion—

VEGETABLE LIFE

RESPIRATION

3. The material world progresses one degree in its ascension towards God—

THE VEGETABLE WORLD.

20. ר

The Judgment

AFFINITIES	SIGNIFICATIONS
Primitive ⎱ The Head of Hieroglyphic ⎰ Man Astronomy Saturn Day Saturday Hebrew letter Resh (double)	ORIGINAL AND DETERMINED MOTION RESPIRATION Vegetable Life
OBSERVATIONS	THE VEGETABLE KINGDOM

LE FOU   LE · MAT

THE FOOL   THE MATE

21. ש

21st Hebrew letter (Shin)

ORIGIN OF THE SYMBOLISM OF THE UNNUMBERED CARD OF
THE TAROT

The *Shin* [1] expresses the same hieroglyphic meaning
as the *Zain* (7th arcanum) and the *Samech* (15th):
this is an arrow, an object directed to an aim. But the
movement which was direct in the *Zain* (ז), and which
became circular in the *Samech* (ס), here takes the form
of a vibration from one pole to the other, with an
unstable point of equilibrium in the centre. The *Shin*
is therefore the sign of relative duration and of the

---

[1] This letter is derived from its vocal י (Yod), when this has
become a consonant; and it adds to its original meaning the
respective significations of the letters ז (Zain) and ס (Samech).—
FABRE D'OLIVET.

movement connected therewith, whilst the *Samech* expresses cyclic movement, and therefore absolute duration.

Shin is one of the three mother letters.

TWENTY-FIRST (UNNUMBERED) CARD OF THE TAROT

The Foolish Man

A careless-looking man, wearing a fool's cap, with torn clothes and a bundle upon his shoulder, goes quietly on his way, paying no attention to a dog which bites his leg. He does not look where he is going, so walks towards a precipice, where a crocodile is waiting to devour him.

This is an image of the state to which unresisted passion will reduce a man. It is the symbol of the *Flesh* and of its gratification. From a moral point of view the following verses of Éliphas Lévi well explain this symbol—

> " Souffrir c'est travailler, c'est accomplir sa tâche,
> Malheur au paresseux qui dort sur le chemin ;
> La douleur, comme un chien, mord les talons du lâche,
> Qui, d'un seul jour perdu, surcharge un lendemain." [1]

1. More rapid return to the Divine World. Personality asserts itself—

THE MOTION OF RELATIVE DURATION

2. The intellect roughly appears under the influence of evolution—

INNERVATION : INSTINCT

---

[1] " Sorrow lessens in work, in fulfilling a task ;
Woe to the sluggard who sleeps on his way ;
Like a dog at his heels pain clings to him fast,
If he leave for to-morrow the work of to-day."

3. The matter of the world attains the maximum of its material progression—

THE ANIMAL KINGDOM

.

21. שׁ

The Foolish Man

AFFINITIES		SIGNIFICATIONS
Primitive Hieroglyphic } The Arrow		THE MOTION of Relative Duration
Hebrew letter { The Shin (one of the 3 mothers)		INNERVATION Instinct
OBSERVATIONS		
		THE ANIMAL KINGDOM

THE WORLD

THE WORLD

22. ת

22nd Hebrew letter (Tau)

ORIGIN OF THE SYMBOLISM OF THE TWENTY-FIRST CARD OF THE TAROT

The *Tau* has the same hieroglyphic meaning as the *Daleth* (fourth card)—that is, the womb; but it is chiefly the sign of reciprocity, the image of all that is mutual and reciprocal. It is the sign of signs, for to the abundance of the letter *Daleth* ד (fourth card), and by dint of the resistance and protection of the letter *Teth* ט (ninth card), it adds the idea of PERFECTION, of which it is the symbol.

In the primitive Hebrew alphabet the *Teth* was represented by a cross (+). This letter is double, and in astronomy it represents the Sun.

TWENTY-FIRST CARD OF THE TAROT

The World

A nude female figure, holding a wand in each hand, is placed in the centre of an ellipsis, her legs crossed (like those of the Hanged Man in the twelfth card). At the four angles of the card we find the four animals of the Apocalypse, and the four forms of the Sphinx: the Man, the Lion, the Bull and the Eagle.

This symbol represents Macrocosm and Microcosm, that is to say, God and Creation, or the Law of the Absolute. The four figures placed at the four corners represent the four letters of the Sacred Name, or the four great symbols of the Tarot.

The Sceptre or *yod* = Fire.
The Cup   or *he*   = Water.
The Sword   or *vau* = Earth.
The Pentacle or *2nd he* = Air.

These affinities can be represented thus—

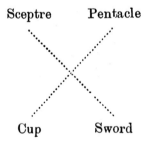

Between the sacred word that signifies GOD and the centre of the figure is a circle or an ellipsis, representing NATURE and her regular and fatal course. From this comes the name of *Rota*, wheel, given to it by William Postel.

Lastly, the centre of the figure represents humanity, ADAM-EVE, the third term of the great series of the Absolute, which is thus constructed :—

The impenetrable Absolute, the EN SOPH of the Kabalists, the PARABRAHM of the Hindus—
The impenetrable Absolute or God   ... 1st septenary.
The soul of the Absolute or Man   ... 2nd septenary.
The body of the Absolute or the Universe 3rd septenary.

This twenty-first card of the Tarot therefore contains in itself a recapitulation of all our work, and proves to us the truth of our deductions.

A simple figure will sum up what we have said.

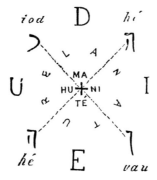

This symbol gives us an exact plan of the construction of the Tarot itself, if we notice that the figure in the centre represents a triangle (a head and two extended arms) surmounting a cross (the legs)—that is to say, the figure of the septenary, thus formed $\Delta\!\!\!+$.

The four corners therefore reproduce the four great symbols of the Tarot. The centre signifies the action of these symbols between themselves, represented by the ten numbers of the minor arcana, and the twenty-two letters of the major arcana. Lastly, the centre reproduces the septenary law of the major arcana themselves.

As this septenary is in the centre of three circles, typifying the three worlds, we see that the sense of the twenty-one arcana is once more determined $(3 \times 7 = 21)$.

The following figure indicates the application of the twenty-first card to the Tarot itself.

We shall also see that this card of the Tarot gives the key of all our applications of the pack to the Year, to Philosophy, to the Kabalah, etc., etc.

THE TERNARY OF TRANSITION

The Elements

Original and
Determined
Motion

The Motion
of Relative
Duration

DIVINE REPRODUCTION

Nutrition   The Mineral Kingdom

Respiration
Vegetable Life   Innervation
Instinct | The Vegetable
Kingdom   The Animal
Kingdom

REPRODUCTION OF MAN.   REPRODUCTION OF THE UNIVERSE

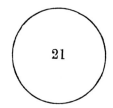

The Absolute
containing in itself
God
Man
The Universe

CHAPTER XIV

GENERAL SUMMARY OF THE SYMBOLICAL TAROT
THEOGONY—ANDROGONY—COSMOGONY

Involution and Evolution—*Theogony*—The Absolute according to
Wronski, Lacuria and the Tarot—Theogony of divers Reli-
gions identical with that of the Tarot—Summary : *Androgony*
—Cosmogony. Table containing the Symbolism of all the
Major Arcana, enabling the Signification of each Card to be
defined immediately.

GENERAL SUMMARY OF THE SYMBOLISM OF THE
MAJOR ARCANA

THEOGONY—ANDROGONY—COSMOGONY

HAVING completed our study of the twenty-two major
arcana, considered separately, we will now review as
clearly as possible the knowledge which may be
gathered from the preceding explanations.

We have already established, from the investigation
of the first card, that three primary principles are
considered throughout their evolution: the Universe,
Man and God.

We need only recall *grosso modo* the sense of each
card of the Tarot to prove the existence of a well-
established progression, which starts from God the
Holy Ghost to end in Matter, while passing through
a number of varying modalities. Another gradation

leads from Matter to God, the primitive origin of all things.

This double current of the progressive Materialization of the Divine, or INVOLUTION, and of the Progressive Divinization of the Material, or EVOLUTION, has been too well studied by our eminent friend CH. BARLET for us intentionally to vary from him in any way; we shall therefore quote his interesting work *in extenso*,[1] and thus enable the reader to see that our conclusions are absolutely identical, although we have been led to them by very different paths.

But our present object is to review as clearly as possible the meanings of the major arcana of the Tarot, regarded from a synthetic point of view. From the preceding chapters it will be seen that this study is really a COSMOGONY, or study of the creation of the Universe, crowned by an ANDROGONY, or study of the creation of Man, and even by an essay on THEOGONY, or study of the innate creation of God.

THEOGONY

The Tarot places at the origin of all things the Absolute undetermined, undeterminable, the ONE, both knowing and unknowing, affirmative and negative, force and matter, inexpressible, incomprehensible to man.[2]

The Unity manifests itself to itself by three terms— the highest and most general which the human comprehension can grasp—terms which form the basis of all theogonies, and which designate the same principles under a multitude of varying names.

[1] See p. 253.   [2] Ch. Barlet, *Initiation*, p 10.

N

1. The first of these symbolizes Absolute Activity in all its acceptations, the origin of all movement, of all masculine creative force.

GOD THE FATHER: OSIRIS—BRAHMA—JUPITER

2. The second of these terms symbolizes Absolute Passivity in all its acceptations, the origin of all repose, of all feminine preserving force. It is the humid principle of Nature, even as the first is the igneous principle.

GOD THE SON: ISIS—VISHNU—JUNO

The third of these terms is the most important to us. Synthetically it blends the two which precede it in UNITY; all study should be commenced thereby, for no being is conceivable unless it be considered synthetically, and the third term is the origin of all synthesis. It is Absolute Union in all its acceptations, the origin of all reality, of all equilibrium, of all equilibrated transforming force. It is the mercurial principle in Nature balancing the two first.

GOD THE HOLY GHOST: HORUS—SIVA—VULCAN

.   .   .   .

It is necessary to give a few explanations before we proceed further, in order that the deductions which follow may be intelligible to our readers.

We have said that no being is conceivable unless it be considered synthetically: we must now explain this sentence.

Let us take Man for our example, and follow the advice of Saint-Martin: "We must explain Nature by man, and not man by Nature."

Man, regarded synthetically, is composed of an acting, animated body.

If we would think of the being Man as a body only, without reference to its animation or to its faculty of acting, its reality immediately disappears; it is no longer a man. We are considering but a phantom created by our spirit, a phantom which we can analyze, study in all its subdivisions, but which, since it conveys no synthetic idea, does not really exist.

If, in the same way, we wish to imagine by itself the principle which animates this body, which makes it live, the reality again disappears. It is impossible for us to separate the life from the idea of the body, to conceive what this thing may be which is called the human Life, if we wish to see in it a kind of metaphysical being. It is on this point that materialistic savants find the most force in their arguments against exclusively idealist thinkers.

The difficulty increases considerably if it be a question of the principle which causes this body to act—of the Will, of the Soul. Analysis here, as elsewhere, can be brought into use, but we cannot possibly conceive what the soul can be like divested of form, that is to say, of a principle that differs from itself. We picture to ourselves a small sphere, a winged head, in fact anything, according to individual fancy, but never the soul considered individually.

On the other hand, the moment we say A MAN, these three terms, thus synthesised, assume consistence and become the expression of a reality; a being, formed of a body, a life and a will, defines itself quite clearly.

This synthetic action, the source of all existence and of all reality, is the innate property of the third term in our Trinity of principles. It is for this reason that the study of all realities should be commenced by this third term. Henri Wronski always adopted the method in question; he named this principle the Neuter Element, and placed it at the commencement of all his studies.

.   .   .   .

Consequently, The Trinity, composed of the three terms which we have specified, should be considered under two aspects.

1. We should first look at the synthesis of this trinity, the cause of its reality. The third term (God the Holy Spirit) contains these conditions in itself.

2. We should then analyze this synthesis by dividing it into its three constituent terms, and by determining the existence of the two opposite terms, active and passive, positive and negative. We must not forget that during this analysis we destroy the reality of the being thus divided into fractions.

Every reality, of whatever kind it may be, is therefore composed of three terms, and these three terms are contained in one whole. This truth is quite as applicable to physics as to metaphysics; the works of Louis Lucas upon physics and chemistry,[1] and of Wronski on mathematics,[2] are an irresistible argument against those who think that a philosophical principle is a foolish idea, without any practical import.

The third term of our theogonic series, or God the Holy Ghost, therefore represents the whole body of God, who can be analyzed in this way—

[1] Louis Lucas, *La Chimie Nouvelle*, Paris, 1854. 18mo.
[2] Wronski, *Messianisme*, 1825, fol.; and above all *Apodictique Messianique*, 1876, fol.

GOD THE HOLY SPIRIT
Synthesis
3

GOD THE SON   GOD THE FATHER
Antithesis   *Thesis*
2   1

To sum up all that we have studied so far, we will say that we have discovered, in the first place—

1. An indeterminable and inexpressible principle, of which we are content to assert the existence only—

2. This synthetic principle, when analyzed, is found to consist of a Trinity thus constituted—

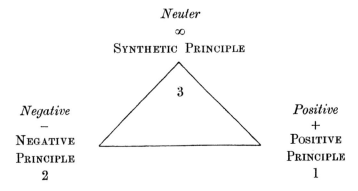

Neuter
∞
SYNTHETIC PRINCIPLE

3

Negative   *Positive*
–   +
NEGATIVE   POSITIVE
PRINCIPLE   PRINCIPLE
2   1

If we would use a common but very suggestive image, we should say—

The constitution of God is thus defined by the Tarot—

The Spirit of God, or *God the Father*.
The Soul of God, or *God the Son*.
The Body of God, or *God the Holy Spirit*.[1]

---

[1] Spirit is here taken in the sense of the superior and creative principle: soul in the sense of median and animator. Since many writers use these words in a different sense, it is useful to explain what is our meaning in this case.

We must now prove that the conclusions which we have reached through the Tarot agree in all points with those of every author who has treated the question on a higher level and with all the superior theogonies of antiquity.

1. THE PRINCIPAL AUTHORS WHO HAVE STUDIED THIS QUESTION.

We have chosen from amongst the authors who have studied this question of first principles, two authors, who—starting from different points of view—support the conclusions of the Tarot: Lacuria and Wronski.

F. G. Lacuria

This eminent writer, in his book on the *Harmonies of Being expressed by Numbers*, starts in his deductions from the three words used by St. John: *Vita, Verbum, Lux*. He analyzes each of these words, establishes the connection that exists between it and the Christian Trinity, and defines each of the elements in this trinity—

"Hereof is the Trinity: the Father, who is life or immensity; the Son, who is word or form, and distinction or variety; the Holy Spirit, who is light and love, or unity. And these three persons are only one God. Their unity is not only in the external fact of their existence, but in the essence of things, for they are inseparable in the thought of man; no one can imagine one without the others" (p. 43).

"In the commencement was BEING; the being is not undetermined, but it is distinct from NON-BEING; it sees that it is being, and these two points of view, participating in the unity of the substance which they affect, produce by their union CONSCIENCE, which is also light or harmony" (vol. ii. p. 333).

+	−
BEING	NON-BEING
The Father	The Son
The Life	The Word

∞

CONSCIENCE
The Holy Spirit
The Light

First principles of Lacuria.

Henri Wronski

This author interests us doubly, for his conclusions not only agree with the data given by the Tarot, but they also throw great light upon them. Let us therefore listen to him (*Apodictique*, p. 5)—

"Thus the reality of the absolute, REALITY in itself or reality in general, is unquestionably the first determination of the very essence of the absolute, and consequently the first principle of reason. Without it as an indispensable condition, as we have just admitted it to be, every assertion made by reason would be valueless. And it is upon this fundamental principle of reason, upon this indestructible and in every way indispensable condition, that we shall now establish absolute philosophy itself with the same infallibility.

"In the first place this reality of the absolute, which we now recognize so profoundly, produces or creates itself; for, as we have already irrevocably concluded, the absolute, this indispensable term of reason, is that which is BY ITSELF. Thus this innate generation, this autogeny of the reality of the absolute, this creation by itself, is manifestly a second determination of the very essence of the absolute ; and the condition by which alone this determination can take place constitutes quite as manifestly, and in all its primitive purity, the faculty which is designated by the name of Wisdom (λόγος, *das Wissen*).

" We therefore discover WISDOM as the second essential attribute of the absolute; this primordial faculty which is the condition of all creation, or rather, which is the creative faculty itself in its highest power, as we have now discerned it, is, if we may thus express it, the instrument of autogeny, that is to say, the faculty of creation by itself. And consequently we discover in Wisdom, shown in this highest creative power, the second principle of reason, quite as infallible as the absolute itself, from which we have now deduced it.

" Moreover, in the reality of the absolute, the necessary result of its wisdom or of its innate creation is PERMANENT STABILITY, because, precisely through being what it is by itself, the absolute could not be other than itself. We can therefore understand that this permanent stability in the reality of the absolute, which is properly its autothesis, constitutes a third determination of the very essence of the absolute, and we shall easily recognize that this stability, this permanent unchangeableness, this innate unalterability, is only that condition of reality which we name Being (ὤν, *das Seyn*).

" Thus we discover, as third essential attribute of the absolute, the condition of Being, the condition of stability in reality, and therefore of its force or innate unalterability, which in the absolute constitutes its autothesis itself. And consequently we find in Being, considered almost in its autothetic origin, the third principle of reason, as infallible as the absolute itself, from which we have deduced it.

"We therefore already possess the three first principles of reason, which, as we have just seen, are the three first determinations of the very essence of the absolute. Moreover, if we notice on the one hand that Wisdom and Being, taking them in all their generality, are opposed to each other, just as autogeny and autothesis—of which they form the conditions— are opposed, or spontaneity and inertia, which form their characters; and if, on the other hand, we notice that Wisdom and Being, those antagonistic conditions, are neutralized in REALITY in general, this reality— according to the deductions which we have given— being the fundamental principle of reason, its primitive basis, we shall understand that the three principles which we have discovered, in the determinations of the essence itself of the absolute, are really the three primitive principles of the supreme Wisdom, or of Philosophy."

+	−
WISDOM	THE BEING
Autogeny	Autothesis
Principle of Motion	Principle of Stability

∞

REALITY
Principle of Existence
FIRST PRINCIPLES OF WRONSKI

2. THEOGONIES OF DIFFERENT RELIGIONS

We have now shown the identity of the three first principles of the Tarot with the philosophical discoveries of some modern authors. We need only revert to the study of the first arcanum to see the conclusions which Fabre d'Olivet and L. C. de Saint-Martin have reached upon the same subject; and we will now add a few words upon the identity of the deductions of the Tarot with the religious ideas of various nations.

EGYPTIAN THEOGONY

Osiris is an emanation of the Great Being; he reveals himself in three persons—

> *Amon*, who brings forth the hidden forms of things, is Power.
> *Ptah* the *demi-urgus*, the eternal workman, embodying the primitive ideas, is Wisdom.
> *Osiris*, the author of being, the source of all life, is Goodness.

"The Egyptian god is called *Amon* when he is regarded as the hidden force which brings all things to the light; he is *Ptah* when he accomplishes all things with skill and truth; lastly, when he is the good and beneficent god, he is named *Osiris.*"—JAMBLIQUE.

Indeterminable Principle
RA
Divine Trinity:

+   –
AMON   PTAH

∞
OSIRIS

HINDU THEOGONY

Indeterminable Principle
PARABRAHM :

+
BRAHMA
Creator

∞
SIVA
Transformer

−
VISHNU
Preserver

Here is an analysis of this conception applied to Cosmogony :—

PRIMITIVE HINDU COSMOGONY, ACCORDING TO THE RIG-VEDA

There was neither being nor no-being, neither ether nor the roof of the heavens, neither enveloping nor enveloped. There was neither death nor immortality; nothing separated the darkness of night from the light of day.

But That One, the HE, breathed alone with HER, whose life was sustained in his breast. Of all those who have existed since that time, no other then existed. The darkness covered them like an ocean, which cannot be lightened. The universe was indistinct, like the fluids mingled with the waters; but this mass, which was covered by a crust, was at last organized by the power of contemplation.

The first wish was formed in its intelligence, and it became the original productive seed. This productive seed became Providence or sensitive souls; and Matter or Elements. SHE who was supported in his breast was the inferior part, and HE who observes was the superior part. Who can know exactly, and who in this world can assert, from whom or how this creation took place? The gods are posterior to this creation of the world.

KABALISTIC THEOGONY

Indeterminable Principle

EN SOPH

The Absolute

Divine Trinity

+		−
Chòcmah		Binah
Absolute Wisdom		*Absolute Intelligence*

∞

Kether

Absolute Equilibrating Power

We might carry these comparisons much further; but it is useless to prolong our studies unreasonably. The curious reader can refer to many works on the ancient theogonies,[1] and see the universal harmony that exists in the primitive principles of all religions.

It will be sufficient if we determine the universality of the Three First Principles, which we name, like the Christians, in order to be clearly understood—

+		−
God the Father		God the Son

∞

God the Holy Spirit

.   .   .   .

These Principles once defined, we shall see them in action throughout creation.

[1] See particularly P. Renand, *Nouvelle Symbolique*, Paris, 1877. 8vo.

The First Principle manifested its existence to itself in the Second Principle, named the Son by Christians. Lastly, these Two Principles embodied themselves in the Third, which gave them substance. This is why we have named the Holy Spirit the Body of God.

Now the same law of creation, acting in the affinities of the First Principle with the Second, will manifest itself in the action of the first ternary upon itself, to give birth to the following trinity—

God the Father, the principle of Will, is entirely self-reflected in the rough ADAM, the principle of Power; God the Son, the principle of Intelligence, is self-reflected in the gentle EVE, the principle of Authority. Lastly, God as a whole, or God the Holy Spirit, clothed these two mystical unities in a body, and made a reality of them in the balanced creation of Adam-Eve, or of HUMANITY.

Humanity, the image of Love, also contains in itself a rough, astringent principle (see Jacob Böhme[1]), and a gentle, insinuating principle (Jacob Böhme). The first of these, symbolized by Adam, is the origin of brute Force, of Power in all its manifestations. The second, symbolized by Eve, is the origin of feminine Grace, of Authority. We have seen that Power and Authority find their equilibrium in Love.

Each man, a reflected molecule of humanity made in its image, contains in himself an Adam, the source of the Will—this is the Brain; an Eve, source of the intelligence—the heart; and he should balance the heart by the brain, and the brain by the heart, to become a centre of divine love.

The same analogy obtains in external and generic

---

[1] Jacob Böhme, *The Three Principles.*

man and woman, represented by Adam and Eve (הוה Eve, the life).

But just as the Father and the Son have become realities in the Holy Spirit, as Adam and Eve are embodied in Humanity, so the third ternary will take rise in the reciprocal action of the other two.

NATURA NATURANS, or creating, will take her birth under the action and the reciprocal reaction of God the Father and of Adam, the two active and passive creative principles. Thus also appears the Universal creative Fluid, balancing and realizing in itself both will and power.

From this again will be born NATURA NATURATA, or preserving, realizing the union of God the Son and of Eve, at the same time that the Universal preserving Fluid, or Universal Life, will appear, balancing and realizing the Intelligence and Authority which define its innate qualities.

Lastly, the Holy Spirit and Humanity, the divine and the human bodies, unite and manifest themselves eternally in the LIVING UNIVERSE, the source of Universal Attraction.

For even as the Holy Spirit was the body of God, the Son his soul, and the Father his Spirit, even as Humanity was the body of Adam, Eve his life or soul, and Adam his Spirit; so also—

The Universe is the body of God;
Humanity is the soul of God;
God Himself is the Spirit of God.

From this we recognize the truth of the opinion of the Pantheists, who declared that God was the Universe; but we also see their error, when they refuse to acknowledge in him any innate consciousness. For as the consciousness of man is independent of the millions of cells which compose his body, so the consciousness of God is independent of the molecules of the Universe and of man which form its body and its soul. We might partly destroy the Universe without in any way diminishing the Divine Personality, even as the four limbs can be cut off a man without his losing consciousness of the integrity of his personality. This is why the conclusions of Schopenhauer and Hartmann are partly erroneous.

Before leaving this study, we must once more express our admiration for this wonderful book, this symbolical Tarot, which thus defines God—

God is the Absolute, the essence of which is impenetrable, formed of the Universe as body, of Humanity as soul, and of Himself as Spirit.

THEOGONY

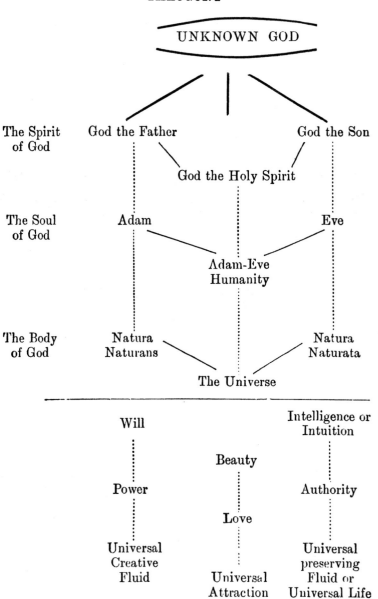

ANDROGONY

Each man contains in himself an Adam, source of the Will, *i.e.* the Brain; an Eve, source of the Intelligence,[1] *i.e.* the Heart, and he should balance the heart by the brain, and the brain by the heart, if he would become a centre of divine love.

In Humanity, the passive Realistic principle of God Himself, the Father and the Divine Son, is represented by Man.

Man accomplishing the functions of God the Creator is the FATHER; the woman accomplishing the work of God the preserver is the MOTHER; lastly HUMAN LOVE realises the whole Divinity in Humanity.

The human family is therefore the representation of the Divinity upon earth. The Tarot also teaches us this fact by its minor arcana (king or father, queen or mother, knight or young man, knave or child); and it was so thoroughly understood by ancient science, that the whole social organization was based upon the family, instead of upon the individual, as it is in modern times.[2] That the social organization of China has been maintained for so many centuries, is solely due to the principle of basing everything upon the family.[3]

The characteristics of the human Ternary are: Adam, Necessity, the image and reflection of Will and Power; Eve, Liberty, the image and reflection of Intelligence and Authority; and Adam and Eve, Charity, the image

[1] Intelligence is here taken in the sense of Intuition, and not in the sense usually attributed to it by the Philosophy of the Universities.

[2] See Saint-Yves d'Alvedyre, *Mission des Juifs*, 1884.

[3] See Simon, *La Cité Chinoise*, 1886. 8vo.

O

and reflection of Love and Beauty given by the constituent terms.

REALIZATION and JUSTICE, balanced by PRUDENCE, indicate the normal constitution of Man, whilst the POSITIVE ASTRAL LIGHT (or OD), the NEGATIVE ASTRAL LIGHT (or OB), and the EQUILIBRATED ASTRAL FLUID (or AOUR), demonstrate the origin of his physical constitution.

Magic Power, Courage and Hope manifest the moral qualities of man, whilst Force, potential in its manifestation, reflected Life, and Force balancing the two preceding qualities, indicate the influence of the Universe in him.

Thus, the law which governs all these manifestations of God in the series of his creations is Emanation.

From the unique but fathomless centre emanates, in the first place, a Trinity of absolute principles which serves as a model for all the posterior emanations of the Being principle itself. Each element of this Trinity manifests itself in two great principles, of which it is the source: from the first principle, or the Father, emanate successively Adam and Nature creating, *naturans*, according to Spinoza; from the second principle, or the Son, emanate Eve and Nature *naturata*, or recipient; lastly, the third principle, or the Holy Spirit, serves as a model to the similar constitution of Adam-Eve, or Humanity and the Universe.

In this way also the Ternary, emanated from the mysterious Unity, constitutes a Septenary formed by the various emanations of these three Principles, like the seven colours of the scale of light formed by the combination of three simple colours, themselves emanated from one single light; or like the seven notes of the musical scale formed by the fundamental trinity of sounds.

The Septenary formed of "two Ternaries in the midst of which the Unity upholds itself,"[1] is therefore the expression of a being completely constituted. This is now confirmed by the recent data given by Hindu Theosophy upon the seven principles of Man and upon the seven principles of the Universe.[2]

We could apply the Tarot to the explanation of these data: but we feel sure that the task will soon be undertaken by others, and we consider it useless to lengthen our work too much.

We will therefore conclude this study upon man by pointing out his constitution as given by the Tarot, which teaches that his body comes from the Universe, his soul from the Astral plane, whilst his spirit is a direct emanation from God.[3]

---

[1] *Sepher Yetzirah* (trans. Papus), chap. vi.

[2] See Sinnett, *Esoteric Buddhism;* H. P. Blavatsky, *Secret Doctrine;* and all the publications of the Theosophical Society.

[3] See for further developments the works of Paracelsus and Van Helmont.

ANDROGONY

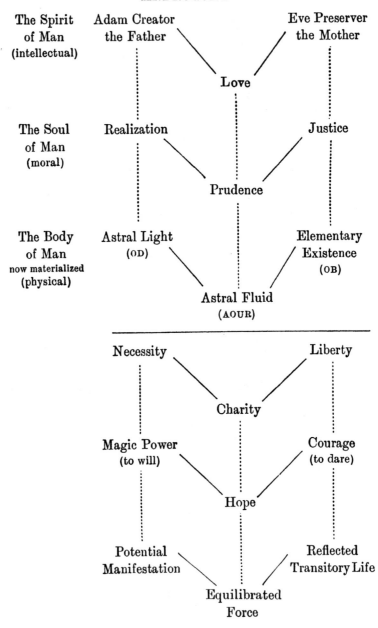

The Spirit of Man (intellectual) — Adam Creator the Father — Eve Preserver the Mother

Love

The Soul of Man (moral) — Realization — Justice

Prudence

The Body of Man now materialized (physical) — Astral Light (OD) — Elementary Existence (OB)

Astral Fluid (AOUR)

Necessity — Liberty

Charity

Magic Power (to will) — Courage (to dare)

Hope

Potential Manifestation — Reflected Transitory Life

Equilibrated Force

COSMOGONY

As we descend the ladder of the emanations of Absolute Being, the principles become more material and less metaphysical. The Tarot teaches us that the Universe results from the participation of the Human in the creative actions of the Divine, a profound mystery, which can throw much light upon the theological theories of the Fall. Jacob Böhme, that sublime visionary shoemaker, and Saint-Martin, his admirer and disciple, give upon this subject some explanations which may be easily understood with the Tarot, and to which we refer curious inquirers.

God manifests himself in the Universe by his third trinitarian manifestation: *Natura naturans*, realized in the UNIVERSAL TRANSFORMING PRINCIPLE, *Natura naturata*, in INVOLUTION; and lastly in the mysterious cyclic force which we have analyzed, in reference to the 15th arcanum, and which we name the FATAL FORCE OF DESTINY. This is the God adored by materialistic science, and we see that unconsciously its homage is offered to the Divinity itself under its most material form, even whilst it foolishly boasts of Atheism.

DEATH, CORPOREAL LIFE and the DESTINY which rules their mutual connection, constitute the preserving principles of the Universe; lastly, PLASTIC FORCE, INDIVIDUAL LIFE and the ASTRAL LIGHT IN CIRCULATION, show us the means of Transformation and of Realization used by the Cosmos.

But these are abstract principles; if we wish to see them in action we must consider the following ternary. The Universal Transforming Principle marks its existence by the DESTRUCTION of beings and of things; but the Opposing Principle, Involution, at once IMMORTALIZES Destruction by the influx of new divine currents into CHAOS.

Adam materialized his nature by the FALL of his spirit into matter, the source of Death; but Corporeal Life, the source of HOPE, arises and provides the means of redeeming the fault, by suffering in the MATERIAL BODY.

Lastly, MATTER itself appears, the final term of involution, after which recommences the grand Evolution towards the primitive centre.

It is unnecessary to say that we have only sought to furnish a rapid sketch of the evidence of the Tarot upon Theogony, Androgony and Cosmogony, without entering into detail. In fact these are very serious questions, which require whole volumes to themselves, and we have no intention of discussing them in a few pages.

COSMOGONY

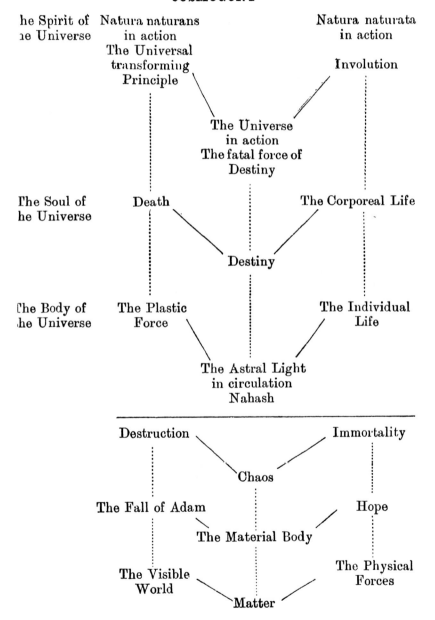

he Spirit of   Natura naturans   Natura naturata
ıe Universe   in action   in action
            The Universal
            transforming   Involution
            Principle

                     The Universe
                     in action
                    The fatal force of
                      Destiny

The Soul of   Death   The Corporeal Life
he Universe

                     Destiny

The Body of   The Plastic   The Individual
he Universe   Force   Life

                 The Astral Light
                 in circulation
                 Nahash

      Destruction   Immortality

                 Chaos

   The Fall of Adam   Hope

              The Material Body

    The Visible   The Physical
     World   Forces

              Matter

Let us now recapitulate a little, so that we may definitely end the involution of the three grand principles:

From GOD THE FATHER have emanated successively—

Adam	*Will*
Natura Naturans	*Power*
Then their form	*The Universal Creative Fluid.*

Adam realized in the Father has produced Realization and the Astral Light; whilst the Will was realized in Necessity, Supreme Power is shown in Magic Power, and the universal creative Fluid in Force potential in its manifestation.

Natura naturans realized in the Universal Transforming Principle has produced Death, and the Universal Plastic Force, with its forms, Destruction, the Fall of Adam, and the visible world.

These are all the principles that have successively emanated from the Father, and which represent Him. We reproduce them thus in a diagram.

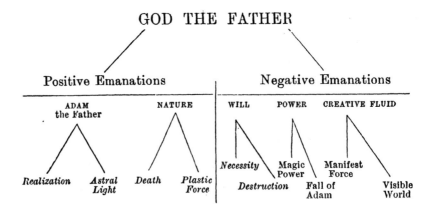

The two following tables, arranged upon the same plan as the present one, give the emanations of the two other principles of the first ternary.

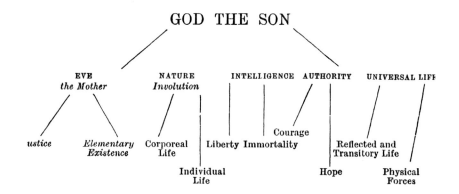

GOD THE SON

EVE
the Mother

NATURE
Involution

INTELLIGENCE   AUTHORITY

UNIVERSAL LIFE

ustice   *Elementary
Existence*   Corporeal
Life   Liberty Immortality   Courage   Reflected and
Transitory Life

Individual
Life   Hope   Physical
Forces

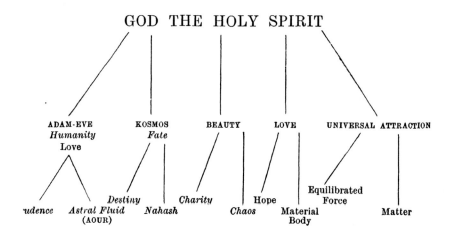

GOD THE HOLY SPIRIT

ADAM-EVE
*Humanity
Love*

KOSMOS
Fate

BEAUTY   LOVE

UNIVERSAL ATTRACTION

udence   *Astral Fluid*
(AOUR)   *Destiny*   Nahash   *Charity*   Chaos   Hope   Material
Body   Equilibrated
Force   Matter

In our introduction to the study of symbolism we have given a numbered figure which enables us to determine immediately the meaning of any card in the Tarot.

If we now apply all that we have said upon the symbolism of each of our cards to this subject, we can condense the whole symbolism of the major arcana in one scheme.

The new table thus formed will give us the sense of all our principles, whatever their number may be, and this is how we obtain their meaning—

USE OF THE TABLE

1. Seek in the horizontal column, to the left of the principle under consideration, the sense written there.

2. Having ascertained this meaning, return to your principle and search in the vertical column at the bottom the great principle (God, Man, or the Universe) which is written there.

3. Combine the meaning first obtained with the name placed in the vertical column, adding to it the word (itself or manifest) written in the vertical column which contains the principle of which you are seeking the meaning.

An example will explain this better.

Let us ascertain the meaning of the MOTHER—

The first term of the 8th arcanum.

1. I look in the horizontal column containing the word MOTHER and I find at the end, to the left, the following meaning—

Active preserving Principle.

The Mother is the Active preserving Principle.   Of what ?

2. In order to know, I seek in the vertical column containing the word Mother, and at the bottom I find Man or Humanity.

The Mother is the Active preserving Principle of Humanity.

3. I add to the word Humanity the word placed in the small vertical column which contains the word Mother. This word is *Himself* if relating to man, or *itself* if we take the sense of Humanity. We should say—

The Mother is the Active preserving Principle of Man himself or of Humanity itself.

This example clearly indicates how the Table should be used.

CREATIVE PRINCIPLE (י) Active י	God the Father	Will	The Father
	1	4	7
CREATIVE PRINCIPLE Passive ה	Adam	Power	Realization
CREATIVE PRINCIPLE Equilibrist ו	Natura naturans	Universal Creative Fluid	Astral Light
PRESERVING PRINCIPLE (ה) Active י	God the Son	Intelligence	The Mother
	2	5	8
PRESERVING PRINCIPLE Passive (ה)	Eve	Authority	Justice
PRESERVING PRINCIPLE Equilibrist ו	Natura naturata	Universal Life	Elementary Existence
REALIZING PRINCIPLE (ו) Active י	God the Holy Spirit	Beauty	Love
	3	6	9
REALIZING PRINCIPLE Passive ה	Adam-Eve, Humanity	Love	Prudence (Be silent)
REALIZING PRINCIPLE Equilibrist ו	Kosmos	Universal Attraction	Astral Fluid (AOUR)
	Himself (י)	Manifested	Himself (ה)
	+	–	+
	G O D	(21)	M A
			HUMA-

Arcana, enabling the definition of any one of these termined. (*See its use on pp.* 218, 219.)

Necessity	Universal transforming Principle	Destruction	The Elements
10	13	16	19
Magic Power	Death	The Fall of Adam	Nutrition
Force potential in its manifestation	Universal Plastic Force	The Visible World	The Mineral Kingdom
Liberty	Involution	Immortality	Innate Motion
11	14	17	20
Courage (TO DARE)	Corporeal Life	Hope	Respiration
Reflected and Transitory Life	Individual Life	The Physical Forces	The Vegetable Kingdom
Charity	Fate	Chaos	The Motion of Relative Duration
12	15	18	0
Hope (WISDOM)	Destiny	The Material Body	Innervation
Equilibrist Force	Nahash Astral Light in circulation	Matter	The Animal Kingdom
Manifested	Itself (ו) Manifested		Return (ה)
–	+	--	to
N (21)	UNIVERSE (21)		the Unity
NITY			

Table indicating the revolutions of yod-he-vau-he *in numbers* (*positive arcana*) : (*yod* = 1, *he* = 2, *vau* = 3, *2nd he* = 4).

(Key to the preceding Table.)

	1	2	3	4
I. 1	$\left.\begin{matrix}1\\2\\3\\4\end{matrix}\right\}$ of 1 in VII. 1	$\left.\begin{matrix}2\\3\\4\\1\end{matrix}\right\}$ of 1 in XIII. 2	$\left.\begin{matrix}3\\4\\1\\2\end{matrix}\right\}$ of 1 in XIX. 3	$\left.\begin{matrix}4\\1\\2\\3\end{matrix}\right\}$ of 1 in 4
II. 2	$\left.\begin{matrix}1\\2\\3\\4\end{matrix}\right\}$ of 2 in VIII. 1	$\left.\begin{matrix}2\\3\\4\\1\end{matrix}\right\}$ of 2 in XIV. 2	$\left.\begin{matrix}3\\4\\1\\2\end{matrix}\right\}$ of 2 in XX. 3	$\left.\begin{matrix}4\\1\\2\\3\end{matrix}\right\}$ of 2 in 4
III. 3	$\left.\begin{matrix}1\\2\\3\\4\end{matrix}\right\}$ of 3 in IX. 1	$\left.\begin{matrix}2\\3\\4\\1\end{matrix}\right\}$ of 3 in XV. 2	$\left.\begin{matrix}3\\4\\1\\2\end{matrix}\right\}$ of 3 in XXI. 3	$\left.\begin{matrix}4\\1\\2\\3\end{matrix}\right\}$ of 3 in 4
IV. 4	$\left.\begin{matrix}1\\2\\3\\4\end{matrix}\right\}$ of 4 in X. 1	$\left.\begin{matrix}2\\3\\4\\1\end{matrix}\right\}$ of 4 in XVI. 2	$\left.\begin{matrix}3\\4\\1\\2\end{matrix}\right\}$ of 4 in XXII. 3	$\left.\begin{matrix}4\\1\\2\\3\end{matrix}\right\}$ of 4 in 4

PART III

APPLICATIONS OF THE TAROT

CHAPTER XV

GENERAL KEY TO THE APPLICATIONS OF THE TAROT

The Principle and the Forms—The Twenty-first Card of the Tarot is a Figure-Principle—The Tarot—·The Year—The Month—The Day—The Human Life.

General Key to the Applications of the Tarot

WE have already stated that the twenty-first card gives the key to the construction of the Tarot. The utility of this arcanum does not end here; we shall now see that it is the key to every application of the Tarot.

Some explanation may be necessary as to the manner in which a symbolical figure can be applied to conceptions of very different orders, without undergoing the least transformation.

Let us take one very simple example, chosen in the realm of experimental science, by applying the analogical method to its study. Let us represent the well-known phenomenon of the decomposition of the white light by the prism.

We place the prism, indicated by a triangular figure, in the centre; the white light, represented by parallel lines, enters it on one side: from the other the colours issue. They are represented by the refracted and more or less oblique lines.

P

The words Prism, White Light and Colours indicate all the phases of the phenomenon.

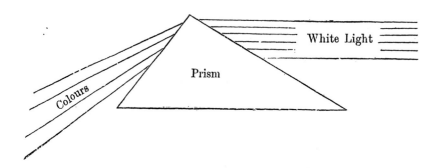

If, however, we reflect that after all it is only a general force (the white light) which undergoes various changes, according to the quantity of matter with which it comes in contact (the different thicknesses of the prism),[1] we shall easily grasp another aspect of the figure.

In fact, the work of Louis Lucas, unconsciously continued by contemporary scientific men, proves by evidence the unity of force in action throughout Nature. The different physical forces, heat, light, or electricity, are only representations of this unique force differently modified, according to the quantity of matter with which it comes in contact.

Thus the white light in contact with the large amount of matter at the base of the prism becomes *violet :* in the same way the unique force coming in contact with much matter becomes *heat,* or placed in contact with little matter becomes *light* or *electricity.*

We can therefore represent this new phenomenon

[1] See Louis Lucas, *Chimie Nouvelle,* chapter upon "Angulaison."

without changing the form of our figure in any way ;
only the words need vary—

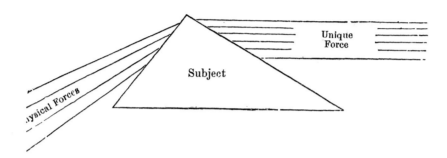

Here the different quantities of matter are represented by the different thicknesses of the prism, the
unique force corresponding with the white light by the
parallel lines, the various physical forces responding to
the various colours by the refracted lines.

If any one should consider that these two examples
belong to the realm of physics, and are therefore insuf-
ficient to generalize a phenomenon to this point, we can
answer by another instance quoted from physiology.

Physiology teaches us that all the organs in man
act under the influence of the blood. Thus the latter,
acting upon the salivary glands, produces the saliva ;
acting upon the stomach, the gastric juice is secreted ;
upon the liver in certain cases it produces bile, etc., etc.

In short, this physiological phenomenon reduces
itself to an unique agent (the blood), acting upon the
different organs (the salivary glands, stomach, liver)
and producing secretions of equally different natures
(saliva, gastric juices, bile).

Can we not therefore represent the different organs
by the different thickness of the prism, the different

transformations of the unique force by the refracted rays, and the unique force itself by the parallel lines?

The correspondence is exact on all points, and the same figure can be used once more—

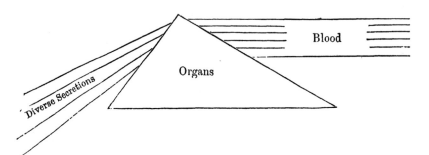

Thus the figure has never changed: only the words applied to its different parts have varied. The basis of all occult science and of the analogical method resembles this example: one fixed and invariable figure, which is always the same (Ex.: the figure), to which various orders of phenomena can be successively applied.

The twenty-first card of the Tarot is a figure-principle of the same nature as the prism which we have just studied, and a few examples of the various methods in which it can be applied will fully enlighten us upon this point.

We have seen that the four figures in the corners of the twenty-first card represent the four animals referred to the Evangelists. In the centre stands a woman, the image of Humanity, and between the two symbolisms is a crown of elliptic form.

This shows us that there will always be four fixed principles in every application of this card (since the symbols placed at the four corners of the square do not move), and a certain number of mobile principles represented by the wheel, *rota*, which occupies the centre of the symbols.

This figure can never change, since it is a figure-principle : the words alone that may be applied to it can vary.

We have in this manner the four following symbols—

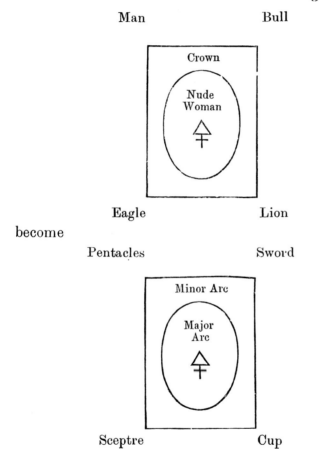

Man   Bull

Crown

Nude
Woman

Eagle   Lion

become

Pentacles   Sword

Minor Arc

Major
Arc

Sceptre   Cup

We see that none of the symbols have changed, but the words only.

The same rule applies to every application of the

Tarot. Thus if we take astronomy, the four figures will be the four seasons, the crown is the zodiac, and the nude figure (Eve) the animating system of the zodiac, the planets; thus—

Winter   Autumn

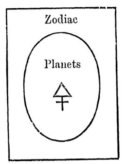

Spring   Summer

This shows us the progress of the sun, as it gives birth to the year. If we wish to know that of the moon as it produces the month, the four seasons would become the four lunar phases, the zodiac would be the twenty-eight houses of the moon, and the centre the sun, which animates the moon; thus—

New Moon   Last Quarter

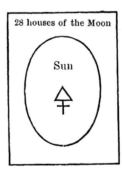

First Quarter   Full Moon

If we wish for the horoscope of a single day we find it in the following figure—

Night   Evening

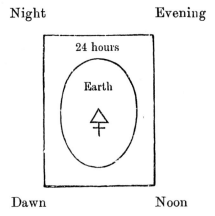

Dawn   Noon

Here the earth occupies the position of the moon in the month and of the sun in the year.

If these astronomical data weary us, we can study the circle of Human Life, and the figure will assume a new aspect.

Old Age   Maturity

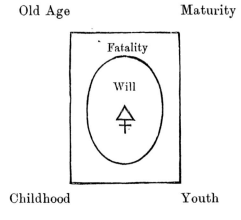

Childhood   Youth

A profound symbol, which indicates that the Human Will creates the fatality in which man moves, under the influence of the providential cycle of the four ages of human life. If we know that Providence (the outer circle) acts upon the Future, Fatality (the intermediate circle) upon the Past, and the Human Will (centre circle) upon the Present, we shall see the basis of the divining Tarot.

We think that these examples are sufficiently clear to enable us to proceed, and we shall now study some applications of the Tarot, leaving to the student the work of discovering a larger number.

To face page 232

CHAPTER XVI

THE ASTRONOMICAL TAROT

Egyptian Astronomy—The Four Seasons—The Twelve Months—
The Thirty-six Decani—The Planets—Absolute Analogy with
the Tarot—Figure containing the Application of the Tarot
to Astronomy—Key to the Astrological Works of Christian—
Oswald Wirth's Astronomical Tarot.

THE ASTRONOMICAL TAROT

In order to demonstrate the accuracy of the principles
upon which the construction of the Tarot is based, we
will take the constitution of the Universe itself, as
shown by Astronomy, for our example of the first
application of its system.

It is known that the Egyptians divided the year into
four seasons, each composed of three months. Each
month contained three decani or periods of ten days,
which gave three hundred and sixty days in each year.
They added to complete it a period of five days, or
Epagomenes, placed after the 30th degree of the Lion
(August).

We must therefore find in our Tarot—

1. The four seasons;
2. The twelve months, or, better still, the twelve
signs of the zodiac;
3. The thirty-six decani.

Moreover each month, or, still better, each zodiacal sign, and each of the decani is ruled by a planet.

1. *The Four Seasons*

The four figures of the Tarot correspond absolutely with the four seasons of the year.

If we then look at the twenty-first card of the Tarot, the origin, as we have seen, of all its applications, we shall see that the four figures in the corners represent the four suits of the Tarot, and in this case the four seasons of the year.

The elliptic space between these four figures and the centre corresponds to the zodiac and its divisions.

Finally, the central portion corresponds to the planets, which influence the whole system.

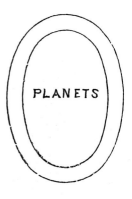

2. *The 12 Signs of the Zodiac*

Each suit represents one season. Each season is composed of three months. How, then, will the months be represented in our suits?

The months will be represented by the figures, and the correspondence is established in this way—

KING.   1st Month or *Active Month* in the Season.
          Creative Month. *Yod.*

QUEEN.   2nd Month or Passive Month in each Season.
          Preserving Month. *He.*

KNIGHT.   3rd Month or *Realizing Month, Equilibrist*
          of the Season. *Vau.*

KNAVE.   Transition from the preceding Season to
          the one following. *Epagomene.*[1]

(Consult, for further details, the first part of our study upon the Tarot.)

We therefore find twelve figures, which respond to the twelve signs of the Zodiac, as follows—

SCEPTRES	King of Sceptres Queen Knight	The Ram The Bull The Twins	}	SPRING
	Knave *Transition*	*Epagomene*		
CUPS	King of Cups Queen Knight	Cancer The Lion The Virgin	}	SUMMER
	Knave *Transition*	*Epagomene*		
SWORDS	King of Swords . Queen Knight	The Balance The Scorpion Sagittarius	}	AUTUMN
	Knave *Transition*	*Epagomene*		
PENTACLES	King of Pentacles Queen Knight	Capricornus Aquarius The Fishes	}	WINTER
	Knave *Transition*	*Epagomene*		

---

[1] Thus the Tarot places one *epagomene*, or complementary day, after each season.

3. *The 36 Decani*

Each season is divided into three months, but each month is divided into three decani, or periods of ten days each.

We need only recall the analogy existing between the figures and the numbers in the minor arcana, to ascertain which cards of the Tarot represent these new divisions.

If we take one of the figures—the King, for instance—we know that this king governs certain cards: the Ace, two, three, and the first ternary.

We then obtain the following analogies—

KING OF SCEPTRES: zodiacal sign, the Ram.

ACE.	1st Decan or *Active Decan* of the Month. *Creative Decan. Yod.*
TWO.	2nd Decan or *Passive Decan* of the Month. *Forming or Preserving Decan. He.*
THREE.	3rd Decan or *Equilibrating Decan. Vau.*
FOUR.	Transition between the third Decan of the actual series, to the first Decan of the following series, which it forms.

The thirty-six decani are therefore represented in the Tarot in the following series—

King $\begin{cases} \text{Ace of Sceptres} & \text{1st Decan} \\ 2 \quad ,, & \text{2nd} \quad ,, \\ 3 \quad ,, & \text{3rd} \quad ,, \end{cases}$ of the Ram

Queen $\begin{cases} 4 \quad ,, & \text{1st Decan} \\ 5 \quad ,, & \text{2nd} \quad ,, \\ 6 \quad ,, & \text{3rd} \quad ,, \end{cases}$ of the Bull

Knight $\begin{cases} 7 \quad ,, & \text{1st Decan} \\ 8 \quad ,, & \text{2nd} \quad ,, \\ 9 \quad ,, & \text{3rd} \quad ,, \end{cases}$ of the Twins

Knave 10 *Transition*   *Epagomene*

King $\begin{cases} \text{Ace of Cups} \\ 2 \quad ,, \\ 3 \quad ,, \end{cases}$ $\left.\begin{array}{l} \text{1st Decan} \\ \text{2nd} \quad ,, \\ \text{3rd} \quad ,, \end{array}\right\}$ of Cancer

Queen $\begin{cases} 4 \quad ,, \\ 5 \quad ,, \\ 6 \quad ,, \end{cases}$ $\left.\begin{array}{l} \text{1st Decan} \\ \text{2nd} \quad ,, \\ \text{3rd} \quad ,, \end{array}\right\}$ of the Lion

Knight $\begin{cases} 7 \quad ,, \\ 8 \quad ,, \\ 9 \quad ,, \end{cases}$ $\left.\begin{array}{l} \text{1st Decan} \\ \text{2nd} \quad ,, \\ \text{3rd} \quad ,, \end{array}\right\}$ of the Virgin

Knave   10   *Transition*   *Epagomene*

King $\begin{cases} \text{Ace of Swords} \\ 2 \quad ,, \\ 3 \quad ,, \end{cases}$ $\left.\begin{array}{l} \text{1st Decan} \\ \text{2nd} \quad ,, \\ \text{3rd} \quad ,, \end{array}\right\}$ of the Balance

Queen $\begin{cases} 4 \quad ,, \\ 5 \quad ,, \\ 6 \quad ,, \end{cases}$ $\left.\begin{array}{l} \text{1st Decan} \\ \text{2nd} \quad ,, \\ \text{3rd} \quad ,, \end{array}\right\}$ of the Scorpion

Knight $\begin{cases} 7 \quad ,, \\ 8 \quad ,, \\ 9 \quad ,, \end{cases}$ $\left.\begin{array}{l} \text{1st Decan} \\ \text{2nd} \quad ,, \\ \text{3rd} \quad ,, \end{array}\right\}$ of Sagittarius

Knave   10   *Transition*   *Epagomene*

King $\begin{cases} \text{Ace of Pentacles} \\ 2 \quad ,, \\ 3 \quad ,, \end{cases}$ $\left.\begin{array}{l} \text{1st Decan} \\ \text{2nd} \quad ,, \\ \text{3rd} \quad ,, \end{array}\right\}$ of Capricornus

Queen $\begin{cases} 4 \quad ,, \\ 5 \quad ,, \\ 6 \quad ,, \end{cases}$ $\left.\begin{array}{l} \text{1st Decan} \\ \text{2nd} \quad ,, \\ \text{3rd} \quad ,, \end{array}\right\}$ of Aquarius

Knight $\begin{cases} 7 \quad ,, \\ 8 \quad ,, \\ 9 \quad ,, \end{cases}$ $\left.\begin{array}{l} \text{1st Decan} \\ \text{2nd} \quad ,, \\ \text{3rd} \quad ,, \end{array}\right\}$ of the Fishes

Knave   10   *Transition*   *Epagomene*

Each decan, governing ten degrees of the zodiacal circle, corresponds to a certain number of days in the month. Consequently each card in the minor arcana, corresponding to a decan, represents a certain fraction of the year—

Ace of Sceptres	21st to 30th of March.
2 ,,	31st of March to 9th of April.
3 ,,	10th to 19th of April, etc.

We need only consult the figure at the end of this study of the astronomical Tarot to see which days correspond to each decan.

This is the basis of the astrological Tarot, and by its cards a horoscope can be drawn out; but since this application lies beyond the purely scientific field to which we have limited ourselves, we must not dwell upon it here.

In short, our minor arcana are fully represented in the astronomical Tarot, and they exactly determine the limits in which move the planets, that we have still to consider.

The Planets

The major arcana are represented in this application of the Tarot by the septenary of the planets acting upon the three worlds ($3 \times 7 = 21$).

Each zodiacal sign and each decan is governed by a planet, and the connection between the planets and these different signs is indicated upon the table which follows.

This table enables us to comprehend all the work that Christian[1] and Ely Star[2] accomplished upon Astrology. Moreover, it indicates the astronomical correspon-

[1] Christian, *Histoire de la Magie*, Paris, 1854. 8vo.
[2] Ely Star, *Les Mystères de l'Horoscope*, Paris, Dentu, 1888. 18mo. (3 fr. 50.)

dence of every card in the Tarot.   Here is an explanation of its construction :—

The four figures of the twenty-first card of the Tarot represent the four seasons of the year and the four suits of the Tarot.

The centre of the twenty-first card responds to the seven planets, which animate the yearly system.

Lastly, the ZODIACAL ELLIPSE revolves between these two terms, and it contains the key to the influence exercised by the major arcana (the planets) over the minor arcana (the signs and decani).

This table is therefore a proof of the accuracy of our system of explaining the Tarot and also a magnificent key to the Tarot itself.

We shall now quote two extracts from J. A. Vaillant (*Les Rômes : histoire vraie des Bohémiens*), which demonstrate the harmony existing between our deductions and the traditional explanations given by the gypsies.

SOME GYPSY TRADITIONS CONCERNING

THE ASTRONOMICAL TAROT

The 21st card, entitled the Universe or Time, is, in fact, the time of the temple and the temple of time.

It represents an oval crown of flowers, divided into four by four lotus flowers, and supported by the four symbolical heads, which St. John borrowed from Ezekiel and the latter from the cherubim and seraphim of Assyria and Egypt.

The four heads are those—

Of the Eagle. The symol of the East, of the morning, of the equinox of spring.

Of the Lion. ,, of the South, and of the solstice of summer.

Of the Bull. ,, of the Evening, the West, and of the equinox of autumn.

Of the Man. ,, of the Night, the North, and of the solstice of winter.

In the midst of this crown, the symbol of the egg of the world, stands a nude woman, the symbol of Eve; one of her feet is raised, symbolizing the flight of time; and she holds two wands of equal length, symbols of the balance and equilibrium of time, of the justice and equity of men, of the equality of day and night, of man and woman.

This Eve is the great Mother (*Ava* or *Ebe*) who pours out to the stars the men-gods of heaven, and to men the star-gods of earth, the nectar and ambrosia of immortality, the shadow and light of eternity (*Aon*), of which the crown that surrounds her is the sea or the ocean, the enclosure or the vase, the ark or the vessel.

This symbol is not new. It was throughout antiquity used to express the nature of the Universe; the synthesis of the arcs of the circle; the union of the arches of the sphere, which the Hebrews made into the ark of the covenant; the modification of the ancient coins of Crete, which took this *arch* of the world; the covenant of the rainbow, for the *principle* of *justice* which gives it its name. And, in fact, the name of *Kudas*, of that *Ebee of Crete*, clearly expresses justice, *saduk*, which makes of this *Melchi sedek*, the spirit of the Lord, and of this spirit (*Eon*) of the sun, the law of the times of the stars, of the life of man; consequently Noah, who is himself the spirit (*Eon*) of eternity (*Aon*) of centuries (*Aion*), has been qualified as *præco justitiæ*, revealer of justice.

.   .   .   .   .

The Tarot is a deduction of the sidereal book of *Henoch*, who is *Henochia;* it is modelled on the astral wheel of *Athor*, who is *As-taroth*, resembling the Indian *ot-tara*, the polar bear or *arc-tura* of the north; it is the major force (*tarie*) upon which is based the solidity (*ferrale*) of the world and the sidereal firmament of the earth; consequently, like the polar bear, called the chariot of the sun, the chariot of David and of ARTHUR, it is the Greek luck (*tuché*), the Chinese destiny (*tiko*), the Egyptian chance (*tiki*), the fate (*tika*) of the Romanys; and the stars, as they incessantly revolve round the polar bear, reveal to the earth ostentation and misery, light and shade, heat and cold; whilst from them flow the good and evil, the love and hatred, which form the happiness (*ev-tuchié*) and the misfortune (*dis-tuchié*) of men.

.   .   .   .   .   .

In truth *Sephora* is one of the harmonies in that triad, s.f.r., which united form the light (*Sapher*), the number (*Sipher*), and the word (*Sephora*) of the Hebrews, from the *Sphere* of the Universe. From this sphere,

of which the light is truth,

the zodiac is the book which contains it, the stars are the numbers and letters which explain it, the *Anaks* have drawn their *Tara*, the Gypsies their *Tarot*, the Phœnicians their *As-tharot*, the Egyptians their *Athor*, and the Hebrews their *Thora*.

But we cannot end our study upon the astronomical

Tarot without some allusion to the work of Oswald Wirth upon this subject. In some respects his conclusions differ from our own; but we are anxious on that account to quote his essay upon it, in order that each reader may judge between us for himself.

ESSAY UPON THE ASTRONOMICAL TAROT
By Oswald Wirth

According to Christian, the twenty-two major arcana of the Tarot represent the hieroglyphic paintings which were found in the spaces between the columns of a gallery, which the neophyte was obliged to cross in the Egyptian initiations. There were twelve columns to the North and the same number to the South, that is, eleven symbolical pictures on each side. These pictures were explained to the candidate for initiation in regular order, and they contained the rules and principles for the Initiate.

The arcana corresponding to the twenty-two letters of the Hebrew alphabet must have been arranged upon the walls of the secret crypts in the temples of Osiris in the following order. (See p. 243.)

This opinion is confirmed by the correspondence which exists between the arcana when they are thus arranged.

It is at once evident that the arcana 2, 3, 4 and 5 form a complete group; this group corresponds to another formed by the arcana 21, 20, 19 and 18. Now in the interpretation of the symbols each arcanum should be studied in its relations with the neighbouring arcana, and particularly with those which are pendant to it in the grouping that we have pointed out. For instance, the 2nd arcanum (ב), or High Priestess, should not only be compared with the 1st

EAST

NORTH

SOUTH

WEST

Hebrew	No.	Card
א	1	Juggler
ב	2	The High Priestess
ג	3	Empress
ד	4	Emperor
ה	5	Pope
ו	6	Lovers
ז	7	Chariot
ח	8	Justice
ט	9	Hermit
י	10	The Wheel of Fortune
כ	11	Strength
ל	12	The Hanged Man
מ	13	Death
נ	14	Temperance
ס	15	Devil
ע	16	The Lightning-struck Tower
פ	17	Stars
צ	18	Moon
ק	19	Sun
ר	20	Judgment
ש	21	Universe
ת	0	Foolish Man

arcanum (א), or Juggler, the 3rd (ג), or Empress, and the 4th (ד), or Emperor; but also with the 5th arcanum (ה), or Pope, with the 21st (ת), or Universe, and even with the 18th (צ), or Moon. By studying each of the twenty-two arcana in this way, we shall discover that the whole are closely linked together, and we shall acquire unexpected light upon the most ancient of all the sacred books which we possess.

It should be noticed that the 7th, 8th, 9th and 10th arcana represent a quaternary, to which a last group corresponds, formed of the 16th, 15th, 14th and 13th arcana. We therefore have sixteen pentacles divided into four quaternaries, which give a definite general meaning. Six other pentacles are placed in pairs at the commencement, the centre and the end of the double series of the arcana of the Tarot. These six arcana appear to frame the others, and this fact gives them great importance. Their signification is easily discovered by their mutual comparison and the judicious application of the laws of analogy supplied by the keys of the Book of Thoth, as well as by those of the Eternal Book that Nature, symbolized under the form of Isis, holds half-opened in the 2nd arcanum (ב), the High Priestess.

But it is necessary to proceed methodically in these researches, by means of a progressive analysis starting from the whole, before we can grasp each arcanum separately, for each one must be carefully examined under the numerous aspects which it presents. When this work of dissection is once accomplished, the student must retrace his steps, and synthetically recompose the whole by a reverse operation.

In applying these principles here, we must first

repeat that the Tarot, considered as a whole, is preeminently the Sacred Book of occult initiation. Now we attain this initiation by two different paths, by one of which we develop the powers that we possess innately to their utmost extent; by the other we subdue ourselves, and thus attain a state of being which renders us susceptible to the action of the cosmic forces that surround us. Although these two methods differ completely, we can accomplish the great work by following either of them. This is the meaning of the Hermetic precept, "that the philosopher's stone can be prepared by the dry path or by the moist, by the red tincture or by the white." Initiation, androgynous as a whole, is therefore subdivided into male and female. It is masculine from the 1st (א) to the 11th (כ) arcana, and becomes feminine in the arcana 21(ת) to 12 (ל). With regard to the arcanum 0 (ש), which is unnumbered in the Tarot, although it is eminently passive in itself, it must not be included in the feminine series, for reasons easily discerned in the study of the exact signification of each arcanum taken separately.

Let us then content ourselves for the moment with asserting that masculine or Dorian initiation starts from א to end in כ, whilst feminine or Ionian initiation starts from ש to end in ל. The two unite and complete each other in the androgynous initiation, which can start from א to end in ש, or start from ש to return to it again, after traversing the whole series of the arcana, taking their numbers in the inverse order.

Initiation can, however, be regarded not only under the double aspect of activity and passivity, represented by the North and South, but it can be also contemplated as light and life, that is to say, as the intellectual instruction as well as the moral education of the

Initiate. In this respect the Tarot is divided by the 6th arcanum (ו), the Lovers, and the 17th (פ), the Stars, into two parts, which represent the West and the East.

This double division produces the four quaternaries of which we have already spoken. Each represents one especial section, its general sense being indicated by its orientation; the North-West thus corresponds with intellectual activity; the North-East with moral activity; the South-West with intellectual passivity, and the South-East with moral passivity. These four sections are also united in the arcana 1 (א) the Juggler; 11 (כ) Strength; 12 (ל) the Hanged Man; and 0 (ש) the Foolish Man.

The 6th arcanum, the Lovers, indicates the passage of intellectual activity to its moral application, the 17th פ. The stars form the transition between passive intellectuality and its practical employment in the exercise of occult powers.

We think that enough has been now said to enable each student to discover for himself the complex signification of every arcanum in the Tarot. We will therefore end this sketch by some classifications, intended to prove that the order in which we arrange the arcana of the Tarot does not form a purely arbitrary system.

It will, in fact, be easily seen that connection in their opposition links the arcana when they are grouped in four quaternaries of different formation from the four first, which we have already examined. (See p. 247.)

The analogy of these significations is particularly striking between the arcana 7 and 16, 10 and 13, which yet present an antagonistic meaning, as soon as 7 is compared with 16, and 10 with 13. It is the same with the other quaternaries represented here, although the

fact may be less visible at the first glance. But we will
now leave a free field to individual investigation on
this point, and pass on to the study of the Tarot from
another point of view.

ב 2 High Priestess	ה 5 Pope	ג 3 Empress	ד 4 Emperor
ת 21 World	צ 18 Moon	ר 20 Judgment	ק 19 Sun
ז 7 Chariot	י 10 Wheel of Fortune	ח 8 Justice	ט 9 Hermit
ע 16 Lightning-struck Tower	מ 13 Death	ס 15 Devil	נ 14 Temperance

*The 22 major arcana of the Tarot compared to
the figures representing the constellations upon
the celestial sphere, according to the Greek and
Egyptian planispheres.*

The Tarot which we possess represents a series of
symbolical images adapted to the ideology of the

fourteenth century, and fixed by the invention of xylography. It is impossible for us to retrace through the darkness of the Middle Ages the origin of the twenty-two significative figures known as *atouts*, in the pack of seventy-eight cards by which the Gypsies claim to reveal the secrets of fate.

Still it has been proved that the major arcana of the Tarot are disfigured reproductions of a primitive model dating from the earliest times. It would be difficult to rediscover this model in its original purity; and if it were possible to do so, it could only be through judicious study of every manifestation of symbolism throughout the history of Oriental mythologies. These have bequeathed to us an hieroglyphic monument of immense importance in the representative figures of the signs of the Zodiac, and of the constellations of the celestial Sphere. But it would be most interesting if we could prove that these allegorical figures absolutely reproduce the 22 major arcana of the Tarot. From this affinity we might obtain great light upon the genesis of human knowledge. For the same identity of origin which manifestly unites the plates of the Book of Thoth to the subdivisions of the Greek and Egyptian planispheres, leads to the conclusion that in both cases we possess a special adaptation, made from documents which we have not yet found, but which may still give us complete information respecting primitive India.

In any case the arcana of the Tarot explain many of the anomalies in Greek mythology. We cannot now enter into any minute details upon this subject, for it would lead us beyond the limits of this book. We must content ourselves with giving the reader a table indicating the constellations which appear to correspond with the 22 major arcana of the Tarot, and therefore with the 22 letters of the Hebrew alphabet, although their correspondence with the latter is much less clearly defined. We will then trace a planisphere grouping the arcana of the Tarot according to the order of the constellations, and we will end by a pentacle in the form of a double hexagram, in which the Hebrew letters will represent the signs of the zodiac, and the circumpolar constellations to which they correspond, according to our first table.

OSWALD WIRTH'S TABLE

No. of the Arcana of the Tarot.	Corresponding Hebrew Letters.	Denomination of the Arcana.	Constellations.
1	א	The Juggler	Orion—The Bull
2	ב	The High Priestess	Cassiopeia
3	ג	The Empress	The Virgin
4	ד	The Emperor	Hercules, Lyra and Boreal Crown
5	ה	The Pope	The Ram
6	ו	The Lovers	Eagle, Antinoüs, and Sagittarius
7	ז	The Chariot	Great Bear
8	ח	Justice	The Balance
9	ט	The Hermit	The Ox-Driver
10	י	The Wheel of Fortune	Capricornus (opposed to Sirius)
11	כ	Strength	Lion (and Virgin)
12	ל	The Hanged Man	Perseus
13	מ	Death	Dragon of the Pole
14	נ	Temperance	Aquarius
15	ס	The Devil	Goat and Coachman
16	ע	The Lightning-struck Tower	Scorpion, Ophiuchus
17	פ	The Stars	Andromeda, the Fishes
18	צ	The Moon	Cancer, Sirius, and Procion
19	ק	The Sun	The Twins
20	ר	The Judgment	The Swan
21	ת	The Universe	Lesser Bear and Pole Star
22	ש	The Foolish Man	Cepheus

PLANISPHERE,

ACCORDING TO THE DATA OF THE PRECEDING TABLE, BY

OSWALD WIRTH

	14 Temperance — Aquarius	10 Wheel of Fortune — Capricornus	6 The Lovers — Sagittarius		
17 Stars — The Fishes	2 The High Priestess — Cassiopeia	0 The Foolish Man — Cepheus	20 The Judgment — The Swan	16 The Lightning- struck Tower — Scorpion	
5 The Pope — The Ram	12 The Hanged Man — Perseus	21 The Universe — Pole Star	13 Death — Dragon	4 The Emperor — Hercules	8 Justice — The Balance
1 Juggler — Bull	15 Devil — The Coachman	7 The Chariot — Great Bear	9 The Hermit — The Ox-Driver	3 The Empress — Virgin	
19 Sun — Twins	18 Moon — Cancer	11 Strength — Lion			

PENTACLE OF OSWALD WIRTH

Signs of the Zodiac and Circumpolar Constellations

Affinities with the Tarot

To face page 252

CHAPTER XVII

THE INITIATIVE TAROT

Ch. Barlet's Essay on this Subject—Involution and Evolution—
The Hours of Apollonius of Tyana—The Phases of Initiation
represented by the Tarot.

THE INITIATIVE TAROT

APPLICATION OF THE TAROT TO THE THEORETICAL AND PRACTICAL DOCTRINES OF INITIATION

OUR friend F. Ch. Barlet has written a very interesting
article upon this subject, which we will quote *in extenso.*
Our readers will then see the exactitude with which his
conclusions harmonize with our own.

INITIATION

Amongst the ancients the scientific men were also the
sages, such as Pythagoras, Plato, Aristotle; in modern
times, on the contrary, science and wisdom are unsuc-
cessfully seeking for each other, or struggling in mortal
conflict over the religious question. That such a
separation is against Nature is easily seen by the study
of those Positivist philosophers whose extensive learning and admirable efforts to build up a synthesis of
scientific wisdom merit high rank in the modern intellectual world. Whilst their fundamental aphorism is

that nothing is attainable by man beyond the world of phenomena, their works display an increasing though unintentional tendency to cross the limits which they seek to impose upon themselves, for they are led by that Nature which they love, and which in its final manifestations they know better than any one else. We may compare them to insects imprisoned behind a window; in despair they beat themselves against the glass, clearly seeing the sunbeam which should lead them to the source of all light, yet unable to follow it beyond the invisible wall of their prison. On the other hand, the Spiritualists are outside, free, and as it were lost in the luminous ocean, wandering without a compass, unable to find the guiding sunbeam which is the despair of the Positivists.

However, a school exists which promises to lead the one, to free the other, and to direct each student towards the centre of Truth so ardently desired; it is an unknown school, little frequented, like every transcendent degree, although its masters have always given proofs of considerable learning—the school of *Theosophy*, a positive spiritualism preserved for ages in the ancient mysteries, transmitted with more or less purity by the Kabalists, Mystics, Templars, Rosicrucians and Freemasons, often degenerate, like every other doctrine prematurely divulged, yet hidden at the root of every religion, and carefully perpetuated in a few unknown sanctuaries, chiefly situated in India.

The secret of Theosophy, in the reconciliation between science and metaphysics, lies in a certain practical development of those human faculties which are best fitted to extend the limits of reliable knowledge. Let us first try to understand this possibility.

An attentive examination of any scientific method, however positive it may be, proves that there is no evidence or certainty save in axioms, and that the fragile and changeable scaffolding of our sciences, built upon this immovable basis, is entirely due to intuition, of which observation and experience are only instruments.

But the field of direct perception in which intuition exerts itself is capable of extension; this fact is now demonstrated by the phenomena of hypnotism and magnetism, the torments of our modern sciences; for by them the limits of opaque matter, of space and time, are suppressed in variable but incontestable degrees.

But still, in this realm of transcendental faculties the perception is not always so reliable as the unvarying certainty which characterizes an axiom; for, in hypnotic or magnetic subjects, material lucidity presents a number of gradations which are reproduced in the intellectual order, and which vary between the fancies of a disordered imagination and the sublime revelations of healthy, inspired genius.

We do not therefore exceed the possibilities given by the reliable evidence of observation and experience, when we assert that the physical or intellectual perception of the human being is capable of extending beyond the limits of ordinary judgments and sensations; and that in the transcendental regions which it can attain it is susceptible of more or less certitude in its impressions. This assertion opens new fields for human knowledge, an hierarchy of new immediate causes, and the prospect of an indefinite progress in science.

Now, Theosophy inspires man with the enthusiasm which enables him to draw near to these transcendent regions of perception, whilst it guards him from illusion, through the forces and the new beings which he will meet there: it is this instruction which constitutes Initiation.

The slight sketch which now follows will at least give some idea of the principles by which Religion and Philosophy, Wisdom and Science, are united in Theosophy. Any defects which the reader may find in it must be attributed to want of skill on the part of the student who has undertaken it.

.   .   .   .

Initiation comprises two different but united sections: (1) the Theory of the resources and necessities of his enterprise, which the neophyte always receives as an inheritance which leaves him absolute liberty of thought—and (2) the Practice wherein he exercises, under the direction of his masters, the physical, intellectual and moral self-control which will render him an Initiate.

The Theory, the primary instruction of Theosophy, is a preliminary definition, consisting almost exclusively of the contents of the Theosophical publications; but a student should not fancy himself one of the Initiates because he possesses these public works; the knowledge of them is an excellent preparation, but nothing more.

This theory is found scattered throughout a number of more or less well-known and accessible books; but there are very few of them which explain it as a whole, simply and methodically enough to satisfy a beginner. This first difficulty, chiefly due to the actual state of many minds, which will not admit regular instruction, also corresponds to the numerous varieties of intelligence which examine them. Some, previously opened to theosophical doctrines, approach every detail with equal profit to themselves; others, on the contrary, who cannot at first accept them as a whole, willingly examine them by means of a secondary door which especially suits them, but which often forces them to make enormous digressions through our sciences and philosophies. The first steps are consequently varied, and the postulants require guidance from some more advanced brother, who is capable of discerning the intellectual and moral state of the neophyte.

This is why no work on the subject can be especially recommended here. An excellent bibliography of theosophic works will be found in the *Traité Élémentaire de Science Occulte*, by Papus. We now add to it a summary list for a series of studies, long but reliable, which will form a gradual transition from Positivism to Theosophy:

For facts. Study: Richet, d'Assier, Liebault, Philipps, Dupotet, Reichenbach, Mesmer, &c.

Hypothesis of the whole: Comte, Stuart Mill, Bain, Ribot, Spencer, Taine, &c.

Philosophers: Du Prel, Hartmann, Schopenhauer, Hegel. Great profit can then be derived from earlier works: Spinoza, Leibnitz, and even from the ancients: Aristotle, Plato, the Neoplatonists, the Pythagoreans; finally, from modern mystic scientists: Wronski, Fabre d'Olivet, Lucas, &c.

The student will then fully understand Theosophy.

This series will, however, require further modifications, according to the character and the scientific aptitudes of the student. We must also point out some features of the theory which are necessary for the comprehension of our principal subject; the reader

R

must only remember that the explanation is entirely due to the author of this article, and he must not impute any of its errors to Theosophy itself.

.   .   .   .

Our positive sciences give the last formula of the visible world in the following words—

There is no matter without force: no force without matter.

It is an indisputable but incomplete formula, unless the following commentary be added to it—

1. The combination of what we call Force and Matter presents itself in various proportions, from that which is called materialized Force (rocks, minerals, simple chemical bodies) to subtilized Matter or Matter-Force (a grain of pollen, spermatozoid, the electric atom). Matter and Force, although we cannot isolate them, therefore present themselves as the extreme and opposing mathematical limits (or contrary signs) of a series of which we see only a few medium terms, abstract but indubitable.

2. The terms of this series, that is to say, the substances of Nature, are never stable; Force, which is characterized by infinite mobility, sways essentially inert matter from one pole to the other, as though it were drawn by a continual current, while matter retorts by a counter-current, which leads it back to its inert condition. For instance, an atom of phosphorus, borrowed by a vegetable from the mineral phosphates, becomes the element of a human cerebral cellule (subtilized matter), and then through disintegration falls back into the inert mineral kingdom.

3. The movement resulting from this unstable equili-

brium is not disorganized; it presents a series of chained harmonies which we call Laws, and which are synthesized in our eyes in the supreme law of Evolution.

One conclusion is forced upon us: This harmonious synthesis of phenomena is the eminent manifestation of what we call a Will.

Therefore, according to positive science, the visible world is the expression of a Will which manifests itself by the unstable but progressive equilibrium of Force and Matter.

It is represented by this quaternary—

I. WILL (simple origin).

III. FORCE (Elements of this polarised Will). II. MATTER.

IV. THE VISIBLE WORLD.

(The result of their unstable, dynamic equilibrium.)

The positive method will not allow us to pause there; we must analyze the Will in its turn. We will abridge this analysis here, for the reader will easily master it with the aid of treatises on psychology; it leads through the two opposing terms of affirmation and negation to a new superior, apparently simple cause, the *Idea*, which analysis again decomposes into consciousness and unconsciousness, gradually remounting to its furthest limit, the absolute term, the One, both conscious and unconscious, affirmative and negative, force and matter, nameless, incomprehensible to man.

Let us designate this supreme term by A, and the material atom by Ω; we shall then have, according to

our analysis, the following series of hierarchical quaternaries as a representation of the Universe—

$+$ (1) A $-$	*Divine World*
(3) *Consciousness* (2) *Unconscious-*	(The Transcendent)
ness	
(4) IDEA	*Intelligible World*
(6) *Affirmation* (5) *Negation*	(Logic)
(7) WILL	
(9) *Force* (8) *Matter*	*Visible World*
(10) KOSMOS	(Positive Science)
Ω	

The extreme terms, a and ω, Spirit and Matter,
equally incomprehensible to human intelligence in
their infinite grandeur and infinite littleness,[1] are not
only linked together by invariable intermediate chains,
but they also make an incessantly descending movement from one to the other, in which the Spirit becomes
Matter by the successive disintegrations which express
the Idea, the Will and Kosmos. This constitutes the
creation.

But since, as our sciences prove to us, the Kosmos
itself is in a state of evolutionary movement, and since
according to their teachings this movement clearly
inclines towards a progressive synthesis, which spiri-
tualizes the living being by entering more and more
into its composition, the preceding scheme expresses
but one-half of the Universe—the one which descends.
We must now add to it a second half, which restores
the atom, ω, to its opposing principle a, through the
progressive synthesis of individual lives. This is
Progress, the sequence of Creation.

1 The first a, *One* and infinitely great; integration of Ω. The
second ω, a multiple composed of an *infinite number* of infinitely
tiny elements; analysis of a.

Thus the Universe appears to us like a circular current, in which the flow is necessarily inverse in the two opposing arcs: from the positive pole a to the negative pole ω the current descends—this is Involution, the descent of the Spirit into Matter; from the negative pole ω to the positive pole a the current re-ascends—this is Evolution, the spiritualization of Matter. We shall describe it presently.

. . . . . .

Let us then infer for man—

The evidence of our sciences shows him to be upon the ascending arc, already far from the negative pole, since he is at the head of the three kingdoms of the terrestrial world. He thus belongs to the visible world of the Universe; the imposing monument of science is a proof of the position which he also occupies in the intellectual world; but at the same time his errors, his doubts, the enormous deficiences in his knowledge, and his passions, sufficiently prove that he is no longer master in this sphere, as he is in the inferior world. As to the divine world, he conceives it, presses towards it; but if he attain it, it will be by faith rather than by science.

Man is then a being who in his re-ascension has reached the middle region, and even the centre of that region; his place is in the centre of the ascending arc, between the superior and the inferior beings of creation, ruling the one, ruled by the others, midway between the Angel and the Beast. It is a situation inevitably painful through the equality of the two opposing forces, that retard his ascension; he has come to a dead stop, which must be overcome by a special effort.

At the present time Initiation is the instrument that

facilitates the development of the human butterfly. We shall soon understand of what it consists.

. . . .

The Ancients, with the usual force of their synthetic genius, have symbolized the whole of Involution and Evolution by a sequence of twenty-two figures, full of hidden significations, which occultists name the Twenty-two Great Arcana.

Taking the ten first as a description of Involution, we find in the others the successive phases of Initiation, such as they are depicted in the twelve hours (or sentences) which form the *Nuctemeron* attributed to Apollonius of Tyana. These we shall now enumerate.

To be perfectly clear we must first return to Evolution for one moment.

As a fact its analysis is not completed by the ten terms which have led us to the Kosmos, the dynamic equilibrium of Force and Matter. This Kosmos can be analyzed in its turn as two principles which, according to all the sciences, are conflicting in every movement of matter: the Active and Passive (male and female of organizations, acid and basis of chemistry, the opposing poles of electricity, &c.). Completely inert matter is only found in their absolute equilibrium in the unattainable pole exactly opposed to the a—the ω of the Universe.

Occultists have represented this 4th tetractys, of which the Kosmos is the first term (the tetractys of the inferior world, *infernum*, hell), by the 11th, 12th, and 13th arcana, the Kosmos being its first term. The arcanum which bears the generally dreaded number 13 requires further notice. It is called DEATH and RESURRECTION, and it represents absolute Inertia, only found in Death; but here Involution stops and Evolution commences, for the equilibrium of the two principles, active and passive, is never prolonged.

This would seem to contradict the preceding remark, that the description of Initiation, that is to say, of the re-ascension, opens with the 10th arcanum, and not with the 14th. This however is not so, because in Evolution the being should retrace in an inverse sense, to complete the synthesis, every stage by which the α has been disintegrated in the course of its Involution. Man is the actual result of a work of this kind anterior to his present state, but of this work which has raised him from the ω to the stage of Will he is quite unconscious; at first he was subjected to it under the fatal pressure of pure Force only, then of instinct, desires and passions; his previous evolution is therefore unknown to him, and yet how can he master any of these worlds without being acquainted with them all? His first work in Initiation must therefore be to re-descend to his first steps in Evolution, to become acquainted with all the degrees, all the forces and all the beings that he has passed through, to penetrate the roots of life to death itself, and learn to dominate them all.

We shall see presently that this is not a figurative assertion; the Neophyte cannot attain any reliable voluntary exercise of the transcendental faculties without first obtaining the mastery over the forces which would produce illusion, which would threaten his life itself; without reaching *Inertia* and conquering it. Like the Christ, the model of regenerate man, he must expire upon the cross and rise again the third day; that is to say, after descending the three last steps represented by the 11th, 12th, and 13th arcana,

into the depths of hell, there to discover Death and
to overcome it.

This fully understood, we will describe the twelve
hours or phases of Initiation.

.   .   .   .

The 10th arcanum, the first hour of the series, corresponds with the stage which man has reached at the
present time. The symbol of this arcanum is the
Sphinx, which guarded the entrance to the Egyptian
world; the Neophyte descended between its paws into
the tunnel which led to the sanctuary, through a series
of tests, the image and novitiate of the descent which
we have just mentioned.

This is then the hour of preparation; it separates
the common life from the transcendental life; in it the
student learns the work that he must undertake, and
prepares himself for it. Let us see in what way.

The human head of the Sphinx, the centre of the
intelligence, says to the Neophyte: "First acquire that
Knowledge which shows the goal, and lights the way
to it." This is the theoretic instruction mentioned above.

Its bull's thighs—image of the rough, persevering
labour of the agriculturist—say to him: "Be strong
and patient in thy work."

Its lion's paws say to him: "Thou must brave all,
and defend thyself against every inferior force."

Its eagle's wings say to him: "Thou must will to
raise thyself towards the transcendent regions, which
thy soul already approaches."

The riddle attributed to the Greek Sphinx, and the
answer required by it, are an equally expressive image
of man, and his aim. He is the animal that in the
morning (that is to say, in the infancy of humanity)

goes on four feet (4 being the number of realization, expresses matter and its instincts, the visible world); at noon (that is to say, in the maturity of his humanity) he walks upon two feet (2, the number of opposition, the image of science, of its contradictions, its doubts, and of the intelligible world); and in the evening (when the day is nearly over) he walks upon three feet (3, the number of the divine world, in which the Trinity gives the solution of all the oppositions, of all the antinomies, by the superior term, the harmonious synthesis of the two adverse terms).

Apollonius describes the same hour in these words: " Here the Neophyte praises God, utters no injurious words, inflicts no more pain," which means that his theoretic knowledge of the Creation is increased, and that he practises self-control. We will now pause and examine the consistency of these various prescriptions.

We have seen that man, having reached the ascending arc, has become the object of dispute between the inferior forces of inertia, which he has traversed under the impulse of instinct, and those active forces which draw him upwards; we have noticed that the struggle must now be decided by the intervention of the Will, sufficiently developed by Evolution and sufficiently free to exert its influence on one side or on the other: man can therefore decide either for the inferior forces of disintegration or for the superior forces of synthesis, under the names of Good and Evil. And truly evil for him if he redescend, for he will meet the terrors of decomposition, of Death! Good, on the other hand, if he ascend, for he will enjoy the realization of his natural aspirations, the knowledge of the Creation and dominion over it!

Now where is the index of the forces of inertia in the human organization?—In instinct, in the passions. Where, on the other hand, is the index of the active forces?—In moral energy, in Virtue.

Where is the index of the forces of disintegration, which lead to inertia in the human organization?—In the tendency to isolation, in egoism. Where, on the other hand, is the index of the integrant forces?—In the tendency to joint responsibility, to altruism, in Fraternity.

The transcendent world is therefore open to him that has sufficient Will (or even artificial impulsion) to triumph over the forces which guard it; but woe to that man who approaches it with a passionate and selfish heart; with lowered head he will fall back into the current of decomposition, where he will be dissolved. Nature destroys all Evil; it is the law of selection!

Only the man whose heart is full of charity can raise himself to the true destination of the human being in the region of Principles.

This is why the Sphinx prescribes, with the persevering will of the Bull, the courage of the Lion, against the forces of the passions; and why Apollonius commands reserve and fraternity, with the Gospels which place self-control at the foundation of all Law.

Such then, with the aid of knowledge, is the preparation for Initiation; we shall soon see the importance of these precepts.

.   .   .   .

The Neophyte, sufficiently exercised in these preliminaries of the first hour, then descends the three lower steps as follows—

ARCANUM XI.: *Strength.*

Second hour of Apollonius: "*The abyss of fire—the virtues of the stars close as a crown through the dragons and the fire*" (*the magnetic chain*).

The Neophyte learns to distinguish universal Force and its double current, positive and negative, in his own organization. The application of this knowledge will be found in the two following hours—

ARCANUM XII.: *The Great Work.*

Third hour of Apollonius: "*The serpents, the dogs, and fire.*"

The first manifestation of force applied externally to inert matter for affecting transmutations; this is Alchemy. The Neophyte having attained this step in practice must be ready morally to make a complete sacrifice of his personality; in the language of the alchemists, he must have destroyed his fixed nature by fire so as to volatilize it.

ARCANUM XIII.: *Death.*

Fourth hour of Apollonius: "*The Neophyte wanders in the sepulchres, and it will injure him; he will experience horror and fear of visions; he should devote himself to magic and to goetia.*" [1]

This is Necromancy, the application of Force to the domination of inferior living beings: Elemental, or organisms ready to synthesize themselves, and Elementary, remains of the dead, on the way to disorganisation.

Morally, the Neophyte should die to ordinary life, to enter the spiritual life; the celestial man will be born from the corpse of the terrestrial man.

The foundations of the Universe are now reached;

[1] The magic which evokes the evil genii who injure man.—A.P.M.

the Neophyte touches the extremity of the terrestrial aura, the sublunar atmosphere which surrounds every planet, like the reservoir of the elements of its life; he has now reached a terrible moment, when he must leave the earth to launch out into the ocean of space; a formidable crisis, to which two periods are consecrated.

The first is transitory.

ARCANUM XIV.: *The two Urns* (the terrestrial and celestial fluids).

Fifth hour of Apollonius: " *The waters above the heavens.*"

Here the Neophyte learns the flow of the astral currents in the planetary aura, just as in the second hour he acquired a preliminary knowledge of Force, before exposing himself to it in the following hour.

ARCANUM XV.: *Typhon* (the electric whirlwind).

Sixth hour of Apollonius: " *Here one must remain quiet, immovable through fear.*"

Unprotected the Neophyte exposes himself to the double and formidable fluid-current of celestial space, by which the ignorant or imprudent is carried away without mercy, but which raises the strong man who has purified himself. Silence, prudence, courage!

According to your deserts, you will be enraptured like St. Paul or you will expose yourself to madness, to the spiritualization of evil or to sorcery. This is the *Sabbat* or the Ecstasy!

The reader cannot pay too much attention to this solemn monument of practical occultism, so well described in Lytton's novel *Zanoni* under the name of the *Dragon of the Threshold;* it is the formidable danger which necessitates so many secrets. This thres-

1old is reached by many artificial paths: hasheesh, narcotics, hypnotics of every kind, the practices of spiritual mediums; but woe to him who attempts to pass it before he has triumphed in the long and laborious preliminary preparation! His fate is foretold in the next arcanum.

ARCANUM XVI.: *The Lightning-struck Tower.*

Seventh hour of Apollonius: "*Fire comforts every living creature, and if some priest, himself a pure man, purloin and use it, if he blend it with holy oil, consecrate it, and then anoint some ailing limb with it, the malady will be cured.*"

The irresistible current has touched the man who exposed himself to its vortex on the terrestrial heights; if he be impure he is threatened with disorganization more or less complete, according to his intellectual or moral unworthiness and his energy (incoherent mysticism, folly, death, or complete disintegration, represented by the genius of evil, the Devil).

If, on the contrary, he be worthy of the higher regions, this baptism of fire renders him one of **the Magi**; the sources of terrestrial life are at his disposition; he becomes a Therapeut.

Having reached this point, he will then learn to know the celestial spheres progressively, as he knows the terrestrial sphere, and to dominate them; three hours are consecrated to this exploration.

ARCANUM XVII.: *The Star of the Magi.*

Eighth hour of Apollonius: "*The astral virtues of the elements, of seed of every kind.*"

This is the region of the principles of the solar

system : in it life becomes clear; its distribution from the solar centre to all the planets and their reciprocal influences are understood in all their details, in what the occultists name the Correspondences. The Initiate is then master of Astrology in every branch of the science, in the widest meaning of its acceptation.

ARCANUM XVIII.: *The Twilight.*

Ninth hour of Apollonius : "*Nothing is finished here.*"
The Initiate now extends his perceptions beyond our solar system, "beyond the Zodiac"; he is in sight of the Infinite; he touches the limits of the intelligible world; the divine light commences to show itself, an object of new terror and danger.

ARCANUM XIX.: *The Resplendent Light.*

Tenth hour of Apollonius : "*The gates of heaven are open, and man is born again, docile in the lethargic sleep.*"
The Idea appears to the regenerate soul of the Initiate, or, in the language of the Occultist, the spiritual sun will rise for him; he will by a new regeneration enter the Divine World, in which man dies no more.

Two steps remain before the highest human destinies can be accomplished.

ARCANUM XX.: *The Awakening of the Dead.*

Eleventh hour of Apollonius: "*The Angels, the Cherubim and the Seraphim fly with rustling wings; there is joy in heaven, the earth rises, and the Sun, which issues from Adam.*"
This is the hierarchy of the Divine world, which

appears upon new earths and new heavens. The Initiate will not pass through death again; henceforth he will live eternally.

ARCANUM XXII.: *The Crown of the Magi.*

Twelfth hour of Apollonius: " *The cohorts of fire rest.*"

Nirvana! Complete return to *a*.

Let us recapitulate these twelve hours of Initiation.

0.—Preliminary studies and tests.		Arcanum X.	1st hour
I.—Transcendental study of the *Visible World.*			
Inferior Manifestations:			
1. Preliminary study of Force.	(*Magnetism*)	Arcanum XI.	2nd hour
2. Application to the inert world.	(*Alchemy*)	Arcanum XII.	3rd hour
3. Application to the animate elementary world.	(*Necromancy*) (*Magic*)	Arcanum XIII. (DEATH)	4th hour
Transitory phase:			
1. View of the superior forces.		Arcanum XIV.	5th hour
2. Entrance into the ultra-terrestrial world.	(*Ecstasy*)	Arcanum XV. (TYPHON)	6th hour
THE DRAGON OF THE THRESHOLD!			
Higher regions:			
1. Application of the higher forces to the terrestrial life.	(*Therapeutics*)	Arcanum XVI.	7th hour
2. The forces in the solar system.	(*Astrology*)	Arcanum XVII.	8th hour
3. The forces of the whole Universe.		Arcanum XVIII.	9th hour
II.—Study of the *Intelligible World.* On the borders of the Infinite.		Arcanum XIX.	10th hour
II.—Study of the *Divine World.* Divine hierarchies		Arcanum XX.	11th hour
Nirvana!		Arcanum XXII.	12th hour

Need we add how much effort and time (years, lives, often centuries) are required for each of these hours, how few there are who pass even the first steps!

And what can we expect from their knowledge? The hope of indefinite progress towards the realization of our most radiant hopes; the desire to attain at least some first realizations, so that we may derive from them the assurance of others; confidence in the instruction of those whom we recognize for masters already far advanced; lastly, the certainty that in these fruitful doctrines we shall find the salvation of suffering peoples, as well as our long-desired individual happiness. And these desires, this confidence, are felt after the first preliminary studies.

To succeed, we need undertake but one work at first—that which the Sphinx depicts to us: moral and intellectual preparations. But only the man who seriously undertakes them can know what immense and persevering efforts they exact! May this rough glimpse of them inspire the reader with the desire and the courage to devote himself to them with all the ardour of Hope!

F. CH. BARLET.

THE DIVINE NAME IN THE TAROT

By Ch. Barlet

THE totality of the symbols which form the Tarot is distributed through a series of 78 plates or cards, instead of being presented in a single figure; the reason for this is, that the signification of this totality is manifold, for it is at the same time theologic, cosmologic, psychologic and divining, which variety is the result of the different combinations which can be produced by the arrangement and comparison of these 78 cards. The multiplying is not one of the lesser beauties of this unique masterpiece, in the sense that it adds movement and consequently life to the usual immobility of every written representation, without counting the diversity of its appliances, which include numbers, words, form and colour.

The Tarot can therefore be made to speak when one of its innumerable combinations has been found; that is to say, when the student knows how to arrange the whole or part of his cards upon the table, in the order necessary to discover the answer which he seeks.

We inquire, for example: " What is the Creation from man's point of view, that is to say, what is the life of the Great All, and how can or should man participate in it ? The whole Tarot, with its 22 greater arcana and 56 minor arcana, will answer us, as we shall show by quoting only a few of the profound interpretations which it provides.

To obtain this information we must remember that the three first cards which express the Trinity form at the same time the key to the 22 great arcana, which, when the 0 is abstracted, are only seven repetitions of this Trinity. We must also notice that card IV., the fourth term of the Divine Tetractys, is both the realization of the Trinity restored to the unity and the first term of the following Trinity. The four first cards thus represent the Divine Name of 4 letters, IEVE (יהוה), so that if we repeat the Trinity seven times, to obtain the sequence of the 21 great arcana, the numbers will correspond to the four letters as follows—

Numbers 1. 2. 3. — 4. 5. 6. — 7. 8. 9. — etc.

Letters... { י ה ו — ה י ה — ו ה י — etc.
            { I E V — E I E — V E I — etc.

We will assume that these letters are thus attached to the corresponding arcana, and this remark will be the first key to the arrangement for which we are looking.

To find a second key, we must re-deal our cards in a given space; at first only their place in the plane will appear; then it will be clearly defined. We know that the Kosmos is conceived as the final expansion of the mathematical point, that is to say, of the Absolute, which before this expansion included all force or potentiality in its nothingness. Let us draw this sphere (see Fig. 1). The centre of it will be represented by one of the cards, 0, the *Foolish Man* or *Crocodile*, which is the pivot of the whole pack, at the same time that it participates in all the other cards, for they include all the properties of our universe. From some point of the sphere, a point which becomes our North Pole, the movement will start, by which the creation will appear on its surface.

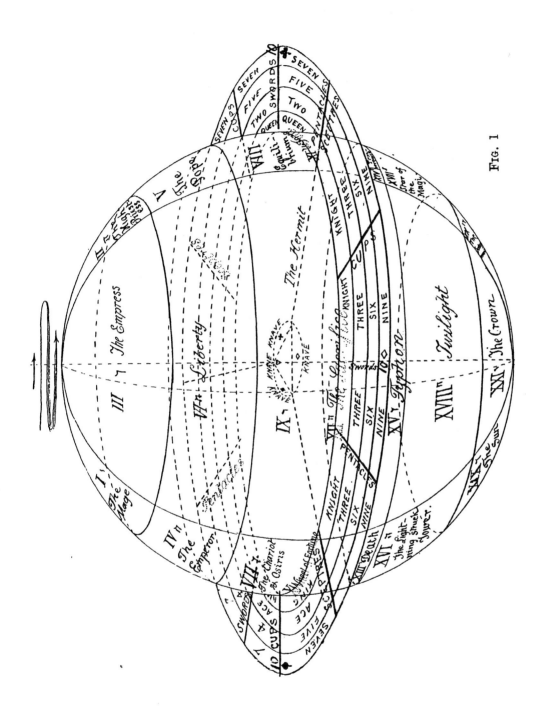

FIG. 1

Around this point upon the sphere, the reflex of the centre, we will place the cards of our 3 first arcana: I. (the Mage, the Spirit, י); II. (Knowledge, Substance, ה); III. (Love, the fertile Power, Being, ו); and in order that this Trinity may be repeated in the whole septenary of our distribution we will make it the root of 3 great divisions, representing the 3 terms of the Trinity, which will divide the surface of our sphere by 3 meridians.

We can then continue the distribution of our cards upon this surface in the following way. The head of each partial Trinity will be in division 1; each second term will be in division 2; each third term in division 3. Consequently our IVth card (the Emperor, ה) will be in I.; the Vth card (the Pope, ו) will be in II.; the VIth card (Liberty, ה) will be in III., and this second sequence will form a new zone upon the sphere. A third, a little inferior, will be formed by cards VII., VIII. and IX.; cards XI., X. and XII. will occupy the Equator, and the 9 cards from XIII. to XXI. will be distributed like the 9 first, in 3 bands placed upon the lower hemisphere, as shown in Fig. 1.

Now that our 22 great arcana are placed, let us pause and look at their significations. Above the Equator we see an ever-increasing expansion of the North Pole, represented by the 3 upper triangles, then by the 6 trapezes which follow, each larger than the one before. Here are the three planes of Creation: The Divine, metaphysic (I., II., III.), the Intelligible, moral (IV., V., VI.), and the physical, that of the generative attributes or elements (VII., VIII., and IX.).

The creation is realized upon the equatorial line (X., XI., XII.), in which the first term, with the preceding cards, represents the 10 sephiroth of the Kabalah.

Below the Equator, in the world of material realization, which is quitted by *Death* (XIII.), this expansion is retracted and synthesized by an inverse and symmetrical movement from above. The arcana which follow represent Initiation carried to its extreme limits, the path by which the creature (X.) returns from its multiplicity to the Unity of the spirit, goes back to the point —the Southern Pole—a new reflex of the Absolute, towards which it re-ascends by the vertical axis of the sphere.[1]

The Neophyte, after his preparation (positive science, magnetism and alchemy, X., XI., XII.), travels through the sublunar world (XIII., XIV., XV.), then through the solar system (XVI., XVII. and XVIII.), and escapes by the sun in the abyss of the Infinite (XIX., XX., XXI.).

We may now end this short explanation of the practical distribution of our 22 arcana upon a plane; it will be easy to imitate it upon a table with a pack of Tarot cards. The student should imagine that our sphere is seen from a considerable distance, vertical upon its axis; for instance, at the distance of the earth from the sun, the upper hemisphere only will appear, the other being seen but transparently; and it will look like a circle, with the Equator for its circumference. The limits of the 3 superposed zones appear like 3 concentric circles; the meridional planes, seen by their dividing lines, only look like 3 equally divided radii, making of the 3 sectors 3 equal arcs. This representation, which geometricians name projection upon the plane of the Equator, gives the second figure (the 4

[1] The details which justify this assertion will be found in the first part of this chapter.

circles of the centre only); to it, for the sake of clearness in the symbols, has been added an equilateral triangle inscribed in the inner circle, with the points posed upon the 3 meridians. The Roman figures inscribed in the circles represent the numbers of the cards arranged as we have said, and, consequently, also indicate their place upon the table. The arcana of the lower hemisphere are shown upon the figure in dotted letters, in the same circles as the preceding; since the lower zones, seen only transparently, might be confused with the upper, through their mutual symmetry.

Here, in broad outline, there is already an answer to our questions: the Spirit descends by three trinities from the Absolute into Matter (upper hemisphere). It is realized by the trinity X. (*Malkuth*), XI. and XII. (the Equator). And it returns to the Absolute by a trinity of growing synthesis, which constitutes human progress (lower hemisphere).

We will presently explain some of the philosophic interpretations which this distribution furnishes; let us first complete it by the 55 minor arcana. They especially represent our solar world.

Since we are now in the world of realization, 4 is its number, its fundamental basis; it is the Trinity realized; the Divine Name of 4 letters IEVE (יהוה). Our cards will be divided into 4 sections: the 4 suits of the pack, spades, hearts, clubs and diamonds, with their hieroglyphic and far more significant names, *Sceptres*, *Cups*, *Swords* and *Pentacles*.

Everything is dual in this world, where equilibrium is unstable, unable to find any rest, except in its return to the Trinity, from which it proceeds. Thus these 4 fundamental divisions will divide into 2 duads—the one spiritual, the other material, each composed of a masculine and feminine principle, namely—

Spiritual duad, the *Sceptre* (spades, a perfect triangle, masculine ; the *Cup* (heart, an open triangle, feminine) : religious attributes ;

Material duad ; the *Sword* (club, a lobed triangle), and the *Pentacle* (diamond, double triangle) ; the attributes of the warrior and of the artisan.

Four other divisions correspond to the 4 suits, those of the pictures which also form 4 duads, namely—

King and Queen ;

Knight or Warrior, and Knave.

As to the numbers which follow these figures, they lead us to another consideration, which is also essential to the distribution of our cards—

If 4 is the fundamental number of these minor arcana, the symbols of our world, we must not forget that it is also connected with the Trinity, from which it emanates ; that it realizes it, and returns thereto. We must then also find the ternary element in it ; after the suits and the pictures, which have provided the basis of our world, the numbers, which are, as it were, the essence of it, will reflect the *Sephiroth* therein, and by them the act of creation. They pause, in fact, at 10, including 3 trinities besides the tenth, *Malkuth*, which unites them.

Our distribution must also take the two numbers 3 and 4 into account, by combining them so as to utilize all the elements which we have just enumerated. This is done as follows (see Fig. 1 upon the plane of the Equator, represented as a ring outside the sphere)—

We will first separate some of the cards : the Knave of each of the 4 suits (ה), which, as the realization of the Trinity, King (י), Queen (ה), Knight (ו), serves as the transition from the quaternary to the ternary; and the 10 of each suit, the unity of complete realization, the multiple unity 1 and 0—*Malkuth*.

The Knaves, by their participation in the quaternary and ternary, and their return to the Unity by the Trinity, have an universality which connects them with the unnumbered card 0 of the great arcana; we will therefore place them round this card, as a cross, in the centre of our equatorial circle. In this way the centre will express: By the card 0—the original unity, the source and aim of creation; by its triangle—the primitive Trinity; by its 4 suits, the quaternary in which it is realized; by the character of the 4 Knaves—the return of this quaternary to the ternary; in short, the whole creation assembled in one point, in potentiality, which is the characteristic of the Spirit.

On the other hand, the four 10 will be placed at the extremities of the cross formed by the Knaves, outside all our circles, as the expression of the Unity multiple, in its last term of differentiation.

As to the other cards, they include first 3 kinds of figures, which correspond with the 3 terms of the Trinity; it is quite simple to distribute them in the 3 parts of our external equatorial plane, corresponding with the 3 divisions of the sphere—

The Kings opposite to division I (י);
The Queens opposite to division E (ה);
The Knights opposite to division V (ו);

and, since there are 4 suits for each of them, 4 subdivisions are naturally produced in each of our 3 principal divisions; these 4 subdivisions, corresponding to the Sceptre ('), the Cup (ה), the Sword ('), and the

Pentacle (ה), also repeat the Divine name of 4 letters (IEVE) (יהוה), and form the passage from the ternary to the quaternary.

Now only the numbers remain to be placed; and these also must correspond with the terms of the Trinity—

The four 1 behind the Kings;
The four 2 behind the Queens;
The four 3 behind the Knights.

Then, in a still more external circle—

The four 4 outside the Kings and the 1;
The four 5 outside the Queens and the 2;
The four 6 outside the Knights and the 3.

Finally, an outlying circle will include the four 7, 8 and 9 in the same order. As to the four 10, they are placed outside, as we have said.

We thus obtain the distribution represented by the figures 1 and 2.

Let us now consider their signification.

The living atom descended upon the sphere has reached the point represented by arcanum X., the wheel of Ezekiel which raises man and lowers the elemental. From this, the atom falls, so to speak, through the material world, which it has just entered. It descends through the spiritual decade (Sceptre and Cup) (see the figure), traversing numbers of increasing complexity: King, 1, 4, 7, then 10. By this 10, the multiple unity, limit of materialization, which unites the two portions of the decade Sceptre-Cup, the atom resumes in an inverse sense, as though by a re-ascending arc, the road which will lead it back to arcanum X., remounting the 4, 7, 10 and King of Cups and Swords, the substantial duad.

This is only one-third of the voyage which the living atom must accomplish in the real world; and, in this first excursion through matter, it has still retained the spiritual character which it received from *Yod* ('), the characteristic of arcanum X.; it must now lose this character for that of the following E (ח). To this end, it passes from arcanum X., which it has just re-entered, to plate XI. (ח), the Hermit, the veiled Lamp, to proceed in the same way as it has already done through the dual series of the Sceptre-Cup, through the Queens, the 2, 5 and 8, passing by the 10 of Cups, and remounting thereby through the second series, Sword-Pentacles, to the arcanum XI., the starting-point of this second excursion.

Finally, from this last arcanum the living atom passes to number XII. (ו), the Sacrifice, descends the neuter series of the Knight, 3, 6, 9 of Sceptres and Cups, crosses the 10 of Swords and the 10 of Pentacles, and remounts by the dual Swords and Pentacles to the intelligible world.

Its journey across the material world is completed; it has travelled over the Zodiac; it will now die; the arcanum XIII. is ready, and will give it access to the spiritual world, to Redemption.

We will now explain some other features of this distribution.

It divides the external circle of the Equator into 3 arcs, subdivided into 4 portions; in all 12 divisions of different characters. These are the 12 signs of the Zodiac. The first is naturally ranked with the first card of the minor arcana in the spiritual sector, *i.e.* the King of Sceptres (Spades); the second corresponds with the King of Cups, and so on to the twelfth.

One observation will suffice to justify the connection between the zodiac and our cards. We must note the 12 divisions of the circle into the triple repetition of the 4 letters of the Sacred Name; an operation legitimized by the remark already made, that the 4 suits correspond with these letters (see Fig. 2, in the intermediate circle, where the signs of the Zodiac are written). We at once recognize the 4 trigons of the Zodiac, corresponding with the elements which the 4 suits also represent, and these trigons are characterized as well as designated.

The fiery trigon (♈, ♌, ♐), corresponding with the Sceptre and the letters יוי, is swayed by the spiritual element.

The earthy trigon (♉, ♍, ♑), corresponding to the Cup and to the letters ההה, namely, two *He's* of the name of 3 letters, and the final *He* of the name of 4 letters—an essentially feminine character, substantial, but of superior order.

The airy trigon (♊, ♎, ♒), corresponding to the Sword and the letters חהו, swayed by the masculine element of the second order.

The watery trigon (♋, ♏, ♓), corresponding to the Pentacle and to the letters ההה, comprising, this time, the final *He* of the name of 4 letters twice repeated, and the *He* of the name of 3 letters—the dominant character, the inferior feminine.

But we must leave the minor arcana to the investigations of the reader—they would lead us too far—and return to some further notice of the great arcana.

Let us first notice how the three chief sectors preserve and reproduce their innate characters in all their divisions.

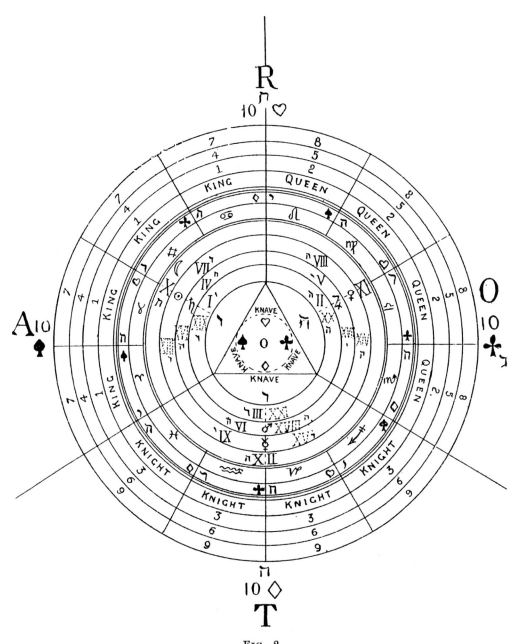

FIG. 2

We find, in the first, that of the letter *Yod* (י), the Spirit, the numbers of the unity, I., IV., VII., X. (repeated in the minor arcana); as figure, the Kings; as suit, the Sceptre; in the Zodiac, the lines of the ascension of the sun above the Equator from the spring to the solstice.

In the second sector (ה) the substantial principle is the feminine numbers II., V., VIII., XI. (repeated in the minor arcana); as figure, the Queens; as suit, the Cup; in the Zodiac, the four signs of the descent of the sun towards the Equator; the season of harvests and vintages, fecundity in all its forms.

In the third sector (ו)—the Son, the Element—are the sacred numbers which participate in the two preceding orders, III., VI., IX.; as figure, the Knight; as suits, the Pentacle of the practical world and the Sword, which close the preceding sector; in the Zodiac, the signs through which the sun passes in the southern hemisphere; our winter, the season for the consumption of the produce of the earth, of renovation for the cycle which follows. Christmas is in the centre; the new birth in the winter of death; the time when the Son was born into an inferior world to reanimate it.

The Divine Name יהוה is not only written in the series of concentric circles; it is also found upon the lines belonging to those circles, either in descending or in remounting.

The first sector gives it without transposition, as we see in Fig. 2.

In the second sector the Divine Name is preceded by the feminine letter *He*, the Mother, and finally pauses at it: E, IEVE, IE. (See the figure.)

In the third, it commences by the letter of the Son

and ends by that of the Father, to which he returns: VE, IEVE, I.

We shall now inquire from the symbols of the cards the different ways of pronouncing the Divine Name, and also the various manifestations in the Kosmos of each of the four letters. Let us question even the spirit of these symbols, instead of their number, colour, or form, which have chiefly occupied us at present.

By first following the regular order of our arrangement we shall find—

In the Divine World: the arcana I., II., III., IV., the Divine Tetractys, comprising: (1) the Absolute Being; (2) the Consciousness of the Absolute; (3) Love or the power of fecundity; (4) the realization of the virtualities of the Absolute.

In the world of laws: arcanum V., the laws of the relation of the Created with the Uncreate (the Initiator, Fear also).[1] VI. (Liberty, Beauty); knowledge of good and evil; knowledge of the Law. VII. (Glory); rule of Spirit over Matter, fertile power of the Law; and VIII. (absolute Justice, Victory), realization of the Law.

In the physical world: arcana IX. (the veiled Lamp), the light extinguished in the darkness of substance, the spirit imprisoned in the material world, *Yesod.* X. (Wheel of Fortune), which raises the fallen spirit to lead it back, with the nature that it has spiritualized, to all its power, by Strength (arcana XI.) and by Sacrifice (arcana XII.).

The phases of spiritualization then follow. XIII.:

---

[1] Consult for the generation and signification of numbers the *Traité Élémentaire de Science Occulte,* by Papus, a learned author, whose good counsels have produced the best part of this article.

First phase: (Death)· to the physical world. XIV. (the two Urns) combination of the movements of life. XV. (*Typhon*) Magic. XVI. (the Lightning-struck Tower); the interplanetary force.

Second phase: XVII. (the flaming Star), the internal light. XVIII. (the Twilight), the aurora of the divine sun. XIX. (the Sun), central; and XX. (the Judgment), after which the supreme realization is obtained, the Crown of the Magi.

We have said that the Divine Name is again enunciated in following the three sectors.

In the first are the arcana I., IV., VII., X. The absolute, the realization of its virtualities, the dominion of Spirit over Matter, and the animating principle of beings. Then, in return, XIII., XVI., XIX., I. Death (Inertia), the astral light, the central sun, and the Ineffable Itself.

This is the account, by principles, of the differentiation and integration of the Absolute.

In the second sector, the one which corresponds to the consciousness of the Absolute or faith, we have the series, V., VIII., XI., XIV. : the Hierophant, or religion ; Justice, Force, and the combination of the movements of life; the image of the Saints; the Mystics of all religions, who by absolute Faith and Justice, receptive, feminine virtues, acquire, without seeking for it, the power of working prodigies.

Lastly, in the third Sector, that of Love or power of fecundity, we have the series: IX., Wisdom and Prudence; XII., the Sacrifice; XV., self-abandonment to astral forces; and XVIII., attainment of the Infinite. The essence of this series of efforts, both active and passive, constitutes Initiation, and Redemption.

Let us once more seek for the Divine Name, through the three divisions at once. We shall find, for instance, the arcana I., II., III., VI., which demonstrate the Divine Trinity, manifesting itself by Beauty and Liberty in the Intellectual world: it is the passage of the Father (ʼ) to the Son (ʼ).

Or again, I., VI., IX., X.: The descent of the Father (ʼ) into the physical world (X.) by the Son (VI.) and by *Yesod* (IX.); the Word made flesh. This is the Redemption, the series which in the *Sepher Yetzirah* represents the Column of the Sephiroth (*Kether—Tiphereth—Yesod* and *Malkuth*.) [1]

But we must limit these examples, which the reader will easily mutiply for himself. Let us only add a few more words upon our second problem: the different manifestations of each of the three persons of the Divine Trinity.

The *Yod* is found in the arcana I., V., IX., XII. and XIII.; in *Kether*, in the Hierophant, in the Wise Old Man; then it presides over death, which will bring the world from the depths of gloomy Inertia to the resplendent crown of the Magi, by the internal light.

It will be noticed, at the same time, that the *Yod* is the only one of the four letters which, by its various positions, forms a complete spiral round the sphere, from the north to the south poles; a symbol which may appear very remarkable to any one acquainted with the mysteries of the life of a planet.

The first He, the celestial Mother (arcana II.), is found in the arcana VI., X., XIV. and XVIII., that

---

[1] The signification of the cards is borrowed from Fabre d'Olivet, Wronski, É. Lévi, Christian, and the *Sepher Yetzirah* (translation by Papus).

is to say, Beauty; Form; the Angel of Temperance, which balances the movements of life and the aurora of the divine Sun; Diana the Moon.

The *Vav*, the Son, is characterized upon the various planes by the arcana III., VII., XI., XV. and XIX.; Love, the fertile power; the Ruler over Matter, Force; then *Typhon*, the mysterious Baphomet of the Templars, which collects the superior forces to spread them over the Earth; and lastly, the central Sun. In a word, the Christ of the Gospel, the Spirit of Love, the Master of the Elements, the Word made flesh to spiritualize the flesh; the divine reflex of the Universal Sun.

Lastly, the second *He;* the terrestrial Mother, is seen in the arcana IV., VIII., XII., XVI. and XX.; the realization of the divine virtualities, and also Mercy, absolute Justice, Sacrifice, the overwhelmed and suffering Spirit, and finally Resurrection; the head of the Serpent crushed beneath the woman's heel, by the force of abnegation and resigned faith.

We need only follow these various arcana upon the sphere, to see once more that the *Yod* has 3 superior arcana (northern hemisphere), and 2 inferior;

That the *Vav* (ᵛ) has only 2 superior and 1 medium (upon the Equator);

And that the *He* has 4 superior—2 inferior and 2 medium.

Let us close these remarks, already too lengthy, by a simple observation upon the general effect of our arrangement.

The three worlds, Divine, Intelligible and Physical, are found not only in the three zones of the sphere, but they are again reproduced in the whole arrangement; the Divine is in the centre, through the Foolish Man of the Tarot, and the cross of four suits; this we have already pointed out.

The Intelligible and its developments are provided by the sphere (Fig. 1), or the circular distribution of the 21 great arcana (Fig. 2).

The physical is seen in the external plane of the Equator (Fig. 1), with the distribution of the 56 minor arcana, representing the Zodiac and the various degrees of the multiplicity of Force through substance to the extreme pole, the negative unity 10.

Moreover, the whole (Fig. 1) reproduces the form of the planet Saturn, with its ring, a form which in itself, according to the theories of our positive sciences, is the clearest manifestation, the proof of the great laws of the formation of the Universe; namely, the concentration of the substance in a radiant state around a point of attraction, producing with a progressive condensation a rotatory movement, particularly accentuated at the Equator, and giving birth to the stars, planets and satellites, thus descending from the nebulous ethereal to the atom, to the solid ultimate; from living nothingness to inert nothingness, from the unit to an infinite multiplicity.

Thus the Tarot, that time-old fruit of the genius of our ancestors, represents not only the creation in its actual state, but its history even in details, and its future with that of the human creature, even to their principles; yet avoiding, by the combination of its analogical symbols, borrowed from natural life, the rock upon which all philosophy breaks—namely, the definition of words, the clear, full expression of the Word in the sublunar world.

CHAPTER XVIII

THE KABALISTIC TAROT

Deductions by Etteila from the Book of Thoth—Example of an Application of the Tarot to the Kabalah—The Hierogram of Adam, by Stanislas de Guaita.

DEDUCTIONS BY ETTEILA FROM THE BOOK OF THOTH

WE will now recapitulate some of the conclusions which Etteila attained in the course of his work upon the *Book of Thoth* (the Tarot).

The *Book of Thoth Hermes* indicates by its name alone that our author had discovered its Egyptian origin. It is composed of 78 leaflets, forming 4 volumes.

The 1st volume contains 12 leaves
The 2nd   „   „   5   „
The 3rd   „   „   5   „
The 4th   „.   „   56   „

Thus the 22 major arcana form 3 volumes, and the 56 minor arcana form the last.

The 56 leaves of the last volume divide in the following way, according to the operation indicated in the first reading of the cards—

$$26 + 17 + 11 + 2 = 56.$$

The 4 divisions of the 56 leaflets (the 4 suits) respectively represent—

1. Agriculture.
2. Priesthood.
3. Nobility, { Magistrates. / Soldiers.
4. People, { Art. / Commerce.

The *Book of Thoth* contains three parts, viz.:

22 Major Atouts.

16 Minor Atouts (the court cards).

40 Small cards.

It is formed like a living being for—

78 is its body;

3 its spirit or mediator;

1 its soul.

If we add the first 12 leaflets of the book together, we shall discover the number of its total—

$$1 + 2 + 3 + 4 + 5 + 6 + 7 + 8 + 9 + 10 + 11 + 12 = 78.$$

If we now look back at the first operation in reading the cards according to our author, new deductions will arise.

Number 78 will be found to represent Salt, or the incorruptible Spirit.

The number 1 (a book) represents Unity, the Divinity; lastly, the number 26, which divides the Tarot into three parts, is exactly that of Jehovah (יהוה).

Yod	=	10
He	=	5
Vau	=	6
He	=	5
Total		26

In the first operation [1] upon the packets of 26 cards, nothing remains, — 0.

In the second operation upon the packet of 17 cards, 1 remains, which represents the point in the centre of the circle zero.

[1] See, for an explanation of these packets and the method of obtaining them, Chapter XX. (6th lesson).

Lastly, in the third operation upon the packets of 11 cards, 2 remain, which represent Man.

To sum up—

0—the Circumference of the Universe.
1—The point of the Centre-God.
2—The Male and the Female. Man.

God, Man and the Universe, obtained by the mystic system of Etteila!

We shall never end if we try to follow our author in all the deductions he makes from the above; let us content ourselves, in closing, with demonstrating the meaning which he gives to the numbers of the packets which have been successively placed on one side.

26-—*The Soul.*
17—*The Spirit.*
11—*The Body.*

Finally, the remainder of the cards $11 + 11 + 2 = 24$ is *Life.*

These few pages will suffice to give the student a glimpse of Etteila's method of proceeding. We have rendered his deductions as clearly, and presented them as methodically, as possible. The curious had better consult his work on the subject—

COLLECTION SUR LES HAUTES SCIENCES, or a theoretical and practical treatise upon the wisdom-magic of the ancients, absolutely complete in twelve books, which contain all that Etteila has written upon the Hermetic philosophy, the art of fortune-telling by cards . . . and particularly the sublime *Book of Thoth.* 2 vols. 8vo, bound, 1780.

EXAMPLE OF THE APPLICATION OF THE TAROT TO THE KABALAH

THE HIEROGRAM OF ADAM

By Stanislas de Guaita

In asserting that the hierogram of Adam conceals the most profound arcana of the living Universe, we shall not astonish those who have made a serious study of the *Sepher Bereshit*. By comparing the admirable translation of Faber d'Olivet with the pentacular revelations of the *Book of Thoth*, it is not impossible to reach the supreme light of truth. Here are a few data which will aid us to reach it.

Adam אדם is written in Hebrew, *Aleph, Daleth, Mem*.

א (1st key of the Tarot: The Juggler). God and man; the Principle and the end; the Equilibrant Unity.

ד (4th key of the Tarot: The Emperor). The Power and the Kingdom; the verbal Quaternary; the Multiplication of the Cube.

מ (13th key of the Tarot: Death). Destruction and Restoration; Night and Day, moral and physical; Eternity and the Ephemeral; feminine Passivity, at once the gulf of the Past, the matrix of the Future.

The ternary analysis of the fathomless principle that *Yod* manifests in its inaccessible and synthetic unity—that is to say, in *Adam*—is, in fact, analogous to the hierogram *Aum*, which is so famous in the sanctuaries of India.

In אדם, *Aleph* corresponds to the Father, the source of the Trinity; *Daleth* to the Son (whom the Kabalah also names the King); and *Mem* to the Holy Spirit, whose ethereal body, devouring yet fertilizing transitory forms, causes life (inexhaustible and unutterable in its essence) to blossom upon the changing hot-bed of Growth.

I have said that אדם is the cyclic analysis of the principle, of which י (*Yod*) is the inaccessible synthesis.

A simple calculation of the numerical Kabalah confirms my assertion. Let us translate the letters into numbers (Tarotic method).

$$\aleph\ 1\quad \daleth\ 4\quad \mem\ 13.$$
$$1 + 4 + 13 = 18. \quad \text{In } 18, 1 + 8 = 9.$$

In Kabalistic absolute numericals the analytical number of Adam is therefore 9. Now we obtain 10 by adding to 9 the specific unity which leads the cycle back to its starting-point and closes analysis in synthesis, and 10 is the number which corresponds to the letter *Yod*: this we were anxious to prove.

The hierogrammatic vocable אדם (Adam) thus represents the ninth evolution of the cycle, which emanated from י (*Yod*), and which closes in 10 by returning to its starting-point: to the principle and end of all, the eternal *Yod*, revealed in its expanded form *tertriune*.

Let us go further still.

We have then the right (noting, however, that Adam differs from *Yod*, or from *Wodh*, as the totality of the sub-multiples differs from Unity),—we have the right to say, pursuing our analogies,

If Adam be equal to 1,

Adam-ah = I-ah; and *Adam Eve = I-eve.* *He* (ה) represents Universal Life, *natura naturans;* יה then represents *Yod* united to Life, and אדמה (Adamah) is Adam united to Life. This is the union of the Spirit and of the Universal Soul at two different degrees (always remembering the distinction noticed above).

Lastly, in יהוה (IEVE), as in ארמ־הוה (Adam-Eve), *Vau* (ו) represents the fecundity of this union, and the last *He* (ה) symbolizes *natura naturata* (issued from *natura naturans*, increased by the mixed principle).

These four letters, יהוה (IEVE), symbolize the quaternary of *Mercavah*; the six letters of Adam-Eve, ארמ־הוה, symbolize the senary of *Bereshith*.

(Fragment of the Serpent of Genesis published in the *Lotus* of March 1880, p. 327, and 328 *note*.)

CHAPTER XIX

LIST OF THE AUTHORS WHO HAVE INTERESTED THEMSELVES IN THE TAROT

Raymond Lully—Cardan—Postel—The Rosicrucians—Court de Gebelin—Etteila—L. C. de Saint-Martin—J. A. Vaillant—Christian—Éliphas Lévi—Stanislas de Guaita—Joséphin Péladan—*The Platonist*—Theosophical Publications—F. Ch. Barlet—Oswald Wirth—Poirel—Ely Star—H. P. Blavatsky—Ch. de Sivry—Mathers.

SOME ACCOUNT

OF THE AUTHORS WHO HAVE SPECIALLY INTERESTED THEMSELVES IN THE TAROT

RAYMOND LULLY (1235–1315), an eminently learned man, the founder of a system of philosophy, but chiefly of logic, entirely based upon the application of the Tarot; this is the *Ars Magna*.

CARDAN (JÉRÔME). Born in Paris in 1501, died in 1576. Professor of Mathematics and Medicine at Milan and Bologna. Travelled through Scotland, England and France, working miraculous cures.

His treatise *On Subtility* (1550) is entirely based on the keys of the Tarot.

POSTEL (WILLIAM). Born at Dolerie (diocese of Avranches) in 1510. Sent to the East by Francis I., he brought back some valuable manuscripts, and was appointed Professor of Mathematics and Oriental Languages in the College of France. Died in the Convent of Saint-Martin des Champs in 1581.

One of the greatest Initiates of the sixteenth century. He discovered the key to the Tarot, but did not disclose the secret, in spite of the promise given in the title to his work, *The Key to the Hidden Mysteries* (1580). He translated the *Sepher Yetzirah* into Latin.

THE MYSTERIOUS FRATERNITY OF THE ROSICRUCIANS (1604). *Fama Fraternitatis Roseæ Crucis* (1615) shows the Initiate that the Rosicrucians possessed the Tarot, which is described thus—

> *They possess a book from which they can learn everything that is in the books already written and to be written.*

We must not forget that the Rosicrucians were the Initiators of *Leibnitz*, and the founders of actual Freemasonry through *Ashmole*.

COURT DE GEBELIN. Born at Nîmes in 1725, died at Paris in 1784. An illustrious scholar, who discovered the Egyptian origin of the Tarot. Consult his *Monde Primitif* (1773–1782).

ETTEILA (1783). We have given a summary of his work upon Fortune-telling with the Tarot, and upon the application of this work to the Kabalah.

LOUIS CLAUDE DE SAINT-MARTIN. The Unknown Philosopher. Born in 1743 at Amboise, died in 1803. The disciple of Martines Pasqualez and Jacob Böhme, founder of the so-called Martinist order. His book, the *Tableau Naturel des Rapports qui existent entre Dieu, l'Homme et l'Univers*, is based upon the Tarot.

J. A. VAILLANT. Lived many years with the Gypsies, and received a great many of their traditions orally : these are contained in his works—

> *Les Rômes, Histoire des vrais Bohémiens* (1857).
> *La Bible des Bohémiens* (1860).
> *Clef Magique de la Fiction et du Fait* (1863).

CHRISTIAN. Librarian of the Arsenal. Has published an occult manuscript upon the Tarot, blending with it his personal reflections upon astrology in—

L'Homme Rouge des Tuileries (1854). See also *Histoire de la Magie* (1876).

ÉLIPHAS LÉVI. Amongst recent Masters of Occultism, he had the greatest knowledge of the Tarot. His work, *Dogme et Rituel de la Haute Magie* (1861, 2 vols., 8vo), is based upon the keys of the Tarot. Éliphas Lévi had a most romantic life, and died in 1870, leaving a son (I believe).

STANISLAS DE GUAITA. Contemporary Kabalistic scholar. He made several applications of the Tarot to the Kabalah. We have given one extract from them already. Consult also, *Au Seuil du Mystère* (1886), and *Le Serpent de la Genèse*.

JOSÉPHIN PÉLADAN. A clever novelist and eminent Kabalist. He has often written upon the Tarot in his works (1885–1889).

THE PLATONIST (1888). Review of American Occultism. It contains a poor study upon the application of the Tarot to horoscopy. This essay has been reproduced in—

Theosophical Siftings. No. 14 (London, 1888).

F. CH. BARLET. One of the most learned and most highly esteemed authorities amongst French Occultists. The summary of one of his works on the *Tarot Initiatique* (1889) is quoted *in extenso*, pp. 253 *et seq.*

OSWALD WIRTH has studied the astronomical Tarot (*see* Chapter XVI.), and has carefully reproduced the twenty-two symbolical figures, according to the most recent information obtainable upon Symbolism (1889).

E. POIREL. Occultist. Editor of the *Tarot d'Oswald Wirth* (1889).

ELY STAR. An author known by his interesting work upon Astrology, the *Mystères de l'Horoscope* (Dentu, 1888). It contains a chapter upon the Tarot.

H. P. BLAVATSKY. This author, rendered eminent by her works upon Theosophy, mentions the Tarot in her books (*Isis Unveiled* and *The Secret Doctrine*), but very superficially and without any synthetic basis.

CH. DE SIVRY. A very talented Occultist, chiefly known by his works upon music. To his kindness we owe the summary of a *Tarot Bohémien* entitled—

Extract from the Sacred Book of the Opâchti tribe, the primitive family, which adored Otchâvâtri, representing the only God Otchawatra. This tribe lived at the foot of the Himalayas.

The book describes the symbolism of the twenty-two arcana, according to the Gypsies, with interesting details upon esotericism.

S. L. M. MATHERS, an English author, has published a short account of the Tarot, which contains nothing very original: it is rather a summary of the principal authors who have studied the question. It is chiefly written as an aid to *fortune-telling by cards.*

This closes the list of authors whose books we have heard of, and who have *alluded to the Tarot, or used its keys.* We may have omitted some of them; if so, we must beg them to excuse us.

CHAPTER XX

THE DIVINING TAROT IN SEVEN LESSONS

Introduction: To our Lady Readers—Astronomy and Astrology—
Intuition—Fortune-telling by the Tarot in Seven Lessons.

1st Lesson: Simplification of the Rules of Fortune-telling by the
Tarot.

2nd Lesson: Minor Arcana—Significations—A good Memory unnecessary for their retention—Key to the Divining Tarot—
Sceptres—Cups—Swords—Pentacles.

3rd Lesson: Major Arcana—Significations from a Divining Point
of View.

4th Lesson: Basis of the Application of this Knowledge—Arrangement of the Cards.

5th Lesson: Reading the Tarot — Rapid Process — Elaborate
Process.

6th Lesson: Etteila's original Method of reading the Tarot (from
one of his rarest works): 1st deal—2nd deal—3rd deal—
4th deal.

7th Lesson: Conclusion—Bibliography.

THE DIVINING TAROT

INTRODUCTION

*To our Lady Readers—Astronomy and Astrology—
Intuition—Fortune-telling by the Tarot in Seven
Lessons.*

THE first part of our study of the Tarot, full of numbers, of Hebrew letters and abstract deductions, is not
calculated to attract the attention of ladies. But if
women enjoy mystery and idealism, prefer and excuse
the flights of a vivid imagination, men exact precision

and method in studies of this kind, and I have therefore built this arsenal of technical arguments for them, confining imagination in the narrow limits of deduction; if it has sometimes escaped and scattered the brilliant gems of illusion over the course of my work, this has been in spite of my efforts to retain it. It is, however, traditional that the future can be read through the Tarot, and our feminine readers will never forgive me if I ignore their natural curiosity on this point.

I have therefore decided to approach the delicate question, and I hope that the pleasure gained by fair inquirers will balance the scepticism of sterner intellects. It is true that I can quote the opinion of all the writers of antiquity, who assert that the Egyptians used the Tarot as a means of predicting the future, and that the Jews also employed it to confirm their prophecies. But in my opinion an important distinction should be made on this subject.

Unquestionably the Egyptians predicted the future through the Tarot; but they used its astronomical applications only. Nothing was left to chance. Thus, knowing that most of the important events which take place upon the earth are determined by the magnetic currents produced by the position of the earth at the moment that the event takes place, these learned men first defined the relations existing between the position of the stars in the heavens and the circumstances which they created upon the earth. Since the stars accomplish fixed revolutions, that is to say, since they return to the same position at the end of a certain number of years, which are mathematically determinable, the Egyptians thought that the same events would be also reproduced at fixed intervals. It would therefore suffice to know the movements of the stars, to predict the coming events. That is why Astronomy was only the commencement of Astrology.

As the Tarot reproduced the movements of the stars upon a table, we can easily guess how the ancients proceeded when they uttered prophecy by its aid. They drew up the Horoscope of the coming year, according to the position which the stars would occupy during its course, and could then at once predict two-thirds of the events likely to occur. Fabre d'Olivet in his works shows that one-third of the events are Determined, another third depend upon the Human Will, and the last third are subject to Providence. As the determining Fatality and the human Will usually unite, almost unconsciously, we see that the astrological Horoscope can predict two-thirds of the events.

Later on, reliable data were lost, and men commenced to read fortunes by chance, without using any scientific method. The astrological system called *onomantic*, that is to say, which uses the numbers formed by the letters of the name and prenames of the individual, is generally false, and produces no practical results. For this reason the astrological system described by Christian can be regarded only as a deceitful, lying dream. The truth of the predictions, then, depends upon the Intuition of the prophet, and this leads us to consider the differences which may be noticed between the predictions of fortune-tellers.

Intuition plays the most important part when the more exact methods disappear, and therefore woman's nature, which is essentially intuitive, is well qualified to make these divinations.

The discussion of the wherefore of all this would lead us much too far from our subject. We cannot teach astrology by the Tarot in a few pages—a whole volume is necessary for this purpose—nor have we the time to handle these difficult subjects. Perhaps we may decide to undertake them at a later day.

However, we see that chance and intuition are the chief instruments in divination by the Tarot, as it is usually practised at the present time. We must therefore aid our readers to attempt it for themselves, and will now explain the most simple principles of the art, dividing them into seven lessons, so as to render them as clear as possible.

We will arrange them so that they may be complete, and therefore it will be unnecessary to read all the preceding abstract studies before using the Tarot from this point of view. Lastly, we will tabulate the principal methods used by masters in the art of fortune-telling, so as to enable our readers to become adepts in the prediction of the future. But we must remind them that science has little empire over the subject, for it is imagination and intuition that reign over this charming domain.

FIRST LESSON

SIMPLIFICATION OF THE RULES OF FORTUNE-TELLING BY THE TAROT

THE great difficulty encountered by a beginner in the study of divination by the Tarot, is the number of meanings to be remembered in reading the cards.

Open any treatise upon this subject, and you will see that you must first master the different significations of the 78 cards. You must then learn the variations in their meaning when reversed, and this does not include the pairings and other complications, which bring up the sum total to about 200 different meanings. All these must be retained in the memory before any one can become a good fortune-teller by cards. Habit only will enable the student to remember such details, and in this case intuition becomes an important aid to the memory.

Now complication of this kind always points to an imperfect system. Nature is synthetic in its manifestations, and simplicity is found at the bottom of the most outwardly involved phenomena. Whilst admitting that our work upon the Tarot may have its errors, no one can deny the absolute simplicity of the constituent principles. We will therefore apply the same method to the divining Tarot, and endeavour to establish a system which will enable us to dispense with memory almost entirely, or at least to reduce

305   U

its work considerably. We shall thus allow a certain scope for scientific data, although we are unwilling to create any prejudice by this influence, considering the subject that we are dealing with.

The first point to retain from the commencement of this study is the necessity for clear, simple rules, by which the divining Tarot may be read. We will explain them in the following lessons.

SECOND LESSON

MINOR ARCANA: SIGNIFICATION FROM THE DIVINING POINT OF VIEW

THE Tarot pack is composed of 78 cards or plates; 22 of them bear symbolical names (the Juggler, Sun, Moon, Hanged Man, etc.), and they should be separated from the 56 others, which are divided into four great series: Sceptres, Cups, Swords and Pentacles.

These four suits each contain 14 cards (King, Queen, Knight, Knave, Ace, 2, 3, 4, 5, 6, 7, 8, 9 and 10), corresponding with the four suits of common playing cards (clubs, hearts, spades, diamonds), but called Sceptres, Cups, Swords, Pentacles. These are the Minor Arcana.

The 22 symbolical cards are the Major Arcana or Great Arcana.

1. MINOR ARCANA, formed of four sequences of 14 cards each, or 56 cards in all.

2. MAJOR ARCANA, formed of 22 cards.

These are the two great divisions which must first be remembered.

We have already said that the minor arcana are divided into four sequences: Sceptres, Cups, Swords, Pentacles. Each of these suits represents one of the four great principles, as follows—

The Sceptres	represent	*Enterprise and Glory.*
The Cups	,,	*Love and Happiness.*
The Swords	,,	*Hatred and Misfortune.*
The Pentacles	,,	*Money and Interest.*

ENTERPRISE, LOVE, HATRED, FORTUNE are the four great principles which must be remembered.

If you now take one of these packets of 14 cards, you will see that it is formed of four pictures, and of 10 other cards, which bear numbers formed by the symbols.

We will first look at the 4 picture-cards—

The King	represents	*Man.*
The Queen	„	*Woman.*
The Knight	„	*A Young Man.*
The Knave	„	*A Child.*

The Man represents the creator, the one who undertakes the enterprises; the woman characterizes love; the young man, conflict, struggle, rivalry, hatred; the child symbolizes the absolute neuter, the second *He*, which varies according to circumstances, money, which addresses itself to all, and applies itself to all, universal transition. Man, Woman, Young Man, Child are therefore the same symbols applied to the family as the four great principles applied to humanity, and to know them in one case is to know them in the other.

To sum up all this, we may say that the first element represents the positive, the second the negative, the third the opposition between the two; finally, the last the absolute neuter; and these elements are symbolized by the four picture-cards of each of the minor arcana.

But even as the cards are divided into two colours, red and black, so humanity is divided into *dark* and *fair*.

The eight picture-cards of Sceptres and Swords therefore represent dark people, and the eight of Cups and Pentacles, fair people.

The picture-cards of Sceptres and Cups are *good;* those of Swords and Pentacles, *bad.*

We shall presently repeat this in connection with each suit, and will now recapitulate the meanings of the four pictures of Sceptres.

```
King of Sceptres : Dark man ; good ; a friend.
Queen       „    : Dark woman ; good.
Knight      „    : Dark young man ; good.
Knave       „    : Dark child or messenger ; good.
```

Besides our four pictures we have to consider the 10 cards bearing numbers. How can we discover the meaning of these 10 cards, and above all how can we memorize it?

We have nothing new to learn, but need only apply all that we already know. We divide our 10 cards into four packets: three packets of 3 cards each, and one packet formed of a single card, the 10th. When this is done we say—

The first packet of 3 cards, formed of the ace, 2, and 3, will have the same meaning as the Man, enterprise, commencement, the creation of some undertaking (enterprise, love, hatred, or money).

The second packet, composed of the 4, 5 and 6, represents Woman, and all the ideas of negation, of reflection, associated with her; that is to say, the contrary of man, antagonism, opposition in any matter.

The third packet signifies the equilibrium which results from the action of the two opposites upon each other, represented by the Young Man.

Lastly, the Child, the absolute neuter, will be represented by the 10th card.

Each of the 3 cards in these packets have the same meaning.

The first card of these 3 packets will indicate the commencement; the second, opposition, antagonism; the third, equilibrium, which gives us the following general sequence in our 10 cards.

KEY TO THE DIVINING TAROT

1. Commencement
2. Opposition   } of *Commencement.*
3. Equilibrium

4. Commencement
5. Opposition   } of *Opposition.*
6. Equilibrium

7. Commencement
8. Opposition   } of *Equilibrium.*
9. Equilibrium

10. Undetermined: The card which follows will explain it.

Thus the three words, Commencement, Opposition, Equilibrium, the synonyms of Thesis, Antithesis, Synthesis, or of *Brahma, Siva, Vishnu*, etc., suffice for the explanation of all the minor arcana of the Tarot. We need only add the words love, hatred, enterprise or fortune to each of the series, and we can define the meaning of every card without wearying the memory. This we will now do.

SIGNIFICATION OF THE FOUR SERIES OF THE MINOR ARCANA IN THE DIVINING TAROT

SCEPTRES

Creation. Enterprise. Agriculture.

KING.
: The King of Sceptres symbolizes a dark man, a friend. He generally represents a married man, the father of a family.

QUEEN.
: A dark woman, a friend. Represents a serious woman, a very good counsellor, often the mother of a family.

KNIGHT.
: A dark young man, a friend.

KNAVE.
: A dark child, a friend. Also represents a message from a near relation.

ACE OF SCEPTRES.
: *Commencement of an Enterprise.*

TWO.
: *Opposition to the commencement of the Enterprise.*
: The Enterprise is commenced when an unexpected obstacle suddenly prevents its execution.

THREE.
: *Realization of the commencement of the Enterprise.*
: The basis of the work is now definitely established, and the undertaking can be fearlessly continued.

FOUR.
: *Obstacles to the Enterprise.*
: Nothing can be accomplished without obstacles. We therefore find them appearing, and must prepare ourselves to overcome them.

FIVE.
: *Opposition to the obstacles. Victory after surmounting them.*

SIX.   *Realization of the opposition.*
            At last the obstacles succeed. *Failure of
            the Enterprise* in the midst of its execu-
            tion.

SEVEN.   *Certain success of the Enterprise.*

EIGHT.   *Opposition to its success.* The Enterprise
            will only partially succeed.

NINE.   *Realization of success.* Success is continued.

TEN.   Uncertainty in the management of the
            Enterprise.

CUPS

Preservation. Love. Instruction.

Knowing the meaning of one series, we know *a priori*
the significations of the three others. We shall however give them in order to facilitate the work.

KING OF CUPS.   *A fair man, a friend.* This card also repre-
                    sents a barrister, judge, or ecclesiastic.
                    It symbolizes a Bachelor.

QUEEN OF CUPS.   *A fair woman, a friend.* The woman
                    loved. The Mistress.

KNIGHT OF CUPS.   *A young fair man, a friend.* The young
                    man loved. The Lover.

KNAVE OF CUPS.   *A fair child.* A messenger. *Birth.*

ACE OF CUPS.   *Commencement of a love affair.*

TWO.   *Opposition to this commencement.* Unim-
                    portant obstacles raised by one of the
                    lovers.

THREE.   *Realization of this commencement.* The love
                    is mutual.

FOUR.   *Serious obstacles to the love.* They arise
                    from other persons, not from the lovers.

FIVE.   *Opposition to the obstacles.* Victory over
                      the obstacles after a struggle.

SIX.   *The obstacles triumph.* Love destroyed in
                      the midst of happiness. *Widowhood.*

SEVEN.   *Success assured to the lovers.*

EIGHT.   *Partial failure of love.* Love only partially
                      succeeds.

NINE.   Motherhood.

TEN.   Uncertainty in the management of the
                      love affair.

SWORDS

Transformation. Hatred. War.

KING OF SWORDS.   *A dark, bad man.* He is a soldier, a
                      powerful enemy, who must be dis-
                      trusted.

QUEEN OF SWORDS.   *A dark, wicked woman.* The card also indi-
                      cates her actions, *gossip and calumnies.*

KNIGHT.   *A young, dark man, an enemy.* He is also
                      a *spy.*

KNAVE.   *A child, an enemy. Bad news. Delay.*

The pictures generally indicate opposition raised outside the house.

ACE OF SWORDS.   *Commencement of enmity.*

TWO.   *Opposition to this commencement.* The
                      enmity does not last.

THREE.   Realization of the enmity. *Hatred.*

FOUR.   Opposition to the hatred. *Success against
                      the enemy.*

FIVE.   *Opposition to this opposition.* The enemy
                      triumphs at the moment one fancies that
                      the victory is secured.

Six.	*Equilibrium of the opposition.* The enemy is rendered powerless at last.
Seven.	*Success assured to the enemy.*
Eight.	*Partial opposition to this success.* The enemy only partially triumphs.
Nine.	*Certain duration of the hatred.*
Ten.	Uncertainty in the enemy.

PENTACLES

Development. Money. Trade.

King of Pentacles. *A fair man,* inimical or indifferent.

Queen of Pentacles. *A fair woman, indifferent* or inimical.

Knight.	*A young, fair man.* A stranger. *An arrival.*
Knave.	*A fair child.* A messenger. *A letter.*

The pictures of Pentacles are inverse to those of Sceptres and Cups, and indicate all that comes from outside, from the country or abroad.

Ace of Pentacles.	*Commencement of fortune.* Inheritance. Gifts. Economy, etc., etc.
Two.	*Opposition to this commencement.* Difficulty in well establishing the first landmarks of good fortune.
Three.	*Realization of this commencement of fortune.* A small sum.
Four.	Opposition of fortune. *Loss of money.*
Five.	Opposition to this opposition. *A success coming which will balance the loss.*
Six.	Realization of the opposition. *Ruin.*

SEVEN.   Success assured.   *A large fortune.*

EIGHT.   *Partial success.*   Great loss of money at
                      the moment apparently of definitely
                      securing the fortune.

NINE.   Equilibrium of Equilibrium.   *A durable
                      fortune.*

TEN.   *Uncertainty in the fortune.*   Great success
                      and great reverses.

As a whole, we see the same series always repeating
themselves.   It therefore requires comparatively little
time to master the meaning of the minor arcana, even
without much memory.   We advise those readers who
anticipate lapses in memory to write the meaning on
the cards themselves.   However, professional card
readers are careful not to do this, for intuition often
leads them to an interpretation which differ from the
exact meaning of the card.

THIRD LESSON

MAJOR ARCANA. SIGNIFICATION FROM THE DIVINING POINT OF VIEW

WE now know the signification of the minor arcana, and need only study the major arcana.

As we have already stated, the major arcana consist of 22 symbolical cards, which we have not yet examined as a means of predicting the future.

Their meaning is very easy to remember, if any one will take the trouble to consider them carefully one by one, as their signification is described.

One general rule will aid the memory in this matter, for the seven first cards chiefly refer to the intellectual side of man, the seven next to his moral side, and the seven last to the various events of his material life.

We will now give the signification of these 22 cards of our Tarot—

1.	*The Juggler*	signifies	MALE INQUIRER.
2.	*The High Priestess*	,,	FEMALE INQUIRER.
3.	*The Empress*	,,	ACTION. INITIATIVE.
4.	*The Emperor*	,,	WILL.
5.	*The Pope*	,,	INSPIRATION.
6.	*The Lovers*	,,	LOVE.
7.	*The Chariot*	,,	TRIUMPH. PROVIDENTIAL PROTECTION.
8.	*Justice*	,,	JUSTICE.
9.	*The Hermit*	,,	PRUDENCE.
10.	*The Wheel of Fortune*	,,	FORTUNE. DESTINY.

11. *Strength*   signifies STRENGTH.   FORTITUDE.

12. *The Hanged Man*   ,,   TRIALS.   SACRIFICE.

13. *Death*   ,,   DEATH.

14. *Temperance*   ,,   TEMPERANCE.   ECONOMY.

15. *The Devil*   ,,   IMMENSE FORCE.   ILLNESS.

16. *The Lightning-struck Tower*   ,,   RUIN.   DECEPTION.

17. *The Stars*   ,,   HOPE.

18. *The Moon*   ,,   HIDDEN ENEMIES.   DANGER.

19. *The Sun*   ,,   MATERIAL HAPPINESS.   LUCKY MARRIAGE.

20. *The Judgment*   ,,   CHANGE OF POSITION.

21. *The Foolish Man*   ,,   INCONSIDERATE ACTIONS.   MADNESS.

22. *The Universe*   ,,   ASSURED SUCCESS.

FOURTH LESSON

BASIS OF THE APPLICATION OF THESE DATA: ARRANGEMENT OF THE CARDS

WE are now in a position to handle the Tarot as a means of divination.

But before we attempt to read it, we must settle how to arrange the cards upon the table.

To know the meaning of the cards is only the first step in the art of cartomancy : to know how to arrange them is still more important. As a fact, the astronomical data should not be lost sight of, and the Tarot ought only to be used to represent the revolutions of the stars, the source of future events; but this is the realm of Astrology, and we must confine ourselves to that of telling fortunes by Tarot cards, and their combinations depend a little upon chance.

We shall, however, give as many reliable elements in this study as possible. We need only look back to the commencement of the third part (Key to the Applications of the Tarot), to see that the human life passes through the four great periods of—

Childhood.
Youth.
Maturity.
Old Age.

If the student is not interested in Human Life and

simply wishes to see the evolution of an event, this will also pass through four great evolutions—

> Commencement.
> Apogee.
> Decline.
> Fall.

We must then first determine, in our arrangement of the cards, four points facing each other in pairs, upon which we can afterwards place the cards which are to reveal the future to us.

This, therefore, is our first point: the determination of the four places which the cards will occupy.

                        4
                     Apogee
                      Youth

        1   3
   Commencement   Decline
     Childhood   Maturity
                        2
                      Fall
                     Old Age

We must notice that the disposition of the points goes from left to right. This is seen by the order of the numbers, whilst the symbols are read from right to left.

The Human Life or the Event moves in three very distinct periods—

> The Past.
> The Present.
> The Future.

This gives us a new figure as follows—

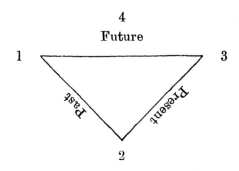

The Inquirer is found in the Centre. The arrangement of the triangle follows that of the figures and not of the symbols.

However, since four points are not enough to reproduce the movement of the sun exactly, we take, for important readings of the Tarot, twelve points which correspond with the twelve months of the year. The figure already obtained will, at any rate, serve as a means of consulting the Tarot upon small events. But we can also get the following figure, which we must remember for the arrangement of our cards when we wish to inquire about great events or the course of a lifetime.

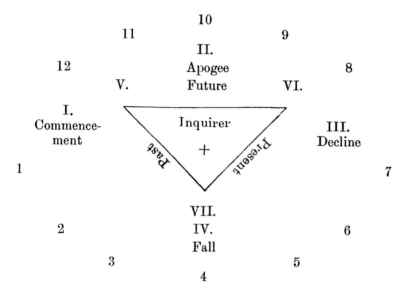

This diagram, which is very important and should be carefully studied, is composed of three circles.

1. An outside circle, formed of twelve houses, filled by the minor arcana. The houses are arranged from left to right; this is shown by the numbers.

2. A second intermediate circle, composed of four houses, arranged from right to left.

3. A central circle, formed by the triangle, and containing a house at each point, giving three houses in the circle.

The last three houses and the four preceding ones will be filled by the major arcana.

The Inquirer will be in the centre of the figure.

X

FIFTH LESSON

FORTUNE-TELLING BY THE TAROT

I.—RAPID PROCESS:

What must we do if we wish to draw out the horoscope of any matter?

1. You should take the minor arcana and separate the suit of cards that refers to the kind of consultation you require.

If it is some business that you are about to undertake, you must take the Sceptres or Diamonds.

If it is a love affair, take Cups or Hearts.

For a law-suit, or any struggle, take Swords or Spades.

In a money matter, Pentacles or Clubs.

2. Shuffle the cards selected; then ask the Inquirer to cut them.

3. Take the four first cards from the top of the pack, and without looking at them place them in a cross in the following way, from left to right, as shown by the numbers.

4

1   3

2

4. Then take your major arcana (which should always be separated from the minor arcana), shuffle them, and let them be cut for you.

5. You then ask the Inquirer to draw out seven cards from the major arcana by chance, and to give them to you without looking at them.

6. Shuffle these seven cards, and when the Inquirer has cut them, take the three top cards, and without looking at them arrange them in a triangle, in the following order—

I.   II.
                III.

You thus obtain the following figure—

4

Major Arcana

I.   .   II.

1   3

III.

Minor Arc.

2

7. Take up the cards so that you can see them and read the oracles, noticing that the card placed at number 1 indicates the *commencement*.

The card placed at number 2 indicates the *apogee*, at number 3 the *obstacles*, lastly, at number 4 the *fall*.

The major arcanum placed at I. indicates the influences that have weighed in the affair during the *Past*.

The major arcanum in II. indicates the influence exerted over the *Present*.

The arcanum at number III. shows the influence which will affect and determine the *Future*.

These cards can be very rapidly deciphered when the habit is once acquired. But one important point should be noted, that when the rapid process is used for fortune-telling, the figures do not exclusively represent persons of especial complexion. The King represents a man, without any other distinction, the Queen a woman, the Knight a young man, and the Knave a child.

II.—A MORE ELABORATE PROCESS:

1. Shuffle all the minor arcana together and let them be cut for you.

2. Take the twelve first cards from the pack, and place them in a circle thus—

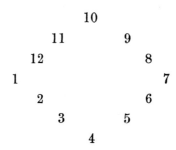

3. Shuffle the major arcana, and let them be cut by the Inquirer, who will then choose seven cards.

4. Take the four first of these cards from the pack, and arrange them opposite the cards placed at numbers 1, 10, 7, 4, thus—

II.

I.   III.

IV.

5. Then place the three others in a triangle in the centre of the figure, thus—

V.   VI.

VII.

You thus obtain the following general figure, which we have already given.

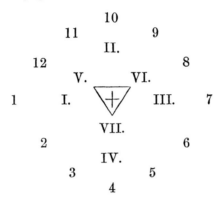

Place the Inquirer in the centre of the figure, unless it has been drawn amongst the other cards. If the Inquirer has been drawn you must place it in the centre, and replace it by another major arcanum chosen by the person whose fate is being studied.

The 12 minor arcana indicate the different phases through which the individual life will pass, or the evolution of the event during the four great periods: Commencement, indicated by the major arcanum I., which displays its character; Apogee (arc. II.); Decline or Obstacle (arc. III.); Fall (arc. IV.).

Lastly, the 3 major arcanum placed in the centre indicate the especial character of the horoscope in the Past (V.), in the Present (VI.), and in the Future (VII.).

The future is indicated in the minor arcana by the cards placed from 7 to 12;

The past by those placed from 1 to 4; and the present by those placed from 4 to 7.

These numbers only indicate the numbers of the

places occupied by the arcana, and never the numbers of the arcana themselves. It is important to avoid the idea that arcanum VII. must always return to the place numbered VII. But our readers are sufficiently intelligent to make any further insistence upon this point quite unnecessary.

The explanation of the meaning of the arcana will be perfectly easy when lessons 2 and 3 have been once read.

Practice will teach these details far better than all the theories in the world.

SIXTH LESSON

Etteila's original Method of Fortune-telling by the Tarot (from one of his rarest works)

WE have explained a method which is original in a great measure, but as we have no intention of monopolizing the art of Cartomancy, we will now say a few words upon the system used by Etteila, the great master in this portion of occultism.

Etteila, whose real name was Aliette, was a hairdresser's apprentice who lived at the time of the French Revolution. Having accidentally found a pack of Tarot cards, he was interested by its eccentricity and began to study it. After thirty years he believed that he had discovered the secret of this Egyptian book. Unfortunately Etteila did not possess any synthetic knowledge, and this ignorance led him to the most erroneous conclusions, though many of his intuitive solutions are really marvellous. There is too much inclination to calumniate this ardent worker; and we must recognize the real truths contained in his works without laying too much stress upon the ignorant simplicity which disfigures them.

However this may be, Etteila devoted all his powers to fortune-telling, and if his contemporaries may be believed, he succeeded wonderfully in his aim. He therefore became the great authority for all fortune-tellers by cards.

We will describe his system in some detail, instead of alluding to those used by his female successors, who as a rule misrepresented without understanding his explanations.

.   .   .   .

Four deals are required before the Tarot can be clearly read according to this method: we will now enumerate them one by one.

FIRST DEAL: Shuffle all the cards of the Tarot, without making any distinction between the major and minor arcana. Then let them be cut, and divide your pack into three heaps, each containing 26 cards.[1]

26   26   26

Take the central heap and place it on your right—

26   26   26   on one side
                                           to the right.

You have still two packets of 26 cards. Take them, shuffle the cards, cut them, and divide them into three heaps, each containing 17 cards—

17   17   17
                    1

One card will remain, but you need not trouble about it.

You then take the central packet and put it on your right hand by the side of the one of 26 cards already there—

17   *   17   17   26 on one side.
          1

You then take the 35 cards which are not on one

---

[1] Etteila quite realised that the number 26 corresponded with the divine name יהוה, the total being 10 + 5 + 6 + 5 = 26.
                                        yod   he   vau   he

side, shuffle and cut them, then divide them into three heaps of 11 cards each—

  11   11   11
        2

Two cards remain, but these are of no consequence; take the central packet as before and place it on your right by the side of those already there—

  11   *   11   11 17 26
       2

This ended, you collect the 24 cards that you have not placed on one side, and you are then ready to explain the oracle.

 . . . .

For this purpose you first take the packet of 26 cards from your right and lay it upon the table card by card, going from right to left—

    26..1

Then take the packet of 17 cards, which you place beneath the others, then the 11 cards, which you also spread out beneath the other two. You then obtain the following arrangement.

Soul 26..1
Mind   17...............................1
Body   11..................1
       Waste packet
        24

You then explain the meaning of the cards, remembering that the lowest line of 11 refers to the body, the centre one to the mind, and, lastly, the upper line of 26 cards to the soul of the Inquirer.

From this system of arrangement Etteila deduced his

subtle arguments upon the creation of the Universe, the Kabalah, and the Philosopher's Stone. But over these we need not linger. We will rather pass on to complete this study of fortune-telling by the Tarot.

SECOND DEAL: Reshuffle all your cards (78) and let them be cut for you.

Take the 17 first cards and arrange them thus—

17.........................1

Look quickly at the 18th card (it will be under your hand when you have placed the 17 first) and the 78th, which will be found beneath the pack.

The meaning of these two cards will tell you whether any fluidic sympathetic communication is established between the Inquirer and yourself.

You can then read the oracles spoken by the line of cards, commencing as usual on the right.

When your line is read, you pass the 17th card to your right and the 1st to your left, then move the 16th and the 2nd, etc., and so on until the cards have all changed places except the one in the centre. This card falls on one side.[1]

THIRD DEAL: Take up all your cards; let them be shuffled and cut for you; then arrange them as shown in the following figure, according to the order of the numbers.

You thus obtain Etteila's great figure, which gives the key to the Past, Present and Future of the person about whose fate you are inquiring. To use this

---

[1] Perhaps we have misunderstood Etteila, who is very obscure in his books, and whom we are trying to explain; but this part of the operation seems perfectly useless.

method successfully, you must follow this figure very
carefully. The best plan is to draw it with all its
numbers upon a table or a large sheet of cardboard,
and then to arrange the cards according to the order of
the numbers.

For reading the results of this figure you must take

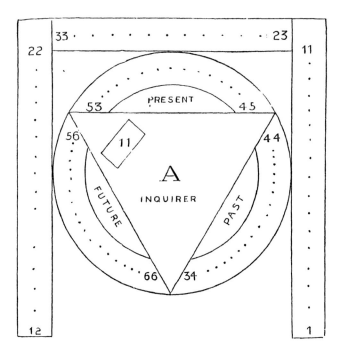

up the cards two by two, the 1st with the 34th, the 2nd
with the 35th, etc., for the Past;

The 23rd with the 45th, the 24th with the 46th . . .
the 33rd with the 55th, for the Present;

The 12th with the 66th, the 13th with the 65th . . .
the 22nd with the 56th, for the Future.

One careful survey of the figure will render it easily
understood.

FOURTH DEAL: The fourth deal is only subsidiary By it answers can be obtained to any questions asked Shuffle all the cards, let them be cut, and then deal out the first seven of the pack thus—

7...........................1

—then read the answer.

The above system of fortune-telling is based upon Etteila's original method. We have summed up, in these few pages, the author's somewhat obscure pamphlet on *The Book of Thoth*. It contains a portrait of Etteila and is very rare, like other works which issued from the same hand. We must add that Etteila's method has never been seriously elucidated by any of his numerous disciples; and we believe ourselves to be one of the first to explain it upon simple principles.

SEVENTH LESSON

CONCLUSION

WE have learnt that intuition and practice are necessities in the art of fortune-telling by cards, now that this art has lost its scientific principles (Astronomy) and launched into empiricism. Having made this reserve in our opinion of its present value, we have studied the best method of applying the Tarot to this curious practice, and with such object we have learnt the meaning of the minor and major arcana, with the best arrangement of the cards for reading them. In respect of this method, which is chiefly the result of our previous studies, we were anxious to give one of the most ancient systems, and have chosen the one used by Etteila, the founder of Cartomancy.

Our readers are therefore able to select whichever system they prefer, and whichever they find most successful. We must repeat that intuition is the great secret of all these divining arts, and that fortune-telling by cards, in water, in earth, or coffee-grounds, is precisely the same thing.

Our intention has been to speak of the modern divining Tarot to render our work more complete, and our lady readers will thank us for not ignoring them in these abstract digressions.

BIBLIOGRAPHY

Mademoiselle Lemarchand, *Récréation de la Cartomancie.* Paris, 1867, 12mo.

Julia Orsini, *Le Grand Etteila, ou l'Art de Tirer les Cartes.* 1853, 8vo.

Madame Clément, *Le Corbeau Sanglant ou l'Avenir Dévoilé.*

The works of Etteila have been already quoted.

CHAPTER XXI

APPLICATION OF THE TAROT TO GAMES

The Royal Game of Human Life played by the Egyptians.
The Unity of Games in the Tarot

THE ROYAL GAME OF HUMAN LIFE,

ACCORDING TO THE EGYPTIANS

1. WHEN the players have chosen their *Magian*, they also choose from amongst the non-players a man and a woman, whom they name *Osiris* and *Isis*.

2. When commencing a game, the Magian having taken the central place, the players settle the amount of the principal fine together (we will suppose it to be one halfpenny), and a basket is placed on the table to receive the money.

3. When all the players are seated, the Magian takes the Book of Thoth, *i.e.* the pack of Tarot cards; he shuffles them, carefully placing their heads alternate ways, but without looking at them. He lets them be cut by some player on his left, and then deals the cards to his right, giving as many as he likes, up to seven, to each player and to himself.

4. Each player should notice that the top of the card (when the Magian deals it) is facing his chest; it is therefore in that sense, and according to the order in which the cards are dealt, that the players should read

335

the oracles traced upon it, which they refer to whomever they choose amongst the persons in the house.

5. When one of the players reads an oracle he assumes the character of an interpreter, and if the person to whom he refers the oracle will not give him a present, he must pay half the fine.

6. When a person has received three veracious oracles upon the past, the present, or according to probabilities the future, and he refuses to reward the interpreter, the players will hold a council, and judge by a majority of voices whether his refusal is justified or not. In the latter case, the Magian must pronounce the word PAMENES, which warns all the household that there is one person present who does not join in the royal game of Human Life, and then Osiris and Isis are obliged to pay for him, for when they accepted these titles, they undertook to diffuse peace and abundance over the heroes who are playing.

7. When one of the spectators asks to buy the hand of one of the players, the Magian fixes its price, which is divided into three parts: the first third is paid into the fine-box; the second to the Magian; and the third to the player, who, however, can avoid parting with his cards by paying the two first thirds of the price fixed by the Magian.

8. When one of the spectators has acquired the hand of one of the players, he takes with it all the player's chances of fines and presents.

9. When one of the players cannot read the oracles, he places his seven cards on one side and pays one-fourth of the fine.

10. If the player, although able to read the oracle, cannot find any one to whom he can refer it, he must

lay his cards upon the table, face upwards, and read the meaning that he sees in them, without paying anything. If, on the other hand, he interprets them badly, according to the judgment of the other players, the Magian condemns him to pay half the fine.

11. When the interpreter has pronounced an oracle, aloud or privately, and has received a present, he can have his seven cards re-shuffled by the Magian, who will return them to him to cut; and finally, if the same cards produce three presents from the same or other persons to whom the oracles have been uttered, all the players, except the Magian, give the interpreter three times the value of the fine. This is the civic crown.

12. The Magian arranges and directs the games as he likes; he awards the fines according to the nature of the faults, such as showing the cards to other players, hiding them from the spectators, any indiscretion in the utterance of the oracles, reading oracles which are not justified by the cards, &c.

13. The spectators can join in the game until the Magian indicates that it is about to end, by saying that in a quarter of an hour, or half an hour, the game will close.

14. If the Magian should forget to announce the coming end of the game, all the spectators have a right to share the fines, which are divided equally amongst all the players, when the expenses have been paid.

THE UNITY OF GAMES

Is it not true that man has displayed more inventive faculties to satisfy his vices, than for anything else?

Y

To convince ourselves of this fact we need only look at the innumerable devices destined to aid him in losing the time which has been so parsimoniously dealt out to us all.

But the human brain acts in accordance with a very small number of laws, and the inventor cannot escape from the effect of this rule. Look at the basis of most games, however they may differ in appearance. Is it not possible to find one single game, from which most of the others are derived?

Follow me in thought, dear reader, over one of the high-roads of Spain or Italy, and let us ask some old Gypsy to leave her camp for a moment and tell our fortunes. Look at the strange cards she draws from her greasy bag: the Universe, the Sun, the Stars, Death, Fortune, Love, are only a few of the names of these eccentric figures, which depict the phases of our daily life with so much simplicity. What is this game? The Gypsy Tarot.

It is composed of our cards with four additional figures called Knights, who are placed between the Queen and the Knave. But its originality lies in the twenty-two supplementary and symbolical figures. Each of them represents an image, a number, an idea. Court de Gebelin, a savant of the eighteenth century, has shown us that this game, as possessed by the Gypsies, is of Egyptian origin, that it also existed in China and India from the earliest antiquity, and we shall see that it is the father of most of the games now known.

It is composed of numbers and figures, which mutually react upon and explain each other. But if we separate the figures and arrange them upon paper in the form of a wheel, making the numbers move in the shape of dice, we produce the Game of Goose, with which Ulysses, according to Homer, practised cheating beneath the walls of Troy.

If we fix the numbers upon alternate black and white squares, and allow the lesser figures of our game to move upon them—the King, Queen, Knight, Foolish Man or Knave, Tower or Ace—we have the Game of Chess. In fact, the primitive chessboards bore numbers, and philosophers used them to solve problems of logic.

If, leaving the figures on one side, we confine ourselves to the use of numbers, the Game of Dice appears, and if we weary of throwing the dice, we can mark the characters upon horizontal plates and create the Game of Dominoes.

If the symbolical figures are in our way, we replace them by black and white draughts, and by using the numbers upon the dice we invent Backgammon, another combination of the Game of Goose.

Chess degenerates in the same way into the Game of Draughts.

Lastly, our pack of cards, instead of first appearing under Charles VI., according to the common report, is of far older date. Spanish regulations were in existence long before this reign, forbidding the nobles to play at cards, and the Tarot itself is of very ancient origin.

The sceptres of the Tarot have become clubs, the cups hearts, the swords spades, and the pentacles or money diamonds. We have also lost the twenty-two symbolical figures and the four knights.

But if all these games are derived from the Tarot, what is its origin and its primitive derivation?

These are grave questions, which for their solution lead the mind into dangerous researches. Let me therefore relate to you a certain confidence upon this subject which I received from a dusty old manuscript, forgotten in a corner of a library. Take it as a romance or as history, whichever you like; it does not matter so long as your curiosity is gratified.

Now, let us transport ourselves in imagination three thousand miles away, into the midst of the wonderful and grandiose Egyptian civilization, which archæologists are each day revealing more fully to our century.

Let us enter one of those cities, of which Paris would form but a district, passing through the defensive outworks guarded by a well-equipped body of soldiers, and let us glide amongst the inhabitants, who are as numerous and as busy as those of our greatest cities.

On all sides immense monuments of strange architecture rise to enormous heights; the terraces of rich houses indicate the first steps of a gigantic staircase, formed by palaces and temples, and dominated by the silent residence of the supreme head of the Empire.

The great cities are everywhere fortified; the Nile is restrained by moles; enormous reservoirs are ready to receive its surplus waters, and thus transform terrible inundations into beneficent irrigation.

All this involves science and savants, but where are they?

At this epoch science and religion were blended in a single study, and all the men of science, engineers, doctors, architects, superior officers, scribes, &c., were called priests or Initiates. We must not confuse the priest of antiquity with the word understood in the modern sense, or we shall fall into many errors, amongst others that of believing that Egypt was given over to clerical despotism in its worst form.

Instruction of every kind was given in the temples in various degrees, according to methods perfectly established, and, at that epoch, imitated in every country in the world.

The highest teaching which man can acquire was given in the great temple of Egypt, and it was there that the great reformers of the future completed their studies—Orpheus, Lycurgus, Pythagoras and Moses amongst many others.

Astronomy was one of the sciences which became the object of constant investigation. We now know through Pythagoras, who has perpetuated the knowledge of the wise men of Egypt, that they were acquainted with the movement of the earth round the sun, as well as with the position of the latter in relation to its satellite planets. Many of the mythological stories relate to these mysteries, and the wise men of the epoch, that is to say, the priests, taught astronomy to their disciples by means of small cards, which represented the months, seasons, signs of the zodiac, planets, sun, &c. In this way they imprinted upon the imagination of students the data which later on they verified in nature.

A time followed when Egypt, no longer able to struggle against her invaders, prepared to die honourably. Then the Egyptian savants (at least so my mysterious informant asserts) held a great assembly to arrange how the knowledge, which until that date had been confined to men judged worthy to receive it, should be saved from destruction.

At first they thought of confiding these secrets to virtuous men secretly recruited by the Initiates themselves, who would transmit them from generation to generation. But one priest, observing that virtue is a most fragile thing, and most difficult to find, at all events in a continuous line, proposed to confide the scientific traditions to vice.

The latter, he said, would never fail completely, and through it we are sure of a long and durable preservation of our principles.

This opinion was evidently adopted, and the game chosen as a vice was preferred. The small plates were then engraved with the mysterious figures which formerly taught the most important scientific secrets, and since then the players have transmitted this Tarot from generation to generation, far better than the most virtuous men upon earth would have done.

Such is the story or the history confided to me by this old manuscript, upon the origin of the father of our great games, and I am very glad that it has given me the means of proving my perhaps paradoxical assertion of their original unity.

CHAPTER XXII

CONCLUSION

HAVING reached the end of our journey we must cast one rapid glance over the road that we have followed, in order to give some account of the scope of our work.

Seeing that materialistic science was giving way, in spite of the desperate efforts of its partisans, under the irresistible pressure of the new era, the impotence of purely analytical methods forced itself upon us, and we were led to search for the possible basis of a synthesis which each day renders more indispensable.

At this moment, the ancient wisdom revealed itself to our investigations, and we find that it contains this synthetic method as the immutable basis of all its scientific, religious and social discoveries.

The secret societies entrusted with the transmission of this sacred deposit have lost its key as well as its ritual; the nomad Gypsies and the Jews only have guarded their Bibles intact throughout the centuries: the latter had the *Sepher* of Moses, the former the Tarot attributed to Thoth Hermes Trismegistus, the triple hierarchic University of ancient Egypt.[1]

The Tarot appeared to us as the Egyptian rendering of the book of initiation, starting as the now missing key to Freemasonry and all occult science.

How could we decipher this series of hieroglyphics?

[1] Consult Saint-Yves d'Alveydre, *Mission des Juifs.*

How discover the mysterious grouping of these plates, now become the property of gamblers?

Wronski teaches us that the faculty to conceive implies the faculty to execute. Strong in this truth, we have questioned antiquity. Its Sphinxes, dumb to the profane, have spoken; its old temples have unveiled their mysteries; its Initiates have re-awakened in answer to our call: four mysterious letters have been revealed to us—

י   ה   ו   ה

Yod   *He*   *Vau*   *He*

—the Sacred Word, which shines upon every initiation, the object of the veneration and respect of all sages.

The study of the Tarot has shown us that it only expresses the combinations of IEVE. However, since we must in these questions guard ourselves above all things from leaving too much scope to the imagination, we chose as the starting-point for our studies a fixed principle, as basis to these immutable combinations, the sole guarantee against all possible error: the number.

We then approached the symbol, and here we again encountered new difficulties. The history of the Tarot has shown us that its figures have often changed in passing through the hands of various peoples, and through different epochs, although its meaning has been preserved in all times and in all places.

It was therefore necessary to find for the symbols a principle as fixed and immutable in its combinations as number itself. The study of the origin of the letters used to inscribe human languages led us back to the determination of the sixteen primitive hieroglyphic signs, the source of the first alphabets. The 22 Hebrew letters, immediately derived from these signs, furnished us with this indispensable basis to all serious researches, as definitely fixed for the symbol as the numbers were for the whole Tarot. We thus had a sure guide, which rendered error still more unlikely.

Thanks to the application of these principles—exact although very general—information was furnished to us upon Theogony, Androgony, and Cosmogony, and we could at last recapitulate the symbolism of the Tarot in a very interesting syllabus.

It was next our desire to show that the Tarot was really the general key which we had pronounced it to be. A few applications proved the fact. Astronomy is unquestionably the most important amongst them, by reason of its fixed principles. Therefore, when we seek to discover how an evolution can advance, but are moving in a labyrinth of inexactitude, Astronomy tells us how the evolution of the sun progresses, and that knowledge gives us the key to every possible evolution.

The gigantic labours of Dupuis were fruitless, because he did not understand that the solar Myth was only a representation of the general law of evolution, and not that of the especial evolution of the sun. The method of occult science is neither induction nor deduction, but analogy, an unknown method at the present date, but one which the Tarot reveals to us in all its splendour.

Afterwards we made other applications of it, and could have accomplished still more, exhibiting the key of Philosophy, of the Holy Kabalah, of Theosophy, of the Physiology of Man and of the Universe in the Tarot; but we have restricted ourselves to giving the key, and to showing the method of its use by a few examples.

We were unwilling to exceed the strict limits of our engagement.

Such as it is, our work still contains some imperfections which we would willingly efface. We are under no illusions on this point, and time alone can remedy it. But we would draw attention to the aim that is visible throughout its pages—the application of the most exact methods possible to occult science.

Through the modern exact sciences we have reached the study of occultism, and starting ourselves from materialism, of which we were one of the most ardent disciples, we felt the necessity of advancing further. But we have retained a single link with our early affections, the taste for method, and it is the absence of this method which spoils occult science. Louis Lucas saw clearly that physics must advance by the side of metaphysics, to serve as its basis: in the same way we have endeavoured to place fixed principles, such as numbers and the Hebrew letters, side by side with the metaphysical data, like symbols or abstract conceptions.

Occultists as a rule are lost through the lack of precision. We have made every effort to avoid this stumbling-block, without however asserting that we have succeeded. An author is not qualified to judge his own work.

Be this as it may, we have been frequently obliged to speak of occult science without the leisure to enter into these explanatory details—this is the reason we have addressed our book

To Initiates.

THE TAROT
CYCLE OF REVOLUTIONS OF IEVE (יהוה)
ABSOLUTE KEY TO OCCULT SCIENCE BY
PAPUS.

HUMANITY

GOD

GENERATION

UNIVERSE

Transformation — Preservation — Creation

Transition — Creation

Generation · Transition · Transformation (Sudra) · Creation (Brahma)

Equilibrium

Transformation · Preservation · Creation · Transition

CUPS

SCEPTRES

SWORDS

PENTACLES

ANDROGONY

COSMOGONY

THEOGONY

GENERATION

KING — QUEEN — KNIGHT — ACE

VII — IV — X — VII — IV

An Initiate is one who possesses the elements of occultism, who is therefore familiar with a whole vocabulary which may well intimidate a man of the world; this is our excuse for words which may sound pretentious to some minds, and this is why we have been anxious to express our ideas quite clearly.

Still, since it is customary for the Tarot to be used for fortune-telling, we have touched upon this subject, and have rendered it as attractive as possible. We have tried to simplify the systems used, so that a woman of moderate intelligence can easily, and with little exercise of memory, amuse herself with this art.

But since our own system may not please all the partisans of Cartomancy, we have summed up the process of the great master Etteila, so that, even in this purely empiric region, we have tried to introduce as much scientific exactitude as possible.

We hope that this recapitulation of the efforts of several years may prove useful to occultism, and to its revival, which becomes daily more pronounced. This is the aim which we have kept in view. May the social disorders which are preparing give rise to an era of peace and harmony amongst the now divided nations, and may the knowledge of these mysteries overthrow European Cæsarism in all its forms! This should be your aim, Kabalists, Theosophists, Martinists, Rosicrucians and Freemasons! On this point believe the humble disciple of your doctrines, who will be only too happy if his work has retained one feeble ray of the Eternal and Holy Truth.

INDEX

Printed in the United Kingdom
by Lightning Source UK Ltd.
9781900001B/3